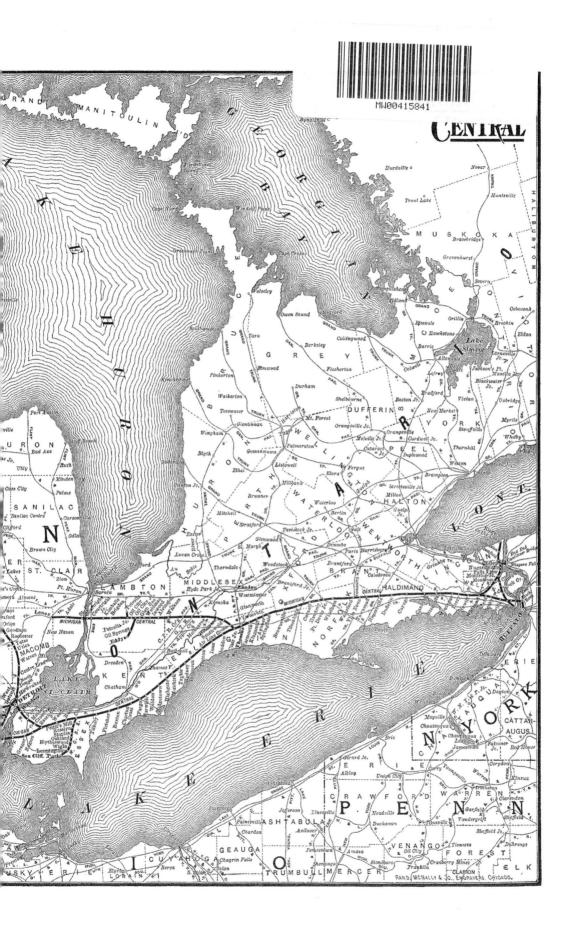

THE MICHIGAN CENTRAL RAILROAD

History of the Main Line
1846–1901

NICHOLAS A. MARSH

For my parents, Barb and Joe

Copyright © 2007, Nicholas A. Marsh

ISBN: 978-0-9798289-0-4

Library of Congress Control Number: 2007932419

Printed in the United States of America

CONTENTS

PREFACE

Some of my earliest memories are of New York Central Railroad (NYCRR) trains thundering through Delhi, Michigan, a small country village a few miles west of Ann Arbor. I lived there as a child and would often return to visit my great grandfather Joseph "Big Joe" Marsh long after we'd moved away from Delhi. My father, grandfather, and Big Joe had all worked on the Detroit to Chicago Main Line between Ypsilanti and Chelsea.

I was nearly a teenager before I realized that the Michigan Central Railroad (MCRR) preceded the NYCRR. When I tried to learn more about the MCRR, I was surprised to find only a few chapters in books dedicated to the NYCRR. I was hungry for more information and started researching. What began as a quest for knowledge to satisfy my curiosity turned into a drive to compile nuggets of information about the MCRR.

During my research I found two main reasons for the absence of a historical text dedicated to the MCRR. One reason is that such a history would be a mammoth undertaking requiring years of research and multiple volumes of text to tell the whole story, even if the whole story could be reconstructed. The other reason is the lack of a central archive of company records, which makes research difficult. Apparently much of the company's archive was lost when the Penn Central moved out in the 1970s and the files at the Detroit depot were dumped. Some records were collected prior to the unfortunate loss, but most of that information is in private hands. Those private MCRR collectors who have pieces of the puzzle tend to prefer not to share the content or location of their treasures.

In an effort to overcome some of these barriers, I looked for help. Luckily, a few dedicated MCRR fans, like Jim Harlow and Dave Tinder, were eager to participate in memorializing Michigan's greatest railroad. Jim, a lifelong collector of Michigan railroad information, is a walking library of railroad facts, and his knowledge was critical to the body of this book. My e-mails and telephone calls to him for leads, clarifications, and verifications number in the hundreds. Photograph collector extraordinaire Dave Tinder has a collection of early Michigan images that is superior to many local libraries and has a special love for railroads. He shared some of his photographs for use here and the book is better as a result.

This MCRR section gang worked the portion of track between Ann Arbor and Delhi. The photo was taken by Paul Richmond near the Farmer's Station in 1900. Front row from left to right: William Riley, Chance Dorman, Henry Marsh, Denny Form, William Roost, two unidentified Italian workers. Back row from left to right: Thomas Riley, Ezra Young, Frank Riley (the section boss), unidentified, Bagley Arnold and Big Joe Marsh. Eight of these men are connected to the author's family tree.

During this research, my father Joseph kept me inspired by telling family railroad stories and answering questions about his time on the Main Line. My brother Kevin helped me by locating records and by doing fieldwork in Washtenaw County. My niece Amanda Marsh and cousin Karen Brewer also helped with research and my daughter Sarah's encouragement helped me stay on course. Most of all, my wife Cheryl supported and encouraged me over the decade of work. In addition to proofreading the manuscript and making suggestions, she was my sounding board every step of the way.

I also relied on help from some long-time friends. Barbara Bell helped with several history projects before, and materials she collected years ago filled holes in this effort and helped to direct further searches. For the last ten years, Ann Arbor historian Wystan Stevens has forwarded bits of MCRR information to me that he found while working on his research projects. I am also indebted to Barbara Rohrer. Not only did she spur me on to finish the project, she reviewed the manuscript and offered helpful edits.

Help was also found at libraries. The Bentley Historical Library in Ann Arbor holds the largest public collection of MCRR records. The library's other holdings, particularly county and local histories, added pieces to the puzzle I struggled to complete. I owe library archivist Karen Jania a special thank you for answering dozens of inquiries over the last several years and helping me locate hard-to-find materials in other locations. University of Michigan digital library supervisor Lara Unger also assisted with helping me locate MCRR records. Reference librarians from Boston Public Library were also quick to respond to questions about the MCRR owners (the "Eastern Capitalists"). Marta H. Pardee-King and Patricia Feeley conducted exhaustive research, as did some anonymous librarians from the New York and Chicago public libraries. Pat Lewis, librarian and researcher from Wayne State University, helped locate some regional material that saved time and trouble. Toni Benson, the librarian at the Van Buren District Library in Decatur, Michigan, found information and referred me to her father who played near a depot as a child. Anne Terpstra, librarian at McKay-Dole Library in Augusta, Michigan, was generous with her time in researching their collection for early photos. Lake County, Indiana, reference librarian Mary Grogan was quick to respond to inquires and led me to other critical resources about stations along the Main Line as did Carol Daumer Gutjahr, manager of the Hobart Township library branches.

Lucy Loomis, director of the Sturgis Library in Barnstable, Massachusetts, was helpful early on with information about the original MCRR directors. Stephen McShane, archivist/curator from the Calumet Regional Archives at the Indiana University Northwest Library, assisted by locating images, as did Richard Lytle, librarian at the Hammond Public Library. Staff at Willard Library (Battle Creek), Buchanan Public Library, Jackson District Library, Edwardsburg Community Library, Comstock Township Library, and the Kalamazoo Library graciously searched their collections.

Historical societies and museums were another source of assistance. Nancy VanBlarcum of the Dexter Historical Society and Museum in Dexter, Michigan, was key to providing research and material on how the MCRR affected a small town on the Main Line. Her assistance in putting together pieces of the puzzle was crucial. Kathy Clark from the Chelsea Historical Society conducted valuable research and located a rare artifact used in this project. Members of the Genealogical Society of Washtenaw County assisted by reviewing their collections for primary source material as did members of the Peninsular State Philatelic Society. Laura Osterhout from the Buffalo & Erie County Historical Society, Buffalo, New York, and Jack Messmer from the Lower Lakes Marine Historical Society in Buffalo, New York, helped locate information on the MCRR steamships. Carrie Supple from the Massachusetts Historical Society was helpful in locating information about the railroad's first directors. Jo Ann Bunce of the Jackson County Genealogical Society searched its collection for material. Carol Bainbridge, director of the Fort St. Joseph Museum, Niles, Michigan, quickly answered an urgent request for help just before the book went to print. Jim Zuleski, historian at the Ella Sharp Museum in Jackson, Michigan, provided assistance with locating antique images, and Judith Groat of the Calhoun County Michigan Genealogical Society provided leads on further research. Charles Baker of the Allen County Ohio Historical Library is curator of the MCRR's copy of the *United States Railroad Administration Property Valuation Study* completed on the nation's rail companies from 1919–1920. It contains photographs of many station houses, freight buildings and other physical property owned by the MCRR at that time. He helped locate photographs and provided tips on locations of other information. Librarian David Kupas of the Senator John Heinz Pittsburgh Regional History Center assisted in research about early iron rail production companies. Claudia Jew, director of photographic services at the Mariners' Museum, in Newport News, Virginia, spent an inordinate amount of time managing a search of its vast holdings.

Private concerns helped too, such as the Mount Auburn Cemetery in Cambridge, Massachusetts, which contains the remains of many souls who were prominent men in the 1800s. Cemetery manager Caroline Loughlin assisted in the search for elusive vital records. Railroad enthusiasts also contributed to the effort. Charles Conn from Centurion Photo in Harbor Springs, Michigan, made some of his personal collection of the property evaluation photos available for this project. Art Lamport, retired railroad employee, provided items from his collection as did author Robert Rosenbaum. Grass Lake historian James Damaron and railroad memorabilia collectors Gary Daniels, John Fowler, Richard Rautio, Frank Passic and David Davis were quick to offer information or pieces of their collections to the effort.

As a member of the Railway & Locomotive Historical Society, Inc., I was able to request information from its vast archive holdings. William F. Howes, Jr., was quick to respond to the inquiry and even followed up with a telephone call.

The people and services mentioned helped ease the problems caused by the lack of a company archive, but one problem had to be faced alone: the project's size. How do you decide what to leave out of a history in trying to make the project manageable yet keep the project true to its purpose? One of the first decisions I made was limit the book's primary focus to the Detroit to Chicago Main Line during the Charter years (1846–1901). The next decision was to exclude most low-interest financial information about stocks, bonds, sinking and floating debt, feeder lines, and freight. An attempt was also made not to print widely distributed illustrations, but include images that have not previously appeared in print, or not been printed lately. Finally, I made the decision to limit the project to one volume of MCRR history, yet provide the type of overview that would make it a reference for enthusiasts, educators and genealogists.

The recent surfacing of *MCRR Construction Distribution Ledger B, July 1848 to July 1851,* and ample evidence that much more material exists in private collections give us hope for more learning about the MCRR. Someday those materials too will see the light of day. Perhaps you have some answers or information that would add to the body of knowledge on the MCRR. If so, I urge you to contact me (mcrrhistory@aol.com) or the Bentley Historical Library in Ann Arbor. Reconstructing the history of the Michigan Central Railroad is a work in progress. Please become of part of that effort.

My purpose in this project was to find and bring together bits of information from a variety of scattered resources and create a more complete and accurate picture of the MCRR. Some of what I found and included presents a different twist on what came before. Mostly this work represents an effort to fill the huge holes, makes corrections, or answers questions about what has been previously recorded. I am under no illusion that this history is complete or even completely accurate. How well this collection of scattered MCRR material represents the company history will be measured by time.

Although this book pays tribute to the mighty Michigan Central Railroad, it is also intended to honor those people who endured the hard labor of bygone days to improve the lives of those who followed. The presence of those pioneers, to which we owe so much, lingers on along the Main Line.

INTRODUCTION

Even though the name of Michigan's most vital railroad company has been gone from rolling stock on the Main Line for nearly a century, the Wolverine State's landscape remains rich with traces of the mighty Michigan Central Railroad. Obvious, hard-to-miss indicators of greatness include the handful of magnificent passenger depots strung out across the lower portion of the state like pearls on a string—with most of the pearls missing. These few remaining architectural jewels have been restored and now house restaurants, museums, or office space. At least 20 MCRR depots still exist—all or in part. The buildings survived because communities had emotional attachments that trumped efforts to demolish the structures when progress forced them into obsolescence.

Less obvious are the railroad bridges, built so well more than a century ago that most still support daily rail traffic. And of course there is the roadway—that long ribbon of steel track that runs from the Detroit River to Chicago, which millions of people cross over, or under yearly on the highways that nearly made the historic roadway obsolete.

Hidden remnants of the Michigan Central Railroad also lie forgotten in bottoms of dresser drawers, attic trunks, corners of barns, and the occasional antique shop. Old company stocks, annual reports, rule books, rail passes, operational forms, timetables, silverware, railroad lanterns, and tools are just a few of the artifacts that railroad collectors can still find by digging through other people's junk. Internet auction sites have helped bring some of the treasures to light. Many of these items carry the Michigan Central name or MCRR initials. Some, like the hand tools of another time, forever bear the imprint of the sweat and smell of heavy labor. To enthusiasts, the life of the Michigan Central Railroad is reflected in all that the company left behind.

But the real treasure left by the Michigan Central is something less tangible. It is a legacy of development and progress comparatively greater in its time than any company has provided Michigan or the region since.

Some of the country's most successful and remarkable men saved the state from economic disaster when they purchased the Michigan Central Railroad in 1846. Partially through overextended internal improvement efforts such as railroad and canal projects, Michigan was on the verge of bankruptcy. Money from the sale of the Central from the state to private developers not only replenished public coffers; it paid off the state's debt. Within two years of the sale, the MCRR brought $6 million to Michigan for investment, where the previous record for investment from outside the state was only $100,000. Taxes from MCRR operations alone paid the entire cost of state government for over a decade. Where are the monuments showing gratitude to the railroad or its builders? Today few people even know the MCRR existed, much less names of men involved.

MCRR stimulated area industry on a large scale by creating a need for locomotives, rail cars, and steamships. Manufacturing plants soon followed and access to natural resources needed to feed these companies was established by another MCRR associated accomplishment—the building of the St. Mary's Canal Locks at Sault St. Marie.

Once Detroit became known as a manufacturing city, it became fused with planning in the minds of industrialists of all kinds, but especially automobile developers. The railroad made it easier for the Dodge brothers, who lived on the MCRR line in Niles, to move to Detroit and first build a machine shop, then engines for Henry Ford, and later automobiles under their family name. It was MCRR wages that helped pay the mortgage on the family farm owned by Henry Ford's parents, and it was a MCRR engine-house that helped inspire young Henry.

It is well documented that prosperity boomed for every village on the Main Line when the railroad arrived, but the MCRR brought development and prosperity to the Michigan wilderness as well. By reaching deep into remote areas with feeder lines, where economic development was stifled due to lack of markets for farm goods, the railroad stimulated industrial and commercial business statewide.

The influence of the MCRR is not limited to Detroit, population centers along the Main Line, the feeder lines, the state of Michigan, or the even the northwest region. The MCRR stimulated an entire nation. Workers who gained experience working for the MCRR played an important part in building many of the country's railroads, including the Atchison, Topeka, & Santa Fe; Northern Pacific; Illinois Central; Maine Central; Chicago; Burlington & Quincy; Hannibal & St. Joseph; the Louisville & Nashville; and the Union Pacific. Former MCRR men became presidents, superintendents, and directors of these major companies and their early exposure of how to run a high-quality efficient railroad unquestionably aided their tremendous success as company leaders later.

Much more about the MCRR is hidden in history. For example, two former MCRR men helped build the transcontinental railroad. The MCRR was one of the first equal opportunity employers to hire blacks as engineers and women as depot agents and telegraph operators. It is long forgotten that the MCRR ran the most luxurious and fastest shipping operation on the Great Lakes in the mid-1800s, or that Michigan's "Favorite Line" was instrumental in building the famous hotel on Mackinaw Island. Sports fans might find it interesting that the MCRR baseball team was runner-up in a Railroad World Series.

Finally we are able to view one volume to see these and other missing portions of MCRR history and answer a few questions about where to go to find more. Who built the railroad? Not only who fronted the money, but also who directed the work? Who labored grading the roadway, erecting buildings and bridges, putting down ties and iron? Who were the earliest engineers, brakemen, conductors, and station agents? How many people were employed building and repairing locomotives and what kind of jobs did they perform? How many steamships did the MCRR operate and what happened to them? Which towns along the Main Line had stations? What did the old depots look like? Why did the company give up its charter? Until recently it has been difficult to provide even partial answers to these questions. Now we have at least some early, verifiable information, which adds to the recorded history of the mighty Michigan Central Railroad.

When reading this version of history, note that all quotes are italicized. All quotes not footnoted are taken from company annual reports. Spelling irregularities found in quotes were not corrected, however, light editing was applied. Recommendations for further readings are found in the footnotes and the bibliography. If the reference cited is incomplete it is because anonymity was requested.

CHAPTER 1

THE DETROIT &
ST. JOSEPH RAILROAD

The history of the mighty Michigan Central Railroad Company began on September 25, 1846, when the company took possession of the state-owned Central Railroad. However, we must look back at least 18 years to 1828 and see what was happening in the Michigan Territory to gain a full understanding of how New Englanders came to build Michigan's premier railroad.

It is easy to understand why Michigan territorial residents were interested in east-west connections. Most residents were from the East and traveling home to visit relatives was as time-consuming as it was arduous. Although improving travel was important to many, the driving force behind transportation development initiatives was the desperate need to market products in the East and develop an economy that would support a state government. In 1828, the Michigan Territory had only half the population needed (60,000) before it could qualify to enter the Union as a state. Politicians and residents were eager to gain statehood for the status, revenue, and subsequent development it would bring to the area.

With statehood far from sight, Michigan's territorial government was desperate for tax revenue to build infrastructure that would attract emigrants. At the time, most westbound people and taxable goods were going around the Great Lakes by ship and avoiding Michigan taxes on freight. This route also prevented travelers from seeing the interior as a possible place to settle. The territory only had four government-built roads into and out of Detroit, and both commerce and its people were confined. The Chicago, Grand River, Fort Gratiot, and Saginaw, popularly called the Pontiac Road, were constructed of clay and practically impassible for three quarters of the year. Farmers and manufactures had a difficult time bringing goods to market. Emigrants had an equally hard time getting out of Detroit to populate the countryside. It was clear to lawmakers that iron rails could be used year round and therefore were the answer their problems.

Territorial Governor Lewis Cass was known for being *indefatigable*[1] in his pursuit of internal improvements, particularly roads. He knew that they would promote the prosperity of the state, but he was worried about another issue. As experiences such as the War of 1812 taught, passable roads were key to providing for the public defense. He knew that the quick and reliable deployment of troops a railroad would provide was important to the safety of settlers.

To illustrate how aggressive territorial lawmakers were in pursuing the new railroad technology on behalf of their constituents, one only needs to note how quickly they responded to developments in the East. On July 4, 1828, the first railroad in the United States, the Baltimore & Ohio Railroad, began construction. The B&O used horses to pull cars for the first two years until the famous engine, the *Tom Thumb,* was built. The Mohawk & Hudson Railroad (M&HRR) was chartered in 1826, but the company engineer had to go to England to learn how to build a railroad, and they didn't break ground until July 7, 1830. It was a year later that the M&HRR put the famous DeWitt Clinton steam engine into service.[2]

Regardless of being unfamiliar with railroads, these New England projects and others in the South sparked an interest across the territory and nation. It is certain that few Michigan residents had any idea what a railroad was, much less had the chance to see one. Yet, although the idea of using iron rail to circumvent muddy, impassable roads was new-fangled, it looked like the answer to several problems. Within a short time Michigan territorial residents were clamoring for their own railroads.

Most of the wealthy citizens in and around Detroit were rich in land, not cash. The state was too young and too poor to have produced any capitalists. The total population of the village in 1830 was only a little over 2,000. But despite the fact that no businessman, no group of businessmen, and not even the young territorial government had the wherewithal to build a railroad at that time, the first railroad charter was made to the Pontiac & Detroit Railway Company in May 1830. The P&DR charter eventually lapsed because it failed to meet its charter requirements, but precedent was set and the public was officially alerted that Michigan was interested in railroads.

So eager was the territory for access to eastern markets, an older mode of transportation and commerce was also promoted in some circles. Canal building had been hugely successful in the east. In 1825 the Erie Canal, for example, cost the state of New York $7 million to build and brought in $1 million in taxes each year thereafter. In addition to filling the public tax coffers, it lowered the price of incoming merchandise residents needed, and enhanced the price of its outgoing agricultural products.

Some Michigan officials, lead by James Kingsley of Ann Arbor, believed that a canal dug across the lower part of the state would realize similar financial rewards faster than waiting for someone to build expensive railroads. In 1830 Kingsley, *and other friends from the interior,*[3] insisted that the state legislative council support the building of a canal or railroad from Detroit to the mouth of the St. Joseph River at Lake Michigan. Thus, the eastern and western terminus of a central transportation route was established early in the mind of officials interested in internal improvements.

By 1830s, however, canals were considered by many to be an old solution to new problems in a new age. The idea could not get traction so it was abandoned. Kingsley then procured a charter for the Detroit & St. Joseph Railroad (D&SJRR), which was given on June 29, 1832. It was the road that would eventually become the Main Line of the Michigan Central Railroad Company.

Twenty-one owners (commissioners) were named in the state-approved railroad charter for the D&SJRR. Most written reports say they were mostly large landowners in Detroit. In fact, 60 percent were from the interior of Michigan and all were prominent men in their regions. They were James Abbott, John Allen, Major John Biddle, Calvin Brittain, Anson Brown, O. W. Colden, Isaac Crary, Samuel W. Dexter, Caleb Eldred, John Gilbert, Job Gorton, E. P. Hastings, De Garmo Jones, Charles Larned, Judge Cyrus Lovell, Dr. Able Millington, Admiral Oliver Newberry, Judge W. E. Perrine, Wm. A. Thompson, Talman Wheeler, and John R. Williams. (See Appendix A for more information about these men.)

The D&SJRR was organized with Biddle as president. Charles C. Trowbridge, Oliver Newberry, E. A. Brush, Shubael Conant, Henry Whiting, J. Burdick, Mark Norris, and C. N. Ormsby were the directors. Lt. John M. Berrien was the chief engineer and Alex I. Center was assistant engineer. The secretary/treasurer was A. H. Adams, *the highly respected cashier of the old Detroit Savings Bank.*[4] They had their charter giving permission to build, but no money to start construction. It appears that Kingsley and the railroad president Biddle, had to solicit money from friends and business associates to secure the initial $400 it would cost to start a survey. The line was to run from Detroit, through the county seats of Washtenaw, Jackson, Calhoun, Kalamazoo, and Van Buren counties, to the mouth of the St. Joseph River for the purpose of running cars *by the force of steam, of animals, of any mechanical or other power, or of any combination of these forces.*[5]

In addition to being chief engineer, Berrien was the surveyor in charge. Berrien was also an Army officer on leave. It was *not an uncommon proceeding, the valuable aid of officers being frequently call into requisition in laying out roads and furnishing drawing of harbors and paper cities.*[6] Berrien, later a colonel, was subsequently hired by the state and, in turn, the Michigan Central Railroad Company to complete the job.

The D&SJRR commissioners were authorized to receive subscriptions for stock fixed at 1.5 million shares at $50 per share. Initially they took pride in the fact that the railroad was a local endeavor with no start-up money coming from outside the state. *Everyone in Detroit who had a hundred dollars at command, present or prospective, subscribed.*[7] But soon it became apparent that adequate start-up money would actually be difficult to secure. Although the charter required road building to start in two years, an extension of two more years was given due to financial difficulties.

Author Alvin F. Harlow (1947) stated that the D&SJRR project would have died of neglect if not for the determination of an Ann Arbor contingent to raise the necessary funding by knocking on doors across the state. *By hard labor $9,000 was raised in Ann Arbor, $70,000 in Detroit and amazingly enough, $100,000 at Ypsilanti.*[8] He gave Ann Arbor and Kingsley the title of *mother and father* of the Michigan Central Railroad, but with an outlay that large perhaps Ypsilanti should be recognized as the mother.

In addition to having the authority to receive subscriptions for stock, the state legislative council authorized banking privileges in its early railroad charters. That is, the D&SJRR charter allowed the company to start a railroad bank to help generate income for road building. Among the many restrictions on the railroad banks, debts were limited to three times the amount of paid-in capital. The purpose of the railroad bank charter was to induce investment to help it meet charter requirements of raising $10,000 in two years and building 10 miles of road in six years, just to name two. The D&SJRR used the banking privilege and printed money, but how much the banking privilege helped is unknown. Surviving banknotes delight collectors today.

In 1836 the Detroit & St. Joseph Railroad Company began construction of its road just months before Michigan was admitted to statehood on January 28, 1837. By then, grading for the track was only complete to Dearborn (then called Dearbornville) a distance of about 9 miles. D&SJRR owners had already *purchased one locomotive, one passenger car and the wheels for some freight cars.*[9] Progress seemed slow to lawmakers and residents alike. Histories written closer to the 1830s support the progress in building track as a fair rate for the period as the forest between Detroit and Ypsilanti was *so dense that it was with the greatest difficulty the surveyors could run a line.*[10]

Even if the delays were justified, many citizens believed more progress should have been made and pressured the legislature to fix the problem of slow advancement. Years before Michigan became a state, representatives had been discussing government involvement in railroad building and slow progress of privately owned companies exacerbated their frustration as pressure from the voters increased.

D&SJRR dollar bill.

The success of the Erie & Kalamazoo Railroad, chartered in 1833 and running at a profit from Toledo to Adrian, the failure of other entrepreneurs to step forward to build railroads with a sense of urgency felt by lawmakers, and the eagerness for the new state government to promote business and growth, all inspired the change to state-sponsored railroad building. Michigan officials understood well how important the railroad was to opening the territory. It was the fastest way to stimulate the overall economy and improve communication and transportation between developing wilderness areas and established centers of population. If the state took over railroads, it would also benefit from controlling the development of internal transportation through guiding where the rail line went, what rates to charge, and what taxes to levy.

Michigan lawmakers soon followed Indiana (1836) and Illinois (1837), by bonding itself for internal improvements—primarily railroads and canals. The state's poor fiscal situation reflected in the fact that it could only manage to bond $5 million, while Indiana and Illinois bonded $10 million and $10.2 million, respectively.

The theory was that taxes from the shipment of goods on canals and railroads would pay for the bonds, making the taxation of the small, rural poor population unnecessary. The plan had merit due to the fact that Michigan's population could not be taxed; that is, the majority were poor dirt farmers who had no money whatsoever. The few who would have a dollar now and then, when land was being purchased for $1.25 an acre, would immediately spend it on expanding the farm. Revenue from freight then traveling from Buffalo to Chicago through the Great Lakes was not taxed. If the same freight went from Detroit to Chicago by canal or rail in less time, businessmen would flock to the route and Michigan tax coffers would be full. Or so the theory went.

On March 20, 1837, just three months after Michigan was admitted to the Union as a state, an act was passed entitled *An act to provide for the construction of certain works of public improvement and for other purposes.*[11] Michigan bonded itself for $5 million and established an internal improvements commission to supervise the construction and operation of state railroads. Governor Stephen T. Mason invited every railroad in the state with a charter to sell it, and whatever improvements, if any, back to the state. The Detroit & St. Joseph, which by now had the right of way purchased just beyond Ypsilanti, and grading completed to Dearborn, sold out for $139,802.[12]

The state takeover of the D&SJRR came just before the state began to feel the effects of the great financial Panic of 1837. This national depression would thwart the state from finishing the road in spite of making a profit each year on what was completed. The state began calling its new enterprise *the Central Rail Road and it was destined to become . . . one of the most important railways in the Western States.*[13]

CHAPTER 2
THE STATE TAKEOVER

Michigan's new Internal Improvements Commission planned for the development of three railroads and was given half a million dollars to start surveying the routes. The three roads were the Northern, which would be built from Port Huron to the Grand River, and the Southern, which would run from the River Raisin near Lake Erie to Lake Michigan along the extreme bottom of the state, and the Central, which would follow the proposed route of the D&SJRR from Detroit to St. Joseph. Due to the work completed by the Detroit and St. Joseph Railroad workers, the Central had the route surveyed to Washtenaw County, construction started, and some rolling stock (cars) purchased. The first of these cars were built in Troy, New York, by the famous Troy Stagecoach Company. But in a short time the Central's rolling stock was being constructed in Detroit. *The first passenger car of the Detroit make was christened the Lady Mason, and was built under the supervision of George and John Gibson.*[1] One of the first projects initiated by the new Central Railroad illustrated a lack of knowledge about railroad operations. The Internal Improvements Commission contracted with Thomas Palmer to build a track from Campus Martius (later called Cadillac Square), the terminus at the time, down Woodward Avenue to the river's edge . . . *with no station or station grounds upon which to do business, and with no plan to acquire any, and with no possibility of doing so for such an approach . . . that part of the road was never used for any purpose and was soon taken up.*[2]

Possibly realizing they didn't know what they were doing, railroad managers went outside state boundaries for assistance. Henry Willis of Pennsylvania agreed to come to Michigan to oversee the building of the road from Dearborn to Ypsilanti and get things started. A small one-story wooden depot was soon built at Campus Martius in Detroit and the Central Railroad (CRR) was soon completed to Ypsilanti. The first trip of cars into town arrived in February 3, 1838, to a great celebration.[3] Lawmakers and other prominent state businessmen were on the train taking a tour of the route and joining in the politically charged festivity. The only locomotive owned by the CRR was named the *Governor Mason* and the governor was among those on the celebration tour. Apparently the engine made it to Ypsilanti without incident, but broke down on the return causing many dignitaries to walk the remaining distance from Dearborn to Detroit in the middle of winter. This 29-mile stretch of track consumed nearly 10 percent of IIC funds. The high rate of expenditure for a relatively short distance foreshadowed money problems to come.

Initially contracts were let to private companies in an effort to save money. The first contractor for the road from Ypsilanti to Ann Arbor was unable to find workers and withdrew. A few months later, in May 1838, the state posted an advertisement in the local Ann Arbor paper looking for a chief engineer to clear the roadway from Ypsilanti to Ann Arbor. John Monroe was given the job and supervised the building of most of the road in the next stretch between Ypsilanti and Jackson. In 1839, for consistency and control, CRR state commissioner William Thompson *resumed construction under direct state management . . . and hired workmen and animals.*[4] The state also hired Jarvis Hurd as chief engineer for the Central road but also retained Capt. John M. Berrien, who was already familiar with the surveyed route to St. Joseph.

Having the state manage road building was likely an error in judgment. Political patronage was a standard operating policy at the time and whenever a party went out of favor, railroad workers affiliated with the outgoing party left as well. Whatever experience was gained by working on the road was lost in the wake of each election.

The CRR reached Ann Arbor in October 1838. A large celebration marked the occasion with processions and parade:

> *. . . on the seventeenth the first passenger train puffed its way into Ann Arbor. All the school children in the village and most of the adult citizens were on hand to welcome the thousand who had come from Detroit and a tremendous ovation was given them. A banquet was spread on the Court House Square, toasts were offered, responses made, and a general good time was enjoyed.*[5]

Lack of funding caused the seven-year delay between the arrival of the railroad and the building of Ann Arbor's first CRR depot in 1845. It was located on Depot Street west of where the famous stone depot stands today, just past Broadway Street. This first depot was on the opposite (north) side of the street but it burned down *in the afternoon of June 4, 1845. . . .* [It] *had recently been completed at a cost of $5,000.*[6]

The coming of the Central Railroad to Ann Arbor was a financial windfall. It was an effect experienced by other towns too. Local historians recorded that it kept the village from suffering from the effects of one of the worse financial panics in our nation's history.

> *Within the years 1837 to 1842 approximately $4,000,000 was spent in Washtenaw County alone . . . and it created a circulation of a large amount of money. As a result it was easy to borrow, interest rates were low, and the outlay for local improvement was extensive. This brought to Ann Arbor an era of prosperity which would never have been possible had the railroad not come.*[7]

While many in the state celebrated the track completion to Ann Arbor, some state representatives were not impressed by little successes. They knew the state could not generate the resources to finish the Central, and they were desperate for the revenue a finished rail line would generate. A few lawmakers were interested in selling the railroad just years after buying the D&SJRR charter, and they pressed for a resolution.

In a speech to the state senate on April 20, 1839, Governor Mason said that he refused to sign a joint resolution *relative to the central railroad, which was a bill to move the railroad project to the private sector.* Mason explained, . . . *it seems to me that the measure contemplated by the resolution before me requires mature deliberation, before my sanction is given to a proposition leasing to individuals the most important public work of the state of Michigan.*[8]

It took almost three years to cover the next ten miles from Ann Arbor to Dexter. The reasons for the slowdown apparently included a change in route. Research indicates that initially the track was to leave Ann Arbor and run parallel and between Dexter and Jackson Roads. This route was taken later by the electric lines, which ran directly west out of town, missing Dexter completely. Apparently Dexter citizens enticed the CRR to come through town by offering free land for the track, as well as passenger and freight houses. Once the route was settled, other land along the Huron River had to be purchased and several bridges had to be built.

The CRR track reached Dexter in the summer of 1841. Like other small villages along the Main Line, it was the biggest thing to ever happen to the small rural community. Judge Alexander D. Crane of Dexter provided an eyewitness description of the July 4, 1841, celebration:

> *Early in the morning of that day the people of the surrounding country came pouring into the village on foot, on horseback, in carriages and wagons, not only to celebrate the anniversary of the Nation's birthday at the same time to celebrate in the completion to our village of the Michigan Central railroad.*[9]

The Dexter celebration was such a noteworthy event that a local area resident wrote to a relative in Ireland about the celebration: *The Rail Road to Dexter was opened on the 5th of July. Five engines came in with long trains crowded with people.*[10]

It is apparent from the size of that first train into Dexter that it was not only area residents who flocked to the railroad celebrations. Much like the earlier Ann Arbor celebration that was attended by thousands, the Dexter event was crowded as well. A Detroit paper tells why the long trains were crowded with people. The event was a day excursion for Detroiters!

> *We understand that there is to be a Railroad and Independent celebration at Dexter on Monday next. Great preparations have been made for the reception of company, and as there is nothing to be done here for citizens will find it a pleasant trip to go out and enjoy the festivities of the day with the Dexterians. They will be well received and well taken care of.*[11]

Dexter was also deemed worthy of being one of the first villages with a CRR depot. The village also received a hand-operated turntable, which turned locomotives around for return trips to Detroit.

To illustrate again how the coming of the Central changed every town it touched, a local historian outlines how it changed Dexter.

> *Up to the time the railroad extended from Detroit to Dexter, times were hard. There was little money in circulation and most business was done by bar-*

tering. There was little market for what farmers raised. Roads were bad and travel slow. The railroad provided an outlet for crops and livestock and Dexter boomed. Soon wheat and other products from neighboring places were brought to the Dexter railroad [station] for shipping. Wagons of wheat were lined up from the Dexter freight house to the Mill Creek Bridge waiting to unload. The mills ran night and day. After the wheat wagons were unloaded, farmers returned to their destinations loaded with freight. Local merchants became merchant princes.[12]

It took only six months to construct the track the next 30 miles to Jackson. The *Detroit Advertiser* announced that cars first reached Jackson on December 30, 1841. When the track finally reached the county seat, the railroad began running regularly and on a schedule:

> *According to the schedule then in use, trains left Jackson at nine o'clock in the morning and reached Detroit about four o'clock in the afternoon. They left Detroit for Jackson at eight in the morning, arriving in Jackson about three o'clock in the afternoon, passing the eastbound train at Ann Arbor. Five cars were hauled from Detroit and from Dexter, but between Dexter and Jackson no more than four were thought necessary.[13]*

At this point, traveling at an average of 12–14 miles an hour, the train ride from Detroit to Jackson took more than five hours. If you were traveling on to Chicago, you had a 24-hour stage ride to St. Joseph and a five-hour steamship voyage from St. Joseph across Lake Michigan still ahead. The state promoted the great efficiency of the route and time saved by claiming the day and a half excursion across the state beat the weeklong trek around the Great Lakes.

The railroad began looking like a viable enterprise, but state revenue shortages made the outlook for continuing state-funded railroad construction seem bleak. Money to pay track construction workers was also becoming increasingly hard to find, and workers were quitting. As early as 1842, the Internal Improvement Warrants, or *state warrants* as workers called them, sunk as low as forty cents to the dollar and the state had no money to back them up. That year one employee wrote to a friend, *I work on the Central Railroad at sixteen dollars a month, but the pay is state warrants which is not worth here more than half in specie* [coin].[14]

Despite these local financial issues, from a national perspective the state was doing better than an adequate job running the railroad. An article from the *American Railroad Journal* provides a national perspective

(1846). The article also gives us insight into the life of an engine named *Dexter.*

> *The engine, which has exceeded all others, is the Dexter, F. Gauriet engineer, exceeding the highest number attained in the previous year, 1,692 miles. Whole number of miles run by this engine is 27,282. We take great pleasure in bearing testimony to the neatness and general good order of the machinery in the hands of the engineers upon the Central road.*[15]

Within a short time, finances forced the IIC to order the work stopped on the Northern Railroad. No track had been laid. Sixty miles of track was in place at the Southern, paid for mostly by the profits earned by the Central, but work there was also stopped. The IIC decided to invest all remaining funds on building the Central Railroad.

With the focus only on the Central, construction picked up and the line reached Marshall in August 1844, Battle Creek on November 25, 1845, and Kalamazoo on February 2, 1846.[16] Here the state ran out of money.

The last village on the CRR line to receive track and depot built by the state was Kalamazoo. The local paper announced the arrival of the first train, reported on the great celebration held by business leaders, and stated that the village's new depot was reportedly *the best in the state.*[17] After reaching Kalamazoo, the state halted all work on the track. *A stage line was organized from there to run to New Buffalo where the passengers would take a steamer for either Chicago or Milwaukee.*[18]

Just like the other villages along the MCRR line, Kalamazoo was profoundly affected by the arrival of the rail line. The exchange of agricultural goods with the outside world allowed interregional trade and the development of civilization in the area. In an 1889 interview a local writer told of the railroad's impact on the village four decades earlier.

> *The year 1846 formed a new era in the growth and prosperity of the village. On the 2d of February, the Central railroad was finished to this place and the influence of this enterprise was at once felt in growth and advancement of business of all kinds. The stage lines run by Davis, Humphrey & Co., had theretofore done a great business eastward, now it was limited to lines south, north and west to Chicago, and the Kalamazoo house was the headquarters.*[19]

Each year, while the state languished in red ink, lawmakers held fast to the hope that when finished, the Central Railroad would provide the revenue to pull the state out of debt. For a short while, their hope was justified. So much business was connected to the 1844 harvest that the Central had its biggest year. Gross proceeds were $211,169 even though it was considered a crop failure year. Because the track was suppose to have been extended more than 40 miles to Kalamazoo during the next year, accountants estimated the gross for 1845 would exceed $275,000 and climb each year thereafter.

The produce harvest was initially abundant enough to allow shipment of the surplus to outside markets. In fact, it was so large the state could barely keep up with demands for shipping. *In the vain attempt to bring forward all the produce, which has been brought to the Central Railroad since the first abundant harvest, 7 locomotives and 96 cars and racks have been running night and day for three months.*[20]

After such progress the year before and a better early harvest in 1845, the state's hopes were high. But as the year progressed, it was apparent that shipping revenues were down and dreams for increased revenue were dashed when profit goals were not met. Facing an increasing need to repair track, replace strap rail with heavy T rail and the Lowell bridge collapse (on the Huron River at Superior Township, Washtenaw County), lawmakers had had enough. Harlow again had an interesting view of this situation.

> *The state had so little money to put into it that as the head crawled forward, the tail was falling apart. It was laid with strap rail, of course, some one-half-inch thick, some three-quarter inch; and the first 30 miles had been based on undersills of oak, elm, anything that was near the right of way, regardless of qualification. It had almost no repairing facilities, few real depots or other buildings, and scanty, ramshackle equipment. It was at the moment about the sorriest looking railroad property.*[21]

It wasn't just the state lawmakers and a few vocal citizens who believed the railway should be put in private hands. Knowledgeable railroad supporters on the national level believed everyone would be better served if it were sold.

> *We perceive that the commissioners consider that a speedy sale of the public works to a company is the only way in which they can be put in a condition to become most useful to the people—thus relieving them from the burden of the public debt, and at the same time increasing their efficiency . . . and the sale should be a liberal one to the companies, in the price and terms of payment, that they may be able, and required to make the roads of the very best character, and to work them at high speed, and low fares and freights in accordance with the spirit of the age.*[22]

It took more than seven years and $2 million dollars to lay 143 miles of track to Kalamazoo. But in 1846, the state had no more money to spend on the Central project and little resolve to push 56 more miles to the terminus at St. Joseph and Lake Michigan. The lack of financial resources, the slow progress on the Central line and tremendous expense sapped the state determination to control its railroading projects. State officials wanted out of the railroading business.

Things were so desperate that the governor stepped in with his own funds.

> The affairs of the Road were in such a strait that it would have stopped entirely, but for the interposition of the Governor [John S.] Barry, who advanced $7,000 in money from his individual means, and became personally responsible for $20,000 more.[23]

The state legislature had discussed cutting losses and getting out of the railroad business for several years before it literally ran out of money. But after work stopped on the Central line, newspaper articles and grumblings of out-of-work track builders brought the state's plight to public light. Prominent citizens too, such as James F. Joy, lawyer from Detroit, wrote letters to the local newspaper editors declaring that the state had no business running a railroad and the state's economy was being ruined with an internal improvement project it could not pay for or complete. The young Auburn & Rochester Railroad superintendent, John Woods Brooks, noticed the letters and decided to travel to Michigan and see the Central Railroad.

On January 6, 1845, in a speech to the state senate, Governor Barry brought up the issue of selling the Central Railroad.

> The sale of the public works . . . has been long a favorite measure with a portion of our citizens and so favorably was it considered at one time, that the Legislature passed an act authorizing proposals to be received for their purchase. Another considerable portion of our fellow citizens, entitled to our confidence and respect, oppose the measure.[24]

The governor was not quite ready to face the political problems that would come with the sale. Finally, a few months later, Judge George E. Hand, a state house representative from Detroit, presented a resolution to form a committee to consider the expediency of providing for the sale of the Central. The governor really had little choice but to accept.

It appears that for at least six years and through three governors' terms (Mason, Woodbridge, and Barry), state lawmakers considered selling the Central to private interests, but political pressures prevented it.

John W. Brooks Arrives

James F. Joy, partner in the Detroit law firm of Porter and Joy, and future president of the Michigan Central Railroad (1867–1877) remembered when Brooks arrived in his office looking for assistance with a grand project he wanted to pursue:

> John W. Brooks was then about 27 years old, a man of great energy and ability, of ideas and industry, educated as a civil engineer and at this time was the superintendent of the Syracuse and Rochester railroad. He wanted to engage in some great enterprise. My letters [to the newspapers promoting the sale to private interests] convinced him that the state would never complete the central railroad . . . [It is likely that these letters also gave Brooks the idea that Joy might be willing to help him make that happen.] Brooks already had some assurances from Boston backers and was prepared to organize a company to purchase the road, complete it and operate it. I consented to act with him, drew a charter for the railroad company and was to endeavor to get the legislature to authorize the sale of the road.[25]

About the same time Judge Hand's resolution to sell the Central reached the governor, Brooks, on the behalf of eastern capitalists and with Joy's help, made an offer on the railroad. Years later, Joy recounted the difficulty in obtaining approval of the sale:

> The legislature met in December. The strongest opposition imaginable was aroused against the bill to sell the Central railroad to a chartered company. The opposition was incited by the jealousies of Monroe and the counties on the route of the Southern road and by Port Huron and the friends of the Northern railroad, and it was urged that if the State abandoned the Central to a private company, the others roads would be crippled, neglected and destroyed. It took until about the last day of the session to pass the bill.[26]

Perhaps it was due to Brooks's youth, but Governor Barry was concerned whether the offer was legitimate. He sent two lawmakers east to confirm that the letters of intent from Boston investor John Murray Forbes and associates were authentic, and that the eastern capitalists could generate the funds to complete the project.

The governor quickly determined the proposal was authentic. It was made by some of the wealthiest men in the country who had been looking for promising regional investments since their opportunities in the China trade had ended years earlier. These eastern capitalists believed the new business of railroad building held the most potential for high returns on their money.

It wasn't surprising that Governor Barry would be concerned. Up to that point in time in the young state's history, never had an amount greater than $100,000 of outside money had been brought in to investment for any purpose. These eastern businessmen were promising to bring in $2 million initially and another $6 million for payment of state debt and track repair and construction. Within a couple of years, the annual taxes alone paid by the Central to the state would exceed *the ordinary expenses of the entire State government.*[27] To understate the situation, state government was about to go from near economic failure to relative comfort.

Although the history of Michigan's experience with government-run railroads had been written as a failure, in hindsight, it actually was a successful venture. Before the state sold the Central, it had operated at a small profit. The track was geographically situated in a way that was attractive to investors. The purchase price was a little below what it cost to build, but the other requirements of the charter more than made up the difference. When the payments made over time were considered, the deal could not have been better for the state. After it was sold, the MCRR provided a large, secure, long-term tax base from which to build a state government.

Nine months prior to the sale, the *American Railroad Journal* (February 7, 1846) listed all 88 railroads that existed at that time in the United States. Of these, only six had more track down than the state-owned Central's 123 miles: Western RR of Massachusetts (156); Baltimore & Ohio RR of Maryland (188); Wilmington & Raleigh RR of North Carolina (161); South Carolina RR of South Carolina (136); Central RR of Georgia (190); Georgia RR of Georgia (147).

CHAPTER 3

THE BROOKS REPORT: ASSETS AND SHORTCOMINGS OF THE CENTRAL RAILROAD

In 1845, a year prior to purchasing the road, John W. Brooks traveled the entire line's length taking notes on the assets and shortcomings of the property. From those notes, he prepared an investment report that he used to sell the idea to eastern capitalists lead by John Murray Forbes. That investment report provides the only real data on the condition of the road and what he thought it needed in terms of repairs and construction. A summary of that report, with copious quoting follows.

On September 23, 1846, the new company took control of its property, which included 143 miles of track, 10 passenger depots (six believed built after his inspection), and a freight depot and engine house. The value of the rolling stock was $67,900 with the following breakdown of what Brooks called *furniture now upon the road:* 7 engines, 8 passenger cars, 4 baggage cars, 114 freight cars, and 25 repairing cars.

The first physical description of the road given in his report deals with the superstructure, or the material and method of laying track to support rolling stock (engines and cars). It is difficult to believe that this superstructure would support anything of substantial weight.

> The superstructure of the road, on the first thirty miles from Detroit, west, is composed of undersills, rough-hewed upon two parallel sides from trees of elm, oak, or any other kind that were nearest at hand, without regard to fitness or liability to decay; their thickness being about seven or eight inches, with bearings from six to twelve inches, and cross-ties of white oak, placed three feet asunder, and spiked to the undersills, into which are let white oak rails, six by six, or five by seven inches square, well secured by wedges or keys; the whole being supported upon short blocks of wood of different lengths, varying according to the distance between the bottom of the undersills and a firm foundation, such blocks being squared at the ends and firmly set as a foundation upon which the superstructure is placed. The rest of the superstructure of the road to Kalamazoo is substantially the same in its manner of construction, excepting that the block foundation is dispensed with, and . . . the workmanship and materials are much improved as the road progresses westward. On the first thirty miles out of Detroit, the superstructure is old and much decayed, having never been renewed, except by such repairs as were absolutely necessary to keep the road in operation; and the iron, which is only ½ by 2 ¼ inches, is practically worn out and very much broken; the next twenty miles has the same sized iron and is very much worn, through somewhat less than the first thirty miles.
>
> The balance of the track to Jackson is ironed with bars of the same size, and were the business of the road such, that iron of that size might be considered suitable, the superstructure would last, without extensive repairs, from two to three years longer. The remainder of the road to Kalamazoo, a distance of sixty-seven miles, is ironed principally with a bar ¾ by 2 ½ inches, and the superstructure is in good order.

Brooks's training and experience as a railroad builder in New York and Maine gave him the wherewithal to compile a thorough estimate of building costs as a selling point for investors. His estimates are detailed and interesting. For example, the estimated cost of one mile of this superstructure is broken down like this:

94+ tons of H rail, weighing 60 lbs. per yard, at $90 per ton, delivered in Michigan	*$8,486*
4,500 lbs. spikes, at 5 ½ cents	*$248*
Joint fixtures, at 50 cents per joint	*$260*
2,500 white oak ties, six inches thick, seven inches bearing, and nine feet long, at 14 cents each	*$350*
Distributing and laying track	*$406*
TOTAL	*$9,750*

At that rate, the 135 miles of superstructure, new and repaired, from Detroit to St. Joseph would cost $1,316,250. Land, equipment and depots would add another $20,000 per mile.

Brooks reported that instead of using cuts and fills to level the road, the state employed *useless bridging of a cheap and perishable nature . . . in place of fills. Just as troubling was the need to raise twenty-one miles of the roadbed between Detroit and Kalamazoo. The sections of track in question were setting on wet material directly on the ground and were constantly under . . . the influence of the clay.*

Not to worry, he told investors, *in all such cases material of a kind easy to be removed is at hand.* He reported that half the dry material needed for the job was within 3 miles of the low spots *and the average haul of the balance not over one mile.* This dry material (sandy loam), he noted, was . . . *very easy to be removed, and quite suitable for a road-bed there, where the frosts of winter are not very severe.* The last phrase indicates that he probably had not spent a winter in Michigan.

The estimated cost of filling up the unstable, dry bridges, reworking these fills between Detroit and Marshall and raising the 21 miles of wet roadbed by 18 inches was calculated at $28,000. Although details were not provided, improvements on the line in the valley of the Huron River were estimated at $18,000.

Buildings for the accommodation of railroad business and protection of property were also *very deficient.* At the time Brooks and his associates took over the line, only 10 depots existed, and Detroit only had a small freight depot and an enginehouse. Worse, the Detroit freight depot was a half-mile from the store houses on the river and the railroad had to pay *a heavy charge for carting as well as for storage or wharfage in its transition from the railroad to the vessels upon the river.* The cost of grading one mile of road to the river and purchasing the right of way to correct the problem was given at $18,000. The necessary passenger and freight depots, with car houses, wharves and lands would cost $75,000, and the estimate to build that huge engine roundhouse we see in old riverfront photographs and nearby the repair shops was set at $45,000. The total for the old riverfront setup was $138,000.

The location of the four depots mentioned in the report has never been given, but a search of local histories along the line gives us some clues. Recorded accounts place these four depots at Detroit (southwest corner of Michigan and Woodward), Ypsilanti, Dexter, and Grass Lake. Brooks was aware of the need for more depots so he added a budget line that said, *Other depots between Detroit and Kalamazoo, including enlargement of water houses, wells, etc., wood houses and other fixtures—$25,000.*

Brooks's estimated budget also called for money to build a Central Station for dealing with rolling stock, but the location was not mentioned. We now know the location to be at Marshall. That location would have a car house, engine house, machine shop, machinery, smith's shop and tools, wood shop, and other fixtures at a cost of $27,600.

On the plus side, Brooks reported that the general width of the cuts and embankments *compare well with most well constructed roads.* And with the exception of the Huron River Valley stretch from Ann Arbor to Dexter, the road was straight and the *curves quite gentle.* Later in the report he noted that 115 of the 145 miles were straight and only one mile of curve had a radius of less than 1,000 feet.

Another positive characteristic of the road was that only five miles of roadway had the steepest grades of 30 feet to the mile, and those descended eastward making them *favourable to the heavier freighting business of the line.* More than half the road was virtually level with grades under 10 feet per mile.

Brooks found no need to be concerned about bridging waterways until looking beyond Kalamazoo. Apparently the eight bridge crossings on the Huron River between Ann Arbor and Dexter were built well enough by the state that they were not worthy of mention in his report.

> *Excepting at St. Joseph . . . there is hardly a bridge required of any magnitude upon the whole line. Should a bridge be built at that place it would be short and could be a pile bridge, there being no stone in the vicinity. It would not be expensive. Crossing the St. Joseph River, unless the bridge was about fifteen feet above the water, would involve the necessity of a draw bridge, as that river is navigable.*

The pro and con section of his report ends here with a couple of statements about building and operational costs. He states that the cost of the right of way thus far averaged $15 per acre, and the future cost to Lake Michigan would likely be less as that section is still is a wilderness. He also points out the hardwood fuel was purchased along the line *from 75 cents to $1 per cord . . .* [but] *it could probably be purchased with cash at an average price of 75 cents.* At the time of his report, the state was paying workers and service providers with state warrants instead of cash.

In summary, *the cost of completing the road from Detroit River to St. Joseph, and placing a T rail of 60 lbs. weight to the yard on all the line, excepting the sixty-six miles of new heavy plate track between Jackson and Kalamazoo, including furniture* [rolling stock] *and every fixture ready for operating the road, the sum of $2,050,000 is needed.* With the addition of the $2 million the investors paid for the road, they also had to be willing to pay the cost of putting the road in operating condition.

The next topic reviewed in the report was the merits of changing the western terminus of the road from St. Joseph to New Buffalo. Brooks pointed out that the question *had not been raised by the state authorities of Michigan.* Although the changes would extend the route by 22 miles, he promoted the idea because it would shorten the water route to Chicago and move the rail line closer to the city.

> *The route via New Buffalo has twenty-two miles more railroad and twenty-eight miles less staging for the winter season, than that via St. Joseph, which amounts to a saving in time of from four to six hours. This savings of time does not appear to compensate but for a small part of the expense of twenty-two miles of railroad; but in the event of the construction of a railroad round the head of Lake Michigan to Chicago and the west, the distance between Detroit and Chicago by railroad would be shortened about six miles, having the present western terminus at New Buffalo.*

Brooks stated that the most important argument for terminating at New Buffalo had to do with produce marketing. By not building the road into St. Joseph, he could cross the St. Joseph River *25 to 40 miles above its mouth, by which means the produce going down the 150 miles of the navigable waters of that river would find a means of getting to market without being obliged to follow the river down to its mouth . . .* and fighting competition for the produce from lake route traffic.

Cutting lake competition for produce from some of the best counties in the state, shortening the time it takes passengers and freight to arrive in Chicago and preparing for a future rail line push to Chicago were three good reasons for contemplating a change of location for the western terminus. However, Brooks casually mentioned one more reason for the adjustment that just might have been a disguised primary factor. *The accommodation* [change from St. Joseph to New Buffalo as the terminus] *rendered . . . by this route would do away with the necessity of continuing the Southern Railroad much farther into the interior.* With this one, short paragraph, Brooks planted a seed that would germinate into a virtual rail business monopoly for the MCRR in southern Michigan.

The final section of the report focused on estimated revenue. How would the company make money? Brooks relied on the state's record of receipts for previous years to show earning potential.

By using the state receipts from 1844, Brooks concluded that on average 85 miles of road generated $206,867 in receipts for passengers and freight—excluding U.S. mail revenue. Perhaps U.S. mail contracts were too unreliable to include in his pitch to investors. This receipt/mile computation showed revenue generated at a rate of $2,433.73 per mile. When the formula was taken to the next step, Brooks used it to declare that when the line is finished to New Buffalo, the 200 miles of line would generate $486,746.

The primary stream of freight revenue for the railroad was the transportation of wheat. It generated 57 percent of the receipts in 1844, and Brooks estimated that it and other rates would increase if prices were reduced from 25 to 33 percent. A barrel of flour shipped in 1844 from Washtenaw County cost the farmer 22 cents. Shipping from the Kalamazoo, the western terminus, cost 55 cents due to the added distance. The 6 to 9 cents in savings from Washtenaw would *bring many articles in large quantities over the road, which are now transported by teams 40 miles to Detroit . . . from mills within sight of the railroad.* Brooks gave freight receipt estimates $346,602.

Using his formula again, he explained that passenger receipts for 1845 with 109 miles of track were $89,128.03 or $817.69 per mile. Looking ahead a year, with 200 miles of track anticipated, receipts could run to $163,538. Brooks concluded the issue of potential passenger and freight receipts by saying, *This view of the matter shows as receipts for the domestic business of the road the sum of $510,140.32.*

Brooks's report next focused on steamboat line income. His research concluded that in 1845 more than 950,000 people traveled west from Buffalo and nearly that many came east from the primary port of departure, Chicago. *The cabin fare between these two places was then $12, and the steerage fare $6.*

He estimated that once the railroad line was completed to New Buffalo the total price of train travel from Detroit would be $6 and on to Chicago by steamboat would cost 75 cents. Even though this proposal was still more than average steerage price, Brooks stated that time saved should shift business to the company.

> *Ordinary passage between Detroit and Chicago by the steam-boats, making no allowance for boisterous weather, which is frequently the cause of serious detention, is three and a half days, and by rail-road and steam-boat, the time would not exceed 15 hours. . . . It is difficult to devise a reason capable of acting as a sufficient inducement to travelers, either upon business or pleasure, to go around through the lakes after the road is completed. . . . Passengers going by the boats would lose, say 2 ¾ days, which for cabin passengers, could not be valued at less than $2 per day, thus involving a loss in time to the value of $5.50.*

Further, Brooks recommended reducing the train travel ticket from $6 to $4.50 as an inducement to those steerage passengers. Those passengers could be placed on a second-class car saving them money and time.

With the inducement of saving time and money, the report estimated that one-third of the passengers traveling west (30,000) would be traveling first class and be willing to pay the railroad $6 for a ticket and save nearly three days traveling. Another one-third would be steerage passengers who would gladly save money and time and pay $4.50 for a ticket west. The total receipts for the 60,000 passengers lured from lake travel is estimated at $300,000 per year.

The Brooks Report then moved from luring passengers off steamships to luring them onto steamships—Michigan Central Railroad steamships.

> *It is not easy to see why steamboats running in direct connection with this railroad would not yield a better revenue than boats working under ordinary circumstances upon the lakes . . . as the public would naturally expect the boats of the company to connect more certainly with their cars, than the boats of other lines. [Should two boats be built] . . . I shall not . . . estimate the net receipts as great even as on many of the boats now in use upon these waters. I will be perfectly safe to put the net receipts . . . at $25,000 each per annum.*

Next Brooks outlined the final operating cost issue for the investors. He estimates the wood to run the locomotives will cost about 6 cents per mile and estimates operating miles for one year at 420,000. Thus, wood could cost a quarter of a million dollars a year to feed the wood burning locomotives.

As the document nears the end, Brooks sums up the report.

It will be seen, from the foregoing estimates, that the domestic or local business of the road will pay the whole expense of operating it, and nearly 7 percent on its entire cost, and this in a new country, just beginning to develop those resources for revenue, which are now steadily increasing at the rate of eight percent per annum. If the population increases at this rate now, it certainly is fair to presume, that after the Central Railroad is completed and in efficient operation this increase would be continued, and possibly in a greater ration.

CHAPTER 4

THE MICHIGAN CENTRAL RAILROAD CHARTER

S ome controversy still surrounds the identity of who actually wrote the Michigan Central charter. The possibilities are numerous. Several Michigan histories state that *a charter for the Michigan Central Railroad was drawn up by Judge Hand.*[1] As a state lawmaker, Hand was instrumental in getting his fellow legislators to approve the document. But a former MCRR president disputed the claim that the judge drew up the charter.

In an 1892 interview, Joy claimed that when Brooks approached him about buying the railroad, *I consented to act with him, drew a charter for the railroad company and was to endeavor to get the legislature to authorize the sale.*[2] Of course Joy was there and he should know, but a third claim also seems to have veracity.

Henry Pearson, author of a John M. Forbes biography, stated that Forbes employed *Daniel Webster to draft a charter embodying the wisdom that had been gleaned from Eastern railroad experience, and to send Brooks back to Michigan to secure the passage of the charter.*[3] The New York Central Railroad concurred with Pearson and believed Forbes hired his friend Webster to write the charter and printed the Webster theory in a company booklet celebrating the MCRR's 100th birthday in 1946.[4] The actual author of the charter has not been determined, but it seems likely that several people contributed to its development.

Regardless of who was involved, the charter was the golden key that unlocked riches for both the state of Michigan and the eastern capitalists. It provided the assurances both entities needed to allow them to continue with the deal. In the interest of brevity the 30-page charter is summarized as follows:

Section 1. The charter begins by outlining the company's powers, which essentially guaranteed that they would be capable of completing the task of building the railroad to Lake Michigan. They *shall be capable in law of taking, purchasing, holding, leasing, selling and conveying estates and property . . .* as long as it was for the purpose of completing the railroad as required. They may also *exercise all powers, rights, privileges and immunities, which are or may be necessary to carry into effect the purposes and object of this act.*

Burned by wildcat banking scandals, the state made it clear that the new MCRR would not enjoy some of the benefits afforded to its predecessor, the Detroit & St. Joseph Railroad. A clause in the charter says that the nothing in the act may be construed to authorize the company to *carry on the business of banking, brokerage, or any other business except what properly belongs to a railroad.*

Section 2. For six months the company had right to purchase *all right, title and interest on the state in and to the Central Railroad, and all its appurtenances, including all machine shops and other buildings, and stock and materials upon said road, of whatever name or kind, and all lands or rights of way which the state has or may have acquired in connection with the said railroad . . . for the sum of two millions of dollars; of which the sum of five hundred thousand dollars should be paid . . . to the State Treasurer, within six months after the passage of this act.*

As mentioned earlier, while the state appeared to drive a hard bargain, the charter shows differently. Further into Section 2 a break for the MCRR appears: *. . . part of the said sum of five hundred thousand dollars, shall be paid in money or in the coupons of the bonds designated in section four of this act.* Forbes, his wealthy friends, and their bankers back east all had access to these bonds that were earning no interest for years. Anyone could buy the bonds from their owners for huge discounts—as much as 30 percent. So, instead of owing the state $500,000, the MCRR could pay $350,000 or less to meet the bill.

A second payment was due *within one year from the payment of the said five hundred thousand dollars, the said company shall pay to the state the further sum of one million and five hundred thousand dollars, with interest on same, at a rate of six percent.*

Section 3. This section outlines the stiff penalties imposed if the MCRR misses the first or second payment. The Michigan Central Railroad would *immediately be and become dissolved.* The *process of dispossession* would be handled by the state supreme court should repossession of the railroad become necessary.

Section 4. This section has less to do with the MCRR and more to do with the lawmakers wanting to ensure that the payments made by the company would be faithfully applied to the state's debt. It outlines which bonds and how much back interest would be paid to creditors.

Section 5. This is one of the more interesting sections. It gave the MCRR the *full power and authority to locate, and from time to time to alter, change and re-locate, construct and re-construct, and fully to finish, perfect and maintain a rail-road with one or more tracks.* A stipulation to this power was that they had to follow the original general route of their predecessor and must *pass through the villages or towns of Ypsilanti, Ann Arbor, Dexter, Jackson, Marshall, Battle Creek, Kalamazoo to some point on Lake Michigan, which shall be accessible to steamboats navigating said lake.* The width of the roadbed was established as *not exceeding one hundred and fifty feet, through the entire line . . . and make take, have and appropriate to their use all such lands so designated for the line . . . upon first paying or tendering . . . damage as shall have been settled by appraisal.*

In addition to setting the width of the road, the additional width of two hundred feet was authorized for constructing depots and shops. Permission was also given for the company to *take and appropriate as much more of land as may be necessary for the proper construction and security of said road . . . and for the obtaining of stone, sand and gravel.*

In addition to providing all the authorizations and removing any hindrance necessary to ensure that the railroad would be completed, competition against the MCRR was also limited. No eastern or southern railroad could be built within five miles of the line west of Wayne County without MCRR consent. No railroad could *commence within twenty miles of the city of Detroit or run within twenty miles of the main line of said Michigan Central Railroad.* This section also made it illegal to build any public road, private road, canal or railroad that would *unnecessarily . . . obstruct the Michigan Central Railroad.* Further, the city of Detroit was to provide right of way on public streets without charge.

Section 6. This section authorized the company to enter into state land to survey, appropriate land for building the road, cut timber, and otherwise clear the right of way as needed to complete or repair the road. Further, the company was directed to make, repair, maintain and alter any fences and *keep in repair any piers, arches or other work in and upon and across any rivers or brooks, for making, using or maintaining the said railroad.*

Section 7. This section gave the company the right to receive donations of lands and rights of way, which one might rightly conclude could influence the route of the railroad or location of depots. It also outlined the lengthy procedure to be used when citizens disagreed with prices paid for land *appropriated* for railroad use.

Section 8. This section addressed railroad crossings and requires the company to build crossings in a manner so *as not to unnecessarily impede the passage of persons or property along the same.*

Section 9. This section specifies the penalty for not providing *wagon way* crossings and keeping same in repair. Those persons damaged may demand a jury trial to seek restitution.

Section 10. To ensure that the railroad would be built as soon as possible and not be hindered by the need to cross other railroads, canals, dam or bridge, the state made it legal for the company to contract with the owner for permission to cross. The company could *vest* with the said company, thereby allowing that company to enjoy the same rights and privileges as the railroad.

Section 11. This section gave the company the authority to purchase *all machines, wagons, carriages or vehicles of any description, which they may deem necessary and proper for the purposes of transportation on said railroad.* It also gave the company the authority to establish rates for transportation and made it unlawful for others to transport anything on the railroad without license or permission of the railroad. It also stated that all improvements, works, profits, machinery, and all buildings shall be vested in the company forever and all capital stock of the company would be considered personal property.

Section 12. This section gave the company the power to regulate the time and manner in which goods and passengers would be transported as well as collecting tolls on transportation and storage.

Section 13. This section gave the company the authority to cross any stream or road lying on the route. However, the company was required to *restore the stream of water . . . or road thus intersected to its former state, or in a sufficient manner not unnecessarily to impair its usefulness.*

Section 14. This section provided authorization to make dividends of profits.

Section 15. This section authorized the company to *fix, regulate and receive the tolls and charges taken for transportation of property and persons on said railroad . . .* while at the same time fixing rates for certain products to a percentage of the rates charged when the state owned the railroad. The company was put at a disadvantage with a provision placing a state officer on a committee to help determine fair rates based on average prices charged on *New England Roads.* Under this provision, rates were to be reviewed after 10 years. Imagine a company today being forced by the state to not change their prices for 10 years. The last part of this section states that the U.S. military equipment and men would take *priority and precedence . . .* over all other traffic.

Section 16. This section authorized the company to charge and collect for storage of goods left in its buildings for more than four days, provided they contact the owner 24 hours before charges begin. Charging otherwise would result in a $50 fine by the state.

Section 17. This section gave the railroad the right to *own, charter or hire, and to employ and use, in the navigation of the lakes and rivers . . . boats or vessels . . . not to exceed eight in number, for the transportation of and carriage of persons and property.*

Section 18. This section gave Detroit the authority to *lay down or construct a track . . . along the streets in front of and near the Detroit river, for the purpose of conveying property* [freight] *to and from said railroad.*

Section 19. This section required the railroad to complete the road to Lake Michigan in three years. Furthermore, it stipulated that the road between Kalamazoo and the lake would be constructed of iron rail with a weight of *not less than sixty pounds to the yard.* The state attached a penalty of $25,000 per year *. . . for each and every year thereafter . . .* that the job was not completed in that time.

Section 20. This section mirrors the preceding stipulation, but focuses on the first 50 miles of road west of Detroit. The road must receive 60-pound rail within two years or the company would face a $50,000 per year fine. The state allowed that if the United States went to war with *any European power . . .* the calendar count would stop for the duration.

Section 21. This section required the company to keep the road open for public use *thenceforth and ever afterward, save on the first day of the week.* So, initially the MCRR was not required to run on Sunday. The company was also forbidden to *engage in the business of purchasing, for sale, produce or any other merchandise or commodity . . . and shall always keep and have upon the said road a supply of motive power, and cars, both for persons and property, sufficient for the expeditious and convenient transaction of all business.*

Section 22. This section set the limit for corporate stock at $5 million with *the privilege of increasing the same to eight million dollars, to be divided into shares of one hundred dollars each.*

Section 23. This section stated that the nine persons first named in the first section of this act shall be the first directors of said Michigan Central Railroad Company, and at their first meeting, they would elect by ballot one of their number to be president. *The notice of the meeting had to be published daily in any newspaper printed in Boston, New York, or Detroit, fifteen days next preceding the time for such meeting.*

Section 24. This section outlined the procedures for receiving subscriptions for capital stock. An interesting provision called for the books to be opened in the city of Detroit *as soon as books are opened elsewhere, for subscription by citizens of Michigan* . . . so that state residents would have an opportunity to share in profits of the railroad. At least $300,000 in stock, or 6 percent, was required to be set aside for that purpose.

Section 25. This section outlined required procedures for the annual election of the president and directors, with requirement that both positions be citizens of the United States and be stockholders of the company.

Section 26. This section specified if, for some reason, an election was not held on the chosen day, those in office would continue to hold office until the election was held.

Section 27. This section specified that the annual meeting of stockholders would be given with 30 days notice and such notice would appear in two newspapers published in Detroit.

Section 28. During such annual stockholders meetings it would be the duty of the president and directors in office for the preceding year, to exhibit a clear and distinct statement of company affairs. During these meetings, a majority in value of all the stockholders could remove any president or any of the directors and elect another in their stead.

Section 29. This section provided for the surrender and sale at auction of any stocks held by a delinquent stockholder who refused to pay whatever sums subscribed to the capital stock, when called upon by the president or treasurer with 30 days notice.

Section 30. This section gave the president and directors the power to hire and fire employees and determine compensation of all such officers, engineers, agents and servants, and write by-laws provided those by-laws were not contrary to the constitution or laws of the United States or Michigan.

Section 31. This section stated that the directors would have full powers to conduct the business affairs of the company according to the acts and company by-laws.

Section 32. This section required that directors shall annually, on or before the twenty-fifth day of January, make a report to the secretary of state, which shall embrace the business of the preceding year stating the length of road; operation cost of construction and company indebtedness; receipts from freight and passengers; expenditures for repairs of the road; repair to engines and cars; the number of engines, passengers, freight, and other cars; average number of men employed; the number of miles run by passenger, freight, and other trains.

Section 33. This section specified that the company would pay to the state an annual tax of one half of 1 percent, upon the capital stock paid in, including the $2 million of purchase money, until the February 1, 1851, and thereafter an annual tax of three fourths of 1 percent, paid in the last week in January each year. In consideration thereof, the company would be exempt from all and every other tax, charge and exaction by any laws in the state.

Section 34. The section specified that the state shall have a lien upon the railroad and all appurtenances and stock for all penalties, taxes, and dues that may accrue to the state and that such a lien shall take precedence against all other claims.

Section 35. The section states that anyone doing harm to any railroad building, construction work, engine, machine, or structure, or doing anything to stop obstruct, impair, weaken, injure, or destroy any person or work on the railroad shall be guilty of a misdemeanor and face fine or imprisonment not exceeding five years or both.

Section 36. This section specified that the state may, at any time after January 1, 1867, purchase and take back the railroad and all appurtenances, in which case the state shall pay the value of the stock plus 10 percent.

Section 37. If the state does repurchase the railroad, all lands and property will also revert to state control, regardless of whether the land was gifted, conveyed, granted, or purchased.

Section 38. This section stated that the railroad must, at all times, if required by the U.S. Post Office, transport the U.S. mail, as often as their cars shall pass thereon, not exceeding twice in each day, for such compensation as agreed upon. Nothing in this act shall be construed to mean that the company has to wait at any office for the change in mail.

Section 39. This section specified that the state reserved the right, at any time after 30 years from the passage of this act, to amend or repeal it. Should this happen, the company would be compensated by the state for all damages sustained by such alteration, amendment, or repeal.

Section 40. This section simply states that the act shall take effect and be in force from and after its passage. (The new charter was formally approved by the state on March 28, 1846.)

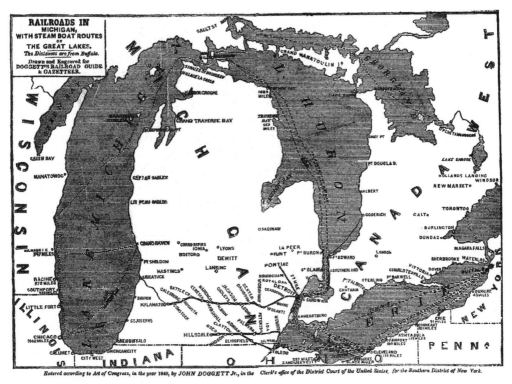

An early map shows the completion of the Central Railroad to Kalamazoo, c. 1848. (Courtesy Library of Congress)

CHAPTER 5

THE NEW ENGLAND CAPITALISTS

With a new charter and Brooks's printed report on the condition of the road in hand, Forbes and Brooks began to collect the $500,000 from those who provisionally agreed to come into the Michigan wilderness railroad construction project that was due to be paid to the state by September 1846. All but two of the original 26 men agreed to come on board. These two men, whose names do appear on that initial charter and are frequently listed as part of the *New England investors* who bought the Central, apparently declined to commit funds after the deal was struck. They were Andrew Duncan, co-owner of New York's accounting house of Duncan, Sherman & Company who became mentor to John Pierpont Morgan, and William Sturgis, a Boston merchant capitalist in the China trading firm of Bryant and Sturgis.[1]

Another wealthy Forbes business partner, John C. Green, replaced the two who withdrew, but his name doesn't appear on the initial charter given to the state because he came in after the deal was approved. The charter did allow the new company to add corporators as desired and once the charter was approved, many other wealthy friends, acquaintances, relatives, and business associates of Forbes joined the investment group.

Michigan was fortunate that Forbes took charge of locating investors for the new company. It could easily be argued that a finer caliber of capitalists could not be found anywhere in the country in 1846. This group included captains of industry, international merchants, mayors, senators, congressmen, and philanthropic heirs to fortunes. Books have been written about several of these interesting fellows. Yet read any existing previously written account of the MCRR and one will only see the phrase "eastern capitalists" or "Boston capitalists" with little or no explanation of who these men were. Omitting this information does not tell us they were from six different states, and not knowing a little history about them deprives us of understanding what influences shaped the mighty Michigan Central.

The following information tells who the men were at the time of purchasing the MCRR in September 1846. Many went on to even greater accomplishments later in their careers and lives.

John Woods Brooks (1819–1881) was born in Stow, Massachusetts. He apprenticed before becoming an engineer on the Boston & Maine Railroad in 1839. By age 24, he was the superintendent for New York's Auburn & Rochester Railroad (1843–45). In 1845, then at 27 years of age and the youngest of the original charter group, he convinced eastern capitalists to purchase the wilderness railroad.

John Carter Brown (1797–1874) was from Providence, Rhode Island. He was the philanthropist son of Nicholas Brown, after whom Brown University was named, and was heir to his father's vast cotton company holdings in the Brown & Ives Company.

John Bryant (1770–1865) was from Boston, Massachusetts. He was a wealthy merchant capitalist in the China trading firm of Bryant and Sturgis.

Cyrus Butler (1767–1849) was from Providence, Rhode Island. He inherited a fortune from his ship-owner father, expanded that wealth through shipping, and became a millionaire philanthropist.

Erastus Corning (1794–1872) was from Connecticut but moved to New York and became a merchant after inheriting his uncle's hardware company. He soon acquired the Albany Iron Works, which at the time was one of the largest industrial establishments in the country. After successes in banking and politics (he was the mayor of Albany), he focused on railroad development, which later culminated in the formation of the New York Central Railroad.

John Perkins Cushing (1787–1862) was from Boston, Massachusetts, and was part of the China trade merchant group of Boston. He was cousin to merchant prince Thomas Handasyd Perkins and also related to John Murray Forbes.

John Murray Forbes (1813–1898) was born in France while his father was on a trading mission, but lived in Boston, Massachusetts. He was the nephew of China trade merchant prince Thomas Handasyd Perkins. John joined the trading firm in 1828, invested his money in land, iron and railroads, and was a wealthy philanthropist by 1840. Trust in him brought investors to the Michigan Central Railroad Company.

Robert Bennet Forbes (1804–1889) was from Boston, Massachusetts. He was ship captain and brother of John Forbes. He worked for his uncle, Thomas Handasyd Perkins, in the China trade firm and partnered in many business ventures with his brother.

George Griswold (1777–1859) was from Connecticut and moved to New York when young. He and his brother, Nathaniel, built one of the largest merchant shipping firms and counting houses in New York and became wealthy in the China trade. He was also the father-in-law of John C. Green, another MCRR initial investor.

Moses B. Ives (1794–1857) was from Providence, Rhode Island. He was the elder son of Thomas P. Ives, who was the co-owner of Brown and Ives Company. Moses was a junior partner in the cotton holdings firm.

Robert H. Ives (1798–1875) was from Providence, Rhode Island. He was the brother of Moses and younger son of Thomas P. Ives.

Edward King (1794–1873) was a lawyer Philadelphia, Pennsylvania, who was an eminent judge known for establishing a system of equity in state law.

Rufus H. King (1784–1867) was originally from Connecticut. He moved to Albany and was a businessman, banker, and state senator.

Gerrit Y. Lansing (1783–1862) was from New York. He became a New York State court judge, a U.S. representative, and a University of the State of New York regent, where he became acquainted with Erastus Corning in 1826.

James K. Mills (1799–1863) was from the Boston area. He was owner of a cotton goods wholesale house named James K. Mills & Company, which controlled seven of the largest cotton mills in New England.

Captain David A. Neal (1793–1862) was a ship owner and sea captain involved in the China trade. He became an investment capitalist from Salem, Massachusetts, specializing in railroad financing and operations.

Thomas Handasyd Perkins (1764–1854) was from Boston. He was a merchant capitalist of China trade fame who was John M. Forbes's uncle and surrogate father. At 82 years of age, he was the oldest investor and known as Boston's greatest philanthropist.

Thomas Handasyd Perkins Jr. (1796–1850) of Boston was the son of Thomas H. Perkins, who became wealthy from the China trade.

Dudley L. Pickman (1779–1846) was from Massachusetts. He was a state representative and a state senator. He died just months after the MCRR purchase.

Josiah Quincy Jr. (1802–1882) was a lawyer, author, mayor of Boston (1823–1828), and president of Harvard University (1829–1845).

Marcus Tullius Reynolds (1788–1864) was Boston's most powerful lawyer. He was also a New York state court judge and U.S. representative.

John Elliot Thayer (1803–1857) was a leading figure in the Boston financial district, owned a banking house and helped establish the Boston Stock Exchange in 1834. His firm raised capital for business and government. He was a distant relative of Forbes and the son of Nathaniel Thayer, a railroad investor and banker who built Harvard's Thayer Hall.

John Townsend (1783–1854) was the mayor of Albany (1829–1831) and owner of Townsend Furnace and Machine Company (foundry). Townsend was also the director of the Mohawk & Hudson Railroad and the president of the National Commercial Bank.

William Fletcher Weld (1800–1881) was from Boston. He was the owner of the William F. Weld & Company, which was the largest firm of ship owners in America at the time. Flying under the Black Horse flag, his ships were the fastest in the world, traveling and trading worldwide.

John Cleve Green (1800–1875) came on board after the charter was issued and the MCRR took control of the railroad, so his name is not on the original list. From New Jersey, he was the great-great grandson of the first Princeton College president. The China trade millionaire was a son-in-law of George Griswold, a MCRR initial investor.

Many of these men were well traveled, most well educated and all highly successful in their business life. Their business practices, morality, personal character, and belief in social responsibility together formed a business ethic that soon made the Michigan Central Railroad the jewel of the industry.

Within a few months of the charter approval, the $500,000 was raised for the first payment, and the company was formed. Forbes invested $200,000 in the company and recalls the day: *About the early days of 1846, having this absurd idea in my head I was led to take an interest, perhaps a tenth, in buying of the State of Michigan its quarter-built road, at seventy cents on the dollar.*[2]

On September 23, 1846, the new company took control of its property. The name of the new firm was the Michigan Central Railroad Company. John Forbes, John Brooks, Erastus Corning, David Neal, and John C. Green were the company's leaders.

CHAPTER 6

THE FIRST YEAR OF MCRR OPERATION

I t is fortunate that the MCRR company charter required full and detailed annual reporting and that company officials took this requirement seriously—at least until the late 1870s. Although locating the annual reports for research may be difficult, in absence of company archives they provide a substantial foundation for a company history. The company was also fortunate to have a stable board of directors over the first 20 years, with only a couple of replacements, resulting in consistent reporting.

The first board of directors included, John M. Forbes of Boston; Robert B. Forbes of Boston; H. H. Hunnewell of Boston; Erastus Corning of Albany; D. D. Williamson of New York; George F. Talman of New York; and Elon Farnsworth of Detroit. For the most part, these men were connected to Forbes through blood or business. The charter required directors to also hold company stock, so these men were also required to become early investors.[1]

Brooks also brought business associates to help him build and operate the new road. Freight agent C. H. Hurd and road master Henry Hopper both came from the Auburn & Rochester Railroad. Reuben N. Rice (secretary to Brooks) came from Massachusetts with F. W. Warren (cashier in the freight department). U. Tracy Howe came from Cincinnati to serve as the local treasurer. Working with a hand-selected team was one of the reasons for Brooks's tremendous success in completing the line in record time.

Other men with insight and experience on the line joined the road-building team. John M. Berrien formerly worked the road under the D&SJRR, the state, and finally the MCRR as construction engineer.[2] Henry's son, George C. Hopper, also worked for the railroad, starting as an office clerk and dock freight handler before he eventually became road master. Fortunately for us, George Hopper provided some memories of the early days through a newspaper interview conducted in the 1890s and some of his thoughts are reflected later in this work.

Another long time MCRR employee, veteran conductor Samuel Skelding, shared his memories of the early days with the company for a 1890s newspaper reporter. Hired prior to the MCRR takeover, he related an unusual story about road master Henry Hopper and a trick he brought from the Auburn & Rochester Railroad. The story of iron strap rail is familiar, but little was known about the MCRR maple strap rail.

> New rails did not come in to replace the flat bars quite as fast as the latter wore out and broke, especially in frosty weather. Mr. Hopper had quantities of maple strips sawed to about the size of the strap rails, and these we fastened to the oak sleepers with eight penny nails. They answered the purpose very well; proved to be quite durable, did not curl up into snake heads and were all right except in rainy weather; then they would warp and split.[3]

Conductor Skelding made a point of mentioning the names of the earliest fellow conductors who worked the road before trains ran after dark. They were, Zenas Tillotson, H. J. Spaulding, Capt. Stone, a Mr. Munger, and a Mr. Wood. He also remembered a few things about operations when Kalamazoo was the end of the line.

> The passenger trains ran through to Kalamazoo. It took 12 hours to make the run from Detroit. The trains stopped at every station. There was no particular time card. "Through by daylight" was the regulation. The meeting and passing points were fixed, subject to variation, because something always occurred to delay or misplace different trains. An allowance of twenty minutes, with five minutes for variation in watches, kept the train for that length of time at the expected meeting place. If the delayed train was not within light or hearing the other set out and always had the benefit of the twenty minutes allowance. Both trains were then "wild."

The first treasurer, George B. Upton, with support of Brooks, the first superintendent, prepared the first annual report given in Detroit in June 1847. Over the next 10 years, Forbes, the first company president, would write an introduction to these annual reports and the company treasurer or the superintendent of the road would write the body of the report.

Before that first meeting of the board, several of the directors, including Forbes and Howe, decided to conduct an inspection of the road. Forbes arrived in Detroit by the steamship *Empire* and started the tour at eight in the morning and arrived in Kalamazoo in the night. He found the road in deplorable condition. He then took a barouche (four-wheeled carriage with two facing double seats) with four horses to St. Joseph and to Michigan City to inspect the harbors. The trip must have been rough as he opted to return by steamship *via the Straits of Mackinaw rather than repeat the journey.*[4]

The first annual report indicates, that under the new management, freight operations started almost immediately on the stretch of road between Detroit and Kalamazoo. Manpower was hard to come by in Michigan at the time, so Brooks likely continued to employ all CRR workers after the MCRR takeover. Available payroll records verify that at least some former CRR men were retained. For example, the Dexter freight agent, E. B. Tyler worked at the CRR depot in 1841 and in 1848, two years after the MCRR takeover.[5] A Jackson County history (1878) states *in 1841, upon the completion of the Michigan Central Railroad to Jackson, Mr. Thompson was appointed freight agent, and continued on the road for a period of ten years.*[6] With these two examples, it appears that at least some men were retained to help keep the line operating.

More men at all levels of skill and experience were hired in anticipation of the great amount of work before the MCRR. The change in ownership also meant a financial inducement to work for the MCRR. Records indicate that when the state was building the road, it paid $16 dollars a month on average with state script worth only half of face value, and the MCRR paid $23 a month in cash. Word spread quickly of the high rate of pay and the challenge of building a road through the wilderness. *About this time there arose a great excitement about the Michigan Central railroad, and everybody with his dog was going there.*[7] Brooks began receiving letters from men seeking employment. For example, nine months after the MCRR took over the road,

Brooks receive a letter from an engineer working for the Hinkley & Drury Locomotive Works. *I am writing to ascertain if you are in want of any more engineers for your road. I have worked for Messers Hinkley & Drury for the last year . . . you have more engines here and . . . one will be finished in a few weeks. If you should think favourable of this I would take an engine on with me when it is finished.*[8]

Brooks continued to receive inquiries about employment throughout the early years, particularly prior to the line being completed to Chicago. One unusual request was for a position of freight agent on the St. Joseph River. *I wish to obtain a situation in your employment. I would prefer the post as freight agent up and down the River, as I suppose you will of course have one on the river. There is a lot of stuff to go down the river this spring and with the proper effort most of it would go over the C. R. Road.*[9]

Another indicator that the MCRR retained most, if not all, of the men on the state CRR payroll, is that operations started immediately after the September 23, 1846, takeover. This could not have been accomplished without experienced men in place. Annual report records show that during the last eight days of September, $9,184 was collected on freight and passengers.

In addition to those eight days, income during the next seven months (reporting ended April 30) totaled $209,300 (freight $146,953; passengers $60,7560; miscellaneous $1,588). The first year's operating expenses totaled $86,169. Expenses were itemized as follows:

Road Repairs	*$21,181*
Building Repairs	*$700*
Shop Repairs	*$215*
Locomotive Repairs	*$13,070*
Car Repairs	*$5,759*
Locomotive Services	*$7,136*
Train Services	*$1,601*
Station Services	*$19,938*
Fuel	*$7,390*
Stationery	*$1,551*
Incidentals	*$750*
Oil	*$4,183*
State Tax	*$2,694*

The 1847 annual report also outlined the steps taken to secure funding to meet the repair, rebuild, and track construction requirements of the charter. Forbes indicated that 22,000 shares of capital stock were subscribed at an estimate of $75 each ($1,650,000) and 7 percent interest had been paid on the first assessment of shares subscribed prior to company start-up.

One of the most startling things in the report was revealed in two paragraphs following the announcement of stock values. It is a familiar bit of MCRR history that $2 million was the purchase price of the road. Therefore, it is not surprising to be further informed that $1,643,106.62 had been paid on account of the railroad purchase by June, 1847, leaving due $356,894. However, it is a little startling to find that MCRR stockholders had already paid the state $1,089,332.46 in cash and in state indebtedness (bonds) toward state indebtedness (as required in Section 4 of the charter). The remaining amount due in cash or state indebtedness was $560,667.

This MCRR receipt, dated April 15, 1847, is for prepayment of shipping fees ($13.20) for 20 barrels of flour from Kalamazoo to Detroit.

These numbers, paid and due, total $3,650,000! It is understood that some of this was paid with discounted bonds, which were selling up to 30 percent below value because the state wasn't paying interest owed on them. Bond owners would sell below face value to anyone who would take them off their hands. If Forbes paid the entire amount in these bonds the total would be $2,555,000. It is apparent that some cash was paid to the State, so the actual total cost of the deal was likely closer to $3 million—not the $2 million figure with which we are all familiar.

The first annual report also mentions something that contradicts other sources claiming that only U.S. funds were used for the railroad. Forbes states that $75,000 in stock was already purchased in Europe and that *arrangements are now making for the purchase in Europe of the balance, or about $250,000,* which will be used toward the purchase price. Consequently, you can still sometimes buy antique, block-printed MCRR stock certificates from sellers in Europe today.

The 1847 report sheds light on another common misconception. The roadway from Kalamazoo to the Antwerp area was graded, but not finished that first year. The report states that rails were not scheduled to *be laid upon this portion of the Road before the close of the next winter.* Thus, there was no new track laid in 1846 or 1847—it was only repaired and replaced.

It also appears that the western terminus location was not yet decided in 1847; at least it was not acknowledged. Forbes stated that, *The surveys from Antwerp to some point on Lake Michigan, are in progress of completion, and a very early determination of the western terminus may be expected . . . by the close of the year 1848.*

Plans for the new riverfront depot in Detroit were outlined for the first time. We do know that the site didn't fully open until 1850, so we can assume that financial or construction problems prevented a prompt completion of the project. One consideration is the project was so large it took that long to purchase materials, find the labor, and to prepare the site.

Finally, Forbes told stockholders in 1847 that contracts were signed to place *upon the Road six passenger and freight engines during the present year* [and build] *an ample supply of passenger and merchandise cars.*

We are lucky to have access to a brief autobiography written by Henry Hall, an employee of the MCRR for 40 years, written after his retirement in 1887. He began working for the MCRR just seven months after Brooks, Forbes, and company took control of the rail-

road. The introduction to Hall's autobiography provides us with another look at operations in the first year.

> *Dexter, Michigan, January 1, 1887*
>
> *I commenced work for the company April 17, 1847, as fireman on a little Baldwin engine, weighing seven tons, eight hundred pounds. She had a frame made of wood, plated with iron, single drivers. The company had six of these; one ten-ton Lowell engine with four drivers, three feet diameter, and two of about fourteen tons, four drivers, I have forgotten the make* [1 Denham & Co and 1 McClung, Wade & Co]. *They had the old style drop hooks and no cut off* [valve to regulate steam] *and wooden cabs. The others had leather cabs that could be rolled up on the sides and front* [weather curtains], *and had two lights of glass* [windows] *forward—one on each side.*
>
> *The small engines run the passenger trains, one daily each way. The western terminus was Kalamazoo. Trains ran into Detroit on what was then called the "Chicago road," now Michigan Avenue, the passengers alighting from the cars, into the street near Woodward Avenue.*
>
> *The engine house was two-story building, standing back of where the new city hall now stands. The machinery for making repairs was one hand lathe with a large band wheel and crank, turned by an old, gray-haired man by the name of Scott.*
>
> *The coaches were of different lengths named after stations on the road. The seats had leather cushions and the backs raised up with a strap across the top to rest the back against.*
>
> *No brakes were used, except the one on the tender. To apply it, we let down a long iron lever outside the tank and stood upon it.*
>
> *Trains were run without time cards; as there was but one passenger train each way, they usually met at one point, but if either one was late, they went on until they did meet: if it was between stations, one backed to the nearest siding to pass. Freight trains ran promiscuously. The two large engines did most of the freighting between Kalamazoo and Marshall. The track was considered unsafe east of Marshall for such heavy engines; the small engines did the work east of Marshall. Sometimes one would go to Ann Arbor and return, sometimes to Jackson and sometimes two or three to Marshall.*
>
> *The engineer was conductor and the fireman was brakeman. When a freight train arrived at a station, the engineer handed the waybills for that place to the agent and the agent unloaded the freight, tended switches, and coupled cars. The cars were four wheeled and carried thirty barrels of flour. An engine would haul from six to eight. There were two men at most of the stations but at some only one. They sawed all of the wood with buck-saws, handled all of the freight, wooded and watered all the engines.*
>
> *There were but four bridges between Ypsilanti and Dexter, two near Ypsilanti, one at Delhi and one near Scio. The road followed the bank of the river all of the way. No night trains were run until the road was completed to New Buffalo.*[10]

Back in those early days the company was especially accommodating to passengers. It had to be because the passengers helped operate the train!

> [W]hen the engineer gave a sudden frantic whistle for brakes, passengers grabbed the nearest wheel and started turning. If a passenger lost his hat, the engineer obligingly stopped the train while he ran back after it, of if a passenger wished to deliver a package . . . to some home along the route, the train would halt while this was done.[11]

These early trains only had three or four cars and the top speed was 12 to 15 miles an hour. It was a while after leaving a station before that speed was reached. It wasn't uncommon for a passenger to miss the departure and be able to run the train down and jump on. One Main Line story from a former MCRR employee provides an illustration about the speed of early trains around Delhi. *My mother told me that the old train through Delhi was so slow she used to jump off to pick some flowers and jump back on.*[12]

These old woodblock prints show how far printing has progressed. This $1,000 stock is dated 1854 and signed by John Brooks and Isaac Livermore.

Newer stocks are plentiful and inexpensive. The orange $5,000 is dated 1896. The blue $10,000 and brown $1,000 are dated 1929.

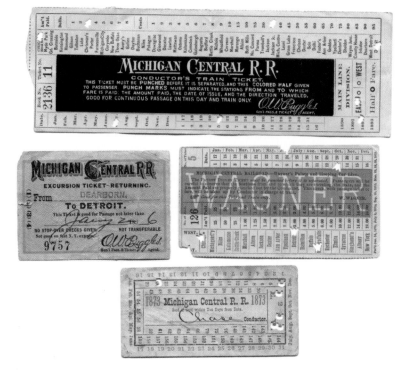

Old MCRR passenger tickets are colorful. The large ticket dates from 1892. The pink ticket is dated 1886. The Wagner Sleeping Car ticket from Chicago to Niagara Falls over the MCRR Main Line and the smaller ticket at the bottom are dated 1873.

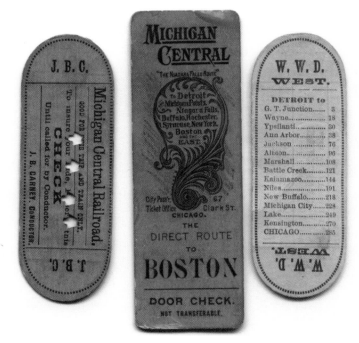

The colorful conductor checks and door check are thought to be from the 1860s and 1870s.

No. F 6268

MICHIGAN CENTRAL
RAILROAD COMPANY.

1000 MILE TICKET
TO BE USED ONLY BY

Mr. *J. M. McVean*

(Whose signature appears on last page).

Only when officially stamped, and when signed by the purchaser.

If Used before *Dec 23* 189*1*

Including transportation of the regulation amount of baggage, and subject to all rules and conditions in regard to baggage transportation and the conditions of this ticket.

THIS TICKET IS NOT TRANSFERABLE.

This ticket will not be accepted for passage on Train No. 19.

O. W. Ruggles

General Passenger and Ticket Agent.

Care should be taken to keep the mileage strip in its original folds within the cover, that it may be more easily handled by Conductor, and not liable to mutilation.

☞ Read all the Conditions and Notices hereon.

Patented June 1st, 1886.

MICHIGAN CENTRAL
RAILROAD.

CONDUCTOR'S TARIFF.

Rates of Fare between

CHICAGO, KENSINGTON
And Intermediate Stations.

		CHICAGO.	22d ST.	HYDE PARK.	GRAND CROSSING.	KENSINGTON.
Chicago	and	...	20	30	40	55
22d Street	"	20	...	20	30	45
Hyde Park	"	30	20	...	20	35
Grand Crossing	"	40	30	20	...	25
Kensington	"	55	45	35	25	...

HENRY C. WENTWORTH,

APRIL 1, 1880. Gen'l Passenger Agent

The 1,000-mile ticket book was purchased in 1891. The conductor's tariff card that was used on the western end of the Main Line is dated 1880.

William Haylow was a telegraph operator at Delhi and his business cards were hand-made and memorable, c. 1875.

Brass switch and door keys are still widely available.

Because the MCRR used so many locks, they are still easily located by collectors. The double lock on the left was made by the Detroit Brass Works in 1867. The steel Adlake model was made after 1900.

Up until 1870 when locomotives changed to coal for fuel, MCRR engineers frequently used brass tokens to pay local providers for wood. This one was from engine 113 for half a cord. They are extremely rare and often counterfeited, c. 1855.

Pressed lead freight car door seals are extremely rare. These date from the late 1840s to the mid-1850s.

MCRR hat badges (c. 1880) are easy to find, but the hats are very rare.

A few lanterns still remain from the old days. Starting on the left is an "Adams" model from the Adams & Westlake Company, 1897, with original tar-like black paint coating. The center lantern is a Dietz model 39 from 1910 and the last lantern is an Adlake (Adams and Westlake merger their name) model 200 from 1908. Earlier models are available but rare and expensive.

These turn-of-the-century kerosene and oil cans are embossed with MCRR.

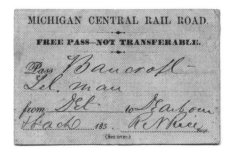 

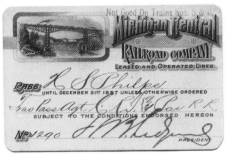 

Early cardstock passes are hard to find and expensive. The printing changed every few years and here are some samples starting in 1856 and ending in 1879.

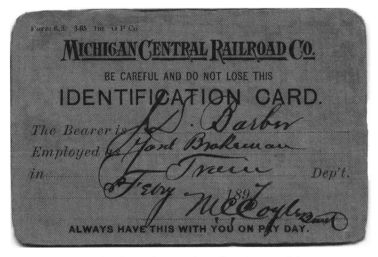

This is a standard employee identification card from 1897.

This set of passes cover styles used from 1892 to 1936. Note that the MCRR name was moved below the NYCRR name in 1936.

MCRR tools are also still around. Here is a depot hatchet with the handle broken off and an open-end wrench. Both are stamped with company initials.

CHAPTER 7

FORBES DRIVES FORWARD

*In year two [1848] new engines began to arrive. First, eight-wheel pas-
senger engines, then ten-wheel freight engines. They were from Hinckley &
Drury's, Boston, with drop hook, independent cut-off, inside connected
passenger engines [with] five-foot drivers; freight [engines had] three and
one-half-foot drivers [diameter of the wheels]; there were no steam gauges
then and we used to hold the safety valve down until they carried steam
enough to haul the train over the hills. I have no doubt they carried at times
two hundred pounds pressure.*

Henry Hall, Dexter, 1887

    The years 1848 and 1849 were filled with facility building, track
construction and rebuilding, and additions to rolling stock. The second annual report shows 16 locomotives, 14 passenger cars, and 268
freight cars were working the line between Detroit and Kalamazoo.
At least ten of these locomotives were purchased from the Boston Locomotive Works in 1848.[1]

June 9	*Herald & tender*	*$7,800*
June 10	*Meteor*	*$7,800*
June 29	*Niagara*	*$8,500*
June 30	*Aetna*	*$8,500*

August 9	*Hecla*	*$8,500*
August 10	*Salamander*	*$8,500*
August 10	*Pioneer*	*$7,500*
August 12	*Rocket*	*$7,500*
September 12	*Vesuvius*	*$8,500*
September 12	*Gazelle*	*$7,800*

Construction was nearing completion on the much-needed Detroit terminal facilities, which now included a new passenger station, freight house, warehouse, machine shop, and engine house. No longer were passengers exiting trains at Woodward Avenue and walking to the river to catch a steamer, and no longer was freight stored outside without means of cartage to and from the riverfront. The new railroad complex at Third Street and the Detroit River were state of the art and reported in newspapers around the world. The *Illustrated London News* made the following report.[2]

MICHIGAN GREAT CENTRAL RAILWAY DEPOT.
The extensive range of buildings presents a specimen of the vast scale upon which railway depots are constructed in the United States. The site of the structures once formed part of the bed of the river Detroit, which has been filled in at a vast expense, and the Depot founded upon piles. It is one of the largest works of its class in the States. Vessels lying at the wharf can directly load and unload from the warehouses, without any cartage.

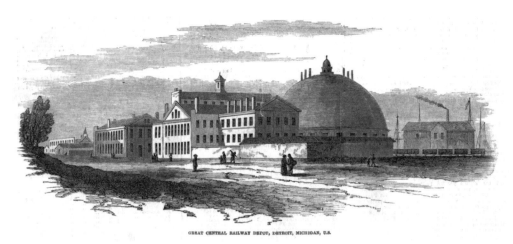

GREAT CENTRAL RAILWAY DEPOT, DETROIT, MICHIGAN, U.S.

Print of the new Detroit depot area from the *Illustrated London News*.

A couple of years later, a Detroiter provided a more detailed description that better illustrates the size of the yard and scope of the operation.

> *They have on these premises upwards of twenty-six hundred feet of dock-front on the river, where vessels can lie in water from twelve to twenty feet deep. They have erected a large Freight Dept, one hundred feet wide, and extending eight hundred feet along the dock, upon the river. This building, in both stories, can store about one hundred thousand barrels of flour. Adjoining that is a Passenger Depot, three hundred and twenty-five feet long and seventy-five feet wide: in one end of which are the Ticket Office, Ladies Room, Baggage Room, & c.: and up stairs, the Superintendent's and Treasurer's Offices, Engineer's Room, & c. Below the Freight Depot, on the river front, are two large two-story warehouses, capable of storing twenty-six thousand barrels of flour. The twenty-two acres are all enclosed by a fence, and have the river on one side for twenty-six hundred feet, and streets upon the other sides. In this enclosure is erected an Engine House, with sixteen stalls for engines. The building is circular, one hundred and thirty feet in diameter, surmounted with a dome eighty-five feet high. Connected with this is a Machine and Blacksmith Shop, one hundred and sixty feet long, sixty feet wide, and two stories high, in which are twenty-three blacksmith's forges, furnished with blast from a fan run by a stationary engine. In the second story of this building, are a large number of lathes, planning machines, work benches, & c., for turning and planning iron, and repairing and fitting up machinery. Adjoining these shops for iron work, is a large shop for building and repairing cars, one hundred and sixty-nine feet long, fifty-five feet wide, and two stories high. In the yard of this company, there is also a Wheat Warehouse, upon the river front, one hundred and twenty feet by sixty, and seventy feet high.*
>
> *This is so arranged as to elevate the wheat from the cards into bins above, and spout it directly into the vessel lying along side the dock, without handling. There are also a Lumber House, a house for storing iron and materials and some smaller buildings. The buildings mostly are of brick and fire-proof from without.[3]*

Brooks, the superintendent and engineer in charge of building the road, was being paid $461.67 a month.[4] His salary equates to roughly $123,000 in today's money. During 1848, he continued to rework the old roadway bringing it up to specifications outlined in the charter and quality levels expected by the directors. That task involved several actions. Straightening out curves in the road, particularly along the Huron River and at Marshall, meant purchasing additional property. Obtaining the property necessary to accommodate the changes at Marshall, for example, cost between $25 and

$75 per lot and less for a right-of-way. Often, land owners did not go willingly along with selling land to the railroad. By law they could not block the progress of the MCRR, but they could appeal the price offered by the railroad. Land owners in the Huron River Valley, near Farmers Station, apparently didn't like the prices offered and appealed to the state.[5] The result was an extra couple of dollars added to the price, which may have been more of a moral victory than a financial one. Satellite photos today still show some places where the original roadbed followed each curve of the river through the Huron River valley from Ann Arbor to Dexter.

After property was purchased, work could then focus on reconstructing old roadbed by raising it off the bare ground with gravel, replacing broken flat rail, preparing the ground for new superstructure and rebuilding bridges to match the new line the track was now taking. Willcox & Colvin had the contract to build new bridges along the Huron River and rebuild the old ones. Brooks spent more than $35,000 for grading, $8,000 for new bridge building, and nearly $14,000 for new superstructure (railroad ties, runners, iron, etc.) in July 1848 alone.[6] Unlike other Michigan strap rail railroads, the MCRR picked up its broken and worn strap rail for resale to iron dealers. That practice makes it nearly impossible today to find older stray pieces of rail along the Main Line, when it is relatively easy to locate along the old Michigan Southern road.

New flat rail was purchased from a variety of bar iron producers and dealers (Wainwright & Laffaw; Brady Bend Iron Co.; C.W. Goddard Co.) in lengths of 15 and 18 feet long for $9.08 per bar. It appears that the first 60-pound "T" rail used for track from Kalamazoo to New Buffalo was purchased from Pennsylvania's Brady Bend firm. All iron was carried to Detroit in brigs, sloops, and steamers with names such as *Gertrude, Kate Howe, West Point,* and *W. A. Cooper.*[7] All ships hauling iron had their cargo insured.

Other new initiatives in year two included selecting Marshall as a rail yard for storing and repairing locomotives and cars. Marshall was approximately in the geographic center of the state, halfway between Detroit and New Buffalo, which was then planned to be the western end of the line.

The directors continued to worry about losing business to steamships carrying freight and passengers from Buffalo and Cleveland to

1849. MICHIGAN CENTRAL RAILROAD COMPANY. 1849.

REGULATIONS

FOR THE

RECEIPT, STORAGE & DELIVERY OF FREIGHT.

AT DETROIT.

The MICHIGAN CENTRAL RAIL ROAD COMPANY will receive at their Depot in Detroit, Freight from the East to be transported over the said Road, which may be consigned to their care, and pay the back charges thereon to Detroit, if delivered at the said Depot,—the account of which will be forwarded with the Freight for collection ; but they will not undertake to settle claims for damages, or matters of disagreement between those interested and the carrier East of Detroit.

Freight which has been transported on the said Road, will be shipped by the Company, if so directed by the written order of the owner or consignor, and if delivered or shipped within twenty-four hours after its arrival at Detroit, no charge will be made except for the transportation. To prevent delay, such order may be endorsed on the Freight bills, which will be transmitted by the respective Freight Agents, or by letter to the Freight Agent at Detroit.

Freight transported as aforesaid, and lying at the said Depot in Detroit more than twenty-four hours, awaiting delivery or shipment, will be charged according to the following

STORAGE RATES.

ARTICLES.		At the beginning of each subsequent week will be added.	Winter storage to the opening of the Lake Navigation.
* Flour, per bbl., within . . . . 4 days,	3 Cts.	1 Ct.	
Corn & other Meal, per 100 lbs., within 4 "	3 "	1 "	8
Wheat & other grains, per 100 lbs. " 14 "	3 "	1 "	
Provisions and Liquors, Lard & Tallow			
per bbl., within . . . . 4 "	5 "	2 "	12
Ashes, per cask, within . . . . 4 "	10 "	2 "	20
Pig Iron, per ton, " . . . . 14 "	25 "	5 "	
Hides, each, "	1½ "	½ "	4
Seeds & Cranberries, per bbl., within 4 "	4 "	1 "	10
Wool, per 100 lbs., within . . . . 4 "	5 "	1 "	10
Lumber, per 1000 ft., b. m., within . . 4 "	37½ "	25 "	
Light & bulky Articles, per B. B., " 4 "	3 "	1 "	6
All other Articles, per 100 lbs., " 4 "	4 "	1 "	10

* Parties who prefer it, by applying at the Freight Office, in Detroit, can have their Flour stored and shipped from the Company's Warehouse, during navigation season, at the uniform charge of one cent per barrel ; such parties would, nevertheless, be charged the regular rates upon such Flour as was held either under their order, or awaiting their order to ship or deliver.

Shipments of property by the Company will be made as far as it is practicable, in the order of its successive arrivals at Detroit, and a copy of the bill of lading of each shipment will be promptly forwarded to the respective owners or consignors, if requested by them.

Transportation and Storage charges on all property to be delivered or shipped at Detroit, must be paid by the owner, or by the master of the vessel receiving the same, before the delivery or shipment.

Storage for property awaiting delivery, will be afforded on the terms mentioned, to the extent of the Company's ability to accommodate ; but should the amount of property received in their Ware-Houses render it inconvenient or impracticable to continue to offer these accommodations, such excess must be promptly taken to other Warehouses : and to prevent delays and embarrassments, owners and consignors generally, who may avail themselves of the facilities offered by the Company for Shipping and Storage, should provide for this contingency, by designating at an early period, the Ware-House in Detroit, to which they prefer the said property shall be delivered.

☞ Arrangements will be made for Winter Storage of Flour and Grain, by special contract.

AT NEW BUFFALO & INTERIOR STATIONS.

Property received at any of the regular Stations West of Detroit, will be forwarded as nearly as is practicable, in the order in which it is received, and without unnecessary delay ; and where the Company have Freight Depots completed, they are ready to receive Freight at such Depots and forward the same without Ware-House charges.

Property offered at any of the said Depots or Stations for transportation on the said Road, must be duly consigned, and the name of the consignee furnished to the Freight Agent at the time when the same is so offered, or it will not be received ; and all property to be transported as aforesaid, should be distinctly and legibly marked, to ensure its safe and prompt delivery.

On property which has been transported, and lying at any of the said Freight Depots of the Company, awaiting delivery, no Ware-

House charges will be made if taken away within FOUR days after its arrival ;—if it remains more than four days, it will become subject to the following

STORAGE RATES.

ARTICLES.	After 4 days and within 11 days.	At the beginning of each subsequent week will be added.
Wheat and other Grains, per 100 lbs., . .	2 Cents.	1 Cent.
Provisions and Liquors, per bbl., ...	6 "	2 "
Pig Iron, per ton, ...	15 "	3 "
Seeds, per bbl., ...	3 "	2 "
Wool, per 100 lbs., ...	5 "	2 "
Lumber, per 1000 ft., ...	25 "	10 "
Light and bulky Articles, per 8 cubic ft.,	2 "	1 "
All other Articles, per 100 lbs., ...	3 "	1 "
Salt and Plaster, per bbl., ...	3 "	1 "

Michigan Central Rail Road Office, }
Detroit, August 1, 1849. }

J. W. BROOKS,

Supt. & Engineer.

Hagg & Harmon, Printers, Detroit.

An early MCRR broadside of regulations for freight related activities, c. 1849.

Detroit and Chicago, so construction started on the company's famous steamship *May Flower*. More about the MCRR and its connection with passenger shipping will follow in Chapter 8.

The MCRR was spending a tremendous amount of money on the railway and needed more capital. The directors authorized another $1.8 million in bonds bearing the high rate of 8 percent. The fact that all bonds were immediately subscribed gives evidence of investor confidence in those running the railroad. The lag time between authorizing bonds and selling them caused a short-term money problem on the line.

> *I was there about one year when the company got behind three months with their pay. The merchants and grocers refused longer credit; the company wanted to pay in scrip due in six months. Grocers and boarding houses refused to take it; and the men struck for their pay—trainmen, shop men and section men—on the whole length of the road. Everything stopped except the mail, which the men carried in a baggage car on time, on the main line and branches. In a few days the president of the road arrived from Boston. He called the men together and said, if the men would go to work, he would commence paying the next week and would keep on as fast as they could, get around until the men were all paid in full. Everything was done according to promise. In about three months, the men were paid in full and I left there and went to Aurora* [Illinois] *to work* [on the Chicago, Burlington & Quincy Railroad].[8]

To further illustrate that money was tight early on, we find that in 1847 Forbes wrote Brooks a letter asking him to *do a favor and approach E. B. Ward,* [the shipbuilder], *and ask him for the money he owes the company. Money is very scarce here and if Capt. Ward will pay us the money on any part of the notes you may allow him 2½% for so doing.*[9]

In 1848 the company decided that they would need to end its line at Chicago instead of Michigan City. Joy was sent to negotiate with the Northern Indiana Railroad for the purchase of its charter. The MCRR wanted to use the charter to cross Indiana and reach the Illinois State line. The asking price was $50,000, but MCRR directors refused to make the purchase as they were not yet convinced of Chicago's importance. The Michigan Southern bought it instead and the race across Indiana to Chicago was on.

Desperate for a means to cross Indiana, Joy then petitioned the Indiana legislature for a charter. As a blocking maneuver, the Southern hired Schuyler Colfax, later to become the vice president of the

United States, to lobby against the MCRR's request. The maneuver worked and a charter was denied. Joy's time in unsuccessfully lobbying the legislature in Indianapolis cost the railroad $5,781.[10]

After Joy left Indianapolis, a small railroad company with an Indiana charter, the New Albany & Salem, contacted the lawyer with a proposal. It offered to let the MCRR use its charter on a perpetual lease for *$599,763*. This time Forbes and company agreed to the purchase with the comment that . . . *he could now easier pay $500,000 than he could have paid the $50,000 when that* [other] *proposal came up.*[11]

Forbes was likely happy to report on progress laying track. The line reached Paw Paw, 16 miles west of Kalamazoo on June 28, 1848, and Niles on October 1, 1848. For some reason, reaching Niles hit the national news. A large portion of a *New York Daily Tribune* front-page newspaper article is reprinted here because it contains a wealth of information about road operations and how the towns along the Main Line felt about the coming of the railroad at the time.

> *Dexter, Mich. Oct. 3, 1848—*
>
> *The road from Kalamazoo to Niles is fifty miles in length, and is as substantial a structure as any in the United States, being laid with the T rail, as is also the greater part of the rest of the road. The special train left Detroit on this occasion at 71/2 o'clock, and was run to Dexter in two hours and five minutes, stopping at Dearborn, Wayne, Ypsilanti and Ann Arbor; this is the first fifty miles of road. Frequently the engineer would suffer the train to run the down grades at the rate of sixty miles to the hour; ay, a mile a minute! The whole distance (200 miles) was run in 8 hours, running time. A band of music mingles with the thousands who greeted the approach of the train. In the evening, the hilarity was heightened by a display of fireworks, rockets, bonfires, a torch-light procession by some of the young Wolverines, kept up till a late hour, and only terminating with a salute of fifty guns from a piece of ordnance.*[12]

Brooks provides interesting figures on the cost of the railroad to date. He estimated that the funds paid out totaled $5,554,633 and another $745,367 was needed to pay outstanding bills, replace the last 16 miles of flat bar between Jackson and Marshall, and purchase equipment needed for the next two years. The list of outstanding bills gives us an idea about costs as related to specific activities. It also tells us that the railroad was fencing the track—a point that would become important in just a year.

Additions at New Buffalo Harbor	*$25,000*
Grading west of Niles	*$10,000*
Complete the enlargement of sidetrack accommodations at several of the stations east of Kalamazoo, with wood sheds and other buildings still required	*$20,000*
Completing buildings and machinery at Marshall	*$13,000*
60 double covered Freight Cars	*$42,000*
Finishing 4 first class Passenger Cars	*$5,000*
4 second class Cars	*$4,000*
3 Freight Engines	*$26,000*
Fencing balance of road	*$25,000*
Balance of Land	*$5,000*
Balance of Iron account and contingencies	*$51,300*
Outstanding accounts unpaid	*$41,566*

Equipment listed in the annual report clearly indicates that freight hauling was the main focus of MCRR. At this point construction was nearly as important. They even had more handcars and gravel cars than passenger cars!

Locomotives	*26*
Freight Cars as single	*471*
Passenger Cars	*20*
Baggage Cars	*4*
Gravel Cars	*44*
Hand Cars	*22*

In 1849 Forbes announced to the directors two momentous events: The road from Detroit to New Buffalo was opened on April 23, 1849, completing the initial phase of construction. He writes that Brooks completed the road *with greater dispatch than has been made in building any other road of equal length.* And even though the road *considerably exceeded the original estimates,* the price per mile is lower than average and it was wise to do the work thoroughly. *We have been able to make our road, so far as completed, with its equipment, depots and land, at once equal to the best roads now in existence in this country.* A chart was provided to make his point:

MCRR cost per mile	$29,000
Syracuse and Utica	$37,000
Utica and Schenectady	$40,000
Boston and Maine	$44,000
Old Colony	$47,000
Fitchburg	$53,000
Eastern	$59,000
Boston and Providence	$63,000
Western	$67,000
Boston and Worchester	$67,000
Albany and Schenectady	$95,000

Possibly stung by the directors for the over-runs needed to complete the road, Forbes went to great effort in explaining to stockholders that he would *endeavor to avoid further calls for money after the construction account is once closed.* In the future, small expenditures legitimately belonging to construction would be taken out of surplus profits instead of bond sales.

The second major announcement was about the much-anticipated steamboat, the *May Flower.* It was completed and put into service on May 28, 1849. More about the *May Flower* follows in the next chapter.

From 1848 to 1850, MCRR experienced a 58 percent increase in passengers (96,070 to 152,674). The wheels on those 20 passenger cars must have never stopped rolling. In regard to movement of passengers to Chicago, Brooks repeats the often-heard concern about competition from lake steamers and the hope that people start taking the train:

> *The passage across from Buffalo to Chicago can be made with regularity, in, from 33 to 36 hours, while the passage round ranges from 4½ to 6 days. With this wide difference, an opposition cannot be permanently maintained, and is only sustained at present, by a system of deception, which, in a little time, will react with power in our favor.*

The company of Hamlin and Fox was awarded the major portion of the contract to lay track between New Buffalo and Michigan City. When the track was completed to New Buffalo on April 23, 1849, the steamer *Pacific* was at the pier to meet the first train and take the passengers on to Chicago. It is fortunate to have a testimonial from someone who traveled the Michigan Central Railroad line from Buffalo to Chicago just months after the route was completed to New Buffalo;

> We left Buffalo on board the fine steamer Atlantic, Capt. Clement, and a better boat or officers in charge we never have been fortunate enough to fall in with. We arrived at Detroit after a pleasant and agreeable passage of seventeen hours; our baggage was removed to the car without any inconvenience or expense to us in fact the only additional expense we were subjected to was 25 cents for a dinner at Marshall—we arrived at New Buffalo after ten hours ride.
>
> We found the cars luxurious, the track smooth and straight, and the conductor attentive and accommodating, and on reaching New Buffalo were immediately transferred without expense on board the fine steamer Sam. Ward. We found on enquiry that there had been but one time since this line of boats commenced running, that they did not make their regular landings and the inhabitants say they have never known a more story season so far.
>
> We left New Buffalo on Sunday morning, and found the Ward all that could be wished for, to make traveling comfortable; her gentlemanly commander, Capt. Charles Cooper, and his subordinates bestowed on us every attention to make the trip pleasant and agreeable. Our passage cost us $7.25 from Buffalo to Milwaukee, and should we have occasion to go east again, we only hope we may come across the same conveyance. In justice to the M.C.R.R. Company, we cheerfully recommend it to those who desire to travel with dispatch and comfort.[13]

To simply say the line to New Buffalo was completed in April 1849 does not tell the full story about the achievement. The track actually went past New Buffalo and out over piers into Lake Michigan one-tenth of a mile. It took months of special preparation to make that happen. Almost a year earlier, the MCRR company established a sawmill on Lake Michigan, north of Union Pier, *and began sawing out timbers and lumber to be loaded on the lake to New Buffalo where a pier was to be built. During the next two years the company spent $250,000 on the pier and improvements at the mouth of the harbor.*[14]

The wooden railroad piers at New Buffalo were parallel to each other, both extended about 800 feet out from the beach into Lake Michigan where the water depth was 18 feet. The northernmost pier ended in a T to make it easy for steamships to dock.

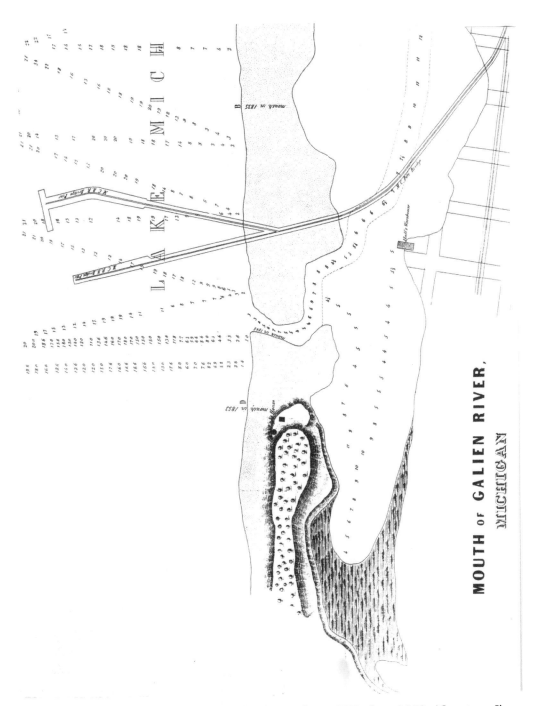

Bowes U.S. Survey Map of New Buffalo shows the MCRR piers, 1853. (Courtesy Jim Harlow)

Behind the thin strip of Lake Michigan beach was Lake Galien, which had to be crossed with a bridge over 800 feet in length. Local folklore tells a story about this railroad bridge. Apparently the original bridge pilings were not driven down deep enough and when the first locomotive attempted to cross the pilings pushed down into the sand taking track and locomotive to the bottom. The lake at that point was only seven feet deep, so perhaps the engineer survived. Although time-honored, the story could not be verified.

The New Buffalo piers and bridge were one the greatest construction challenges faced by the engineers and are almost never mentioned in historical text. Perhaps it is because it was virtually abandoned within a couple of years of its completion.

The 9.5-mile extension of the Main Line from New Buffalo to Michigan City was completed on October 30, 1849. The harbor there would allow ships to dock nearly right in front of the depot, making the pier set up at New Buffalo obsolete. Although ships did continue to use the piers at New Buffalo for a couple of years, they soon belonged only to fisherman and swimmers. Eventually lake ice destroyed the piers but remnants could still be seen 100 years later.

The 1850 annual report lists the 1849–1850 gross earnings at $698,876, which was $271,000 more than 1848–1849. The largest

Photograph of New Buffalo pier, c. 1865. (Courtesy Art Lamport)

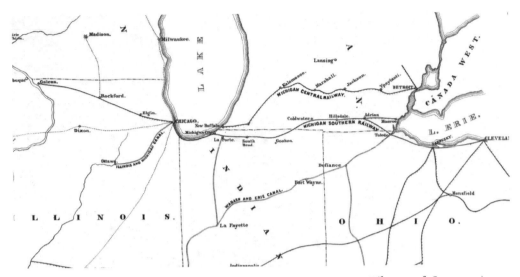

Map showing progress toward Chicago, 1850. (Courtesy Library of Congress)

jump was in through passengers with an increase of $143,000 from through passengers (anyone with a one-way ticket to Chicago).

An 1892 interview with former MCRR conductor Eralsy Ferguson provides some interesting reminiscences of how company rail yards operated in 1846–1849. Mr. Ferguson actually entered railroad work as a night watchman (seven shillings per night) two years before the MCRR took over. He then became a freight handler.

> There were no yard engines in those days and the freight trains were made up by horses. The trains did all their running in the day time and were loaded and unloaded at night. All my work, therefore, was done after dark, and that, too, without a light of any kind. I had to work in all sorts of weather, and many a time I have labored away in mud up to my knees trying to get my work done. After a time, I was promoted to baggage master.[15]

Contractors, not permanent MCRR employees, built the road to New Buffalo, a fact that sometimes caused problems. In 1849 the contractor in charge of grading the road near Pokagon took the payroll and ran away. Officials had to replace the stolen money and pay the men for their work.[16]

What happened to the area economically as the contractors cleared the way started long before the trains came and illustrates how the region was affected. A great example of this process can be found near the town of Three Oaks in Berrien County, Michigan.

Under normal circumstances, contractors would win the contract and place their workers in whatever housing was available in the area. When contracts were issued in the fall of 1847 for the clearing of the 150-foot right of way between Niles and New Buffalo, only one house, the home of Moses Chamberlain, was found along the line. Mr. Chamberlain allowed the contractors to use it as a headquarters.[17] At other locations, log cabins were built to house workers on the track right-of-way.

Contractors had to have food for their workers, so they contracted out to locals to provide it. John Love had the food contract in the Three Oaks area and brought workers their grub by hauling it out on flat skids with oxen.[18] Love purchased the garden products from local settlers, giving them a source of income.

After the right-of-way was cleared, more teams of workers came to prepare the ground and lay the track. They needed railroad ties,

This 54-pound iron T rail was purchased by the MCRR for use on sidetracks as the state charter required 60-pound rail on the Main Line. This half-inch iron strap rail was originally placed on the state railroads prior to the MCRR Company purchase. Old iron items are rarely found on site as these were.

and tie making became a large income source for locals. *Ties were cut nine feet long and were hewn on the upper and lower faces. They had to be at least six inches thick and six inches wide on the hewn faces. Each cross-tie brought twelve and a half cents.*[19]

Soon the railroad let contracts for wood to fuel its locomotives and steamboats on the big lake. They had specific requirements. The cordwood had to be only straight pieces of the best hardwood (beech, maple, white ash, and hickory). Each piece had to be split and piled beside the tracks. Chamberlain's siding was built here for easy loading of the wood. It first appeared in 1855 station listings.[20]

The economic activity around Chamberlain's farm began to attract settlers. In 1854 he and Joseph G. Ames built several buildings near the new track. One, a two-story warehouse, was soon purchased by the MCRR and used as a passenger and freight house. Chamberlain became a MCRR mail agent.

When the post office came in the late 1857, it was named after the only landmark in the area—three large oaks. The MCRR renamed the station Three Oaks, which was on the station schedules well into the 1900s.

CHAPTER 8

STEAMSHIPS AND STAGECOACHES

From the beginning, Brooks was in favor of building steamboats to further the business interests of the railroad. He believed transporting passengers from Buffalo to Detroit on a steamship flying the MCRR flag would promote travel on its overland route to Chicago. As previously noted, the public perception would be that the schedules of boats owned by the MCRR would directly connect with those of its trains at Detroit. The Erie Canal ended at Buffalo and thousands of potential MCRR passengers would be dockside looking for connections to Chicago and points west.

Brooks, and subsequently Forbes, felt so strongly about the benefits of boats to the railroad, they insisted that their new Michigan charter give them the authority to build and operate steamboats. You may remember from Chapter 4 that Section 17 of the Charter gave the railroad the right to *own, charter or hire, and to employ and use, in the navigation of the lakes and rivers . . . boats or vessels . . . not to exceed eight in number, for the transportation of and carriage of persons and property.*

The MCRR's first effort at shipbuilding was meant to make a statement because the company built the most magnificent vessel on the Great Lakes. That palatial ship was called the *May Flower,* and it was ultimately a testament to the financial power of the company and the wealthy men who ran it.

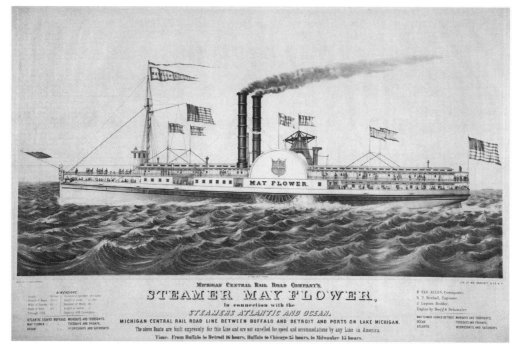

May Flower Lithograph, 1852. (Courtesy The Mariners' Museum, Newport News, Virginia)

The 1849 annual report tells that the steamship was launched on May 28, 1849, and it had the following dimensions: length of deck, 290 feet; depth of hold, 13.5 feet; breadth of beam, 35.5 feet; extreme width on deck, 65 feet; tonnage, 1,354 tons.

Forbes's understatement at the end of the 1849 annual report indicates that he may have been attempting to play down the steamboat's opulence and cost to stockholders. *The finishing, furniture, general equipment and speed of the boat, are such as to compete well with any steamer on inland waters in this country. It will probably not be necessary for the Company to construct another boat at present.*

The *May Flower* was huge for the time, the largest passenger and most plush steamship on the lake, costing the company approximately $150,000 to complete. Her engine, built by Hogg & Delamater (who later built an engine for the famous Civil War ship, the *Monitor*) of New York for $30,405, was a walking beam engine.

The most common ship steam engine of the time, a walking beam engine was a huge one-cylinder steam motor that powered an apparatus that looked like a giant teeter-totter. The walking beam pivoted on top of an A-frame that rose from the keel through the roof of the upper deck. A shaft to the engine linked one end of the beam, and the other end of the beam was linked to a crank that drove the paddle wheels. This up-and-down motion of the beam gave the walking engine its name.

To give some perspective on the size of this huge engine, the diameter of the *May Flower*'s cylinder was 72 inches, or about the size of a round kitchen tabletop. The length of the engine's up-and-down stroke was 11 feet, and the diameter of the paddle wheel was 35 feet. *Length of bucket* was the term used to describe paddle wheel width and the *May Flower*'s was 11 feet. Cartage from New York to Detroit on this monster motor was as much as shipping a locomotive, $575.[1]

To round out the ship's description, the 1849 annual report said she had three wood-burning boilers, 9.5 feet in diameter and 30 feet long. The sides of the hull were strengthened with an iron lattice, riveted at the crossings, and bolted to every frame, giving the whole ship great strength and stiffness. She had about 85 staterooms, and accommodations for about 300 cabin passengers and from 300 to 500 steerage and deck passengers.

New York's Josiah Lupton (often mistakenly listed in histories as "I. Lupton") supervised building the ship in Detroit. Samuel Foster, George Schuel, J. E. Dixon, Samuel Palmer, and many others were paid for laboring on the steamship. MCRR construction records show the company made every effort to make the *May Flower* more than mere transportation across Lake Erie; it was built as an attraction and traveling on her was an event. Imagine the passenger who, upon approaching, saw a figurehead of a pilgrim woman carved by the nationally renowned Charles J. Dodge of Boston, who also carved the figurehead on the U.S.S. *Constitution*.[2] Looking up you would see the walking beam and surrounding ironwork painted bronze and shining in the sunlight. Upon entering the vessel, you would notice the life-sized mural representing the landing of the pilgrims, painted by noted artist John G. Taggart. Perhaps the silk and velvet curtains, 13 crystal chandeliers (with drops), the copper whale oil lanterns adorning the walls or the beautiful stained glass throughout would make you feel like you were someplace special.

Further examination of below decks would find polished copper pipe, gilded columns, painted boilers and engine, and a couch in the engine room to sit and observe the apparatus in motion. At the dining room you would be served meals on monogrammed plates, with monogrammed silverware and napkins all marked *MCRR Co. Steamer May Flower.*[3] After retiring to your room you would notice quilts and pillowcases, all monogrammed with the name *May Flower.* A trip to the washroom would reveal Italian marble slabs and monogrammed towels. Perhaps the final touch, for first class passengers at least, would be that someone left you a pair of monogrammed slippers at your bedside.

Those who would be operating the steamship were hired to conduct a final check prior to the completion of construction. First mate on the *May Flower* was William Caverly, who was paid at a rate of $70 per month. Stephen T. Newhall was first engineer receiving $80 per month in salary. Captain George Willoughby's salary was not listed in construction records.

The MCRR protected its floating jewel by purchasing policies with three insurance companies: the Hartford Insurance Company, of Massachusetts; the Columbus Insurance Company, of Ohio; and the Lexington Insurance Company, of Kentucky. One month's premium was $41.25.[4]

May Flower was assigned to the northern route across Lake Erie, the fastest and more direct express route from Detroit to Buffalo with no stops between. This route was called the North Shore Line and the *May Flower* was the only MCRR owned steamship on the lake. Three other routes on Lake Erie offered passage on *connecting* steamship lines doing business with MCRR. White chinaware on ships working the North Shore Line was marked with *MCRR Co. North Shore Line* in green lettering.

In just a few months of service, the *May Flower* had become the belle of the lake, giving the MCRR command of passenger traffic. Her first year was not without trouble, however. At the end of the fifth month running, a mechanical accident shortened the ship's first season. While leaving Buffalo, the engine came apart and damaged the ship. The incident was so destructive that it could not be fixed right away, and the ship had to be dry docked until the spring of 1850. The cost of fixing the engine alone was $9,057.

The MCRR didn't construct a second passenger steamship *independently* for at least five years. (The statement frequently seen about MCRR never constructing another steamboat is incorrect.) Instead, they contracted for the services of ship builders such as Captain Samuel Ward and his nephew Eber B. Ward, using ships the uncle and nephew built for passenger service on the Great Lakes. These ships were either chartered by the MCRR, or paid a sum for each passenger and ton of freight hauled to Detroit and Buffalo.

The first Ward-owned boat put in service by the MCRR was the 1,100-ton, 267-foot-long passenger steamer, the *Atlantic,* which was completed in Marine City (formerly Newport), Michigan, also in 1849 and built by J. L. Wolverton. At the time of the *Atlantic*'s completion it was the largest and most beautiful steamship on the Great Lakes until the *May Flower* came along. Samuel Ward was heard to say that nothing built by the MCRR would be as *gingerbread* [5] as the *Atlantic.* But at 23 feet longer and 200 tons heavier, the *May Flower* bested the *Atlantic* in size and beauty when completed. *The [MCRR] built a floating palace, called the May Flower. She was magnificent.* [6]

When the *May Flower* and *Atlantic* were ready to start the shipping season, the *Detroit Free Press* announced to the public to get ready for something special.

> *May 26, 1849—Sixteen and eighteen hour trips from here to Buffalo would have frightened travelers a few years since, but there is no telling in this progressive age what will be done next. It is not expected that the first trips of these two*

The *Atlantic.*

boats will be made as quick as they can do it—the machinery and works being new, but when they "get the hang of things," hold on to your hats.

The building of these two magnificent steamships had the desired effect on the traveling public. Passenger patronage was so high it required the MCRR to add ships during peak months. The *Henrick Hudson,* the *London,* and the *Canada* all helped the *May Flower* and *Atlantic* carry the overload on the North Shore route across Lake Erie. The *Canada* was assigned temporary duty and only worked a few months until it was moved to Lake Michigan to make room for another new steamship, the *Ocean.* By May 1850, the 900-ton *Ocean* (she was paid according to the number of passengers and tons of freight hauled), also a magnificent large steamship built by the Wards in Marine City, Michigan, was added to the route.

Forbes gives us an overview of the steamship operation in the 1850 annual report:

> *We started our Lake Erie Line late in the spring, with only two Boats to do the work of three—a distance of two hundred and seventy miles per diem, and although they performed admirably, it naturally required time to gain the reputation for speed and efficiency, which they have now established. We found so much competition from the Upper Lake boats, upon which the public had become accustomed to travel, that we considered it expedient to reduce our cabin fares during the Summer to $5, at and under which price our competitors were carrying their passengers from Buffalo to Chicago.*

A vintage broadside from 1852 provides the ships' departure schedule from the MCRR wharf in Buffalo. The *Atlantic,* under Captain J. B. Petty left Buffalo on Mondays and Thursdays. The *May Flower,* under Captain Geo. E. Willoughby left Buffalo on Tuesdays and Fridays, and the *Ocean,* under Captain D. H. McBride, left on Wednesdays and Saturdays. Even though all three could make the trip in under 17 hours, the *Atlantic* was the fastest of the three ships and held the speed record between the two cities for many years (16.5 hours).[7]

To add to the status of the line, advertising presented the ships as *U.S. mail carriers.* They were also advertised as the only line of steamers that run directly through without landing. The northern route across Lake Erie was also touted as the *cheapest, safest and quickest route to Detroit, Chicago, Milwaukee, Sheboygan, Kenosha, Racine, Waukegan and other ports on Lake Michigan.*[8] It may have been the safest route, but it certainly was not totally safe for passengers or ships.

In December 1851, the *May Flower* was stranded on a sandbar on the coast of Pennsylvania and could not be recovered until spring. At great expense a barrier was built around it to keep the winter ice from destroying the hull. The cost of repairs to the boat was more than $40,000, and the cost of the building the barrier and hiring a wrecking crew and equipment to lift it off the sandbar cost more than $25,000.

Finally, at the end of the 1854 season on November 24, her five-year run as the queen of Lake Erie ended. She left Detroit on a Friday night and while running in a thick fog she ran too close to shore and was grounded on the west side of a sandbar near Point Pelee, Ontario. The *May Flower*'s passengers were picked up right away by the *Ocean* and the *Pearl* stayed with her ready to offer assistance. Initial reports had her hull smashed and soon *gone entirely to pieces . . .*[9] taking cargo of mostly iron rail worth $100,000 with her, but the report of her demise was premature.

For the first several days the weather was so horrible that efforts to free the *May Flower* were not possible. The *Detroit Daily Free Press* followed her plight.

A rare photograph of the steamship *May Flower* taken in January 1852 when she went ashore on Lake Erie just below Conneaut, Ohio. (Courtesy Lower Lakes Marine Historical Society)

> *November 29, 1854—The steamer Ocean passed the May Flower yesterday, on her passage up from Cleveland, but could learn nothing new, except that it was thought her arches were broken. The wind was blowing so hard that it was impossible to do anything for her. The Pearl is still with the May Flower, and the Ocean left again last night, intending to stay with her and render her all the assistance possible.*

The newspaper ran daily reports with information obtained from passing ships. The report on November 3 said she *had begun to open across mid-ships and her stem and stern had both sunk considerably below the level of her middle.* On December 2, they told the public, *hopes are entertained that the old favorite will again reach our docks in a few days.*

Finally, on December 5, the *Detroit Daily Free Press* reported that the *Ocean* and *Pearl* came up to Detroit from the *May Flower* with a final report. *The idea of getting the May Flower off has now been pretty generally abandoned . . . her planking midship is strained apart some six or eight feet. She is undoubtedly broken in two across the middle.* The *Pearl* had waited two weeks for the weather to clear enough to get next to the *May Flower.* Finally, the lake gave her and the *Ocean* a day and a half to salvage what they could. The December 5 report went on to say that *the* Ocean *and* Pearl *brought up large loads of her furniture and such other stuff that could be moved away and are to return today with the necessary implements to get her engine and machinery.*

We know that when the *Ocean* and *Pearl* returned for the engine, the lake was again rough and prevented them from removing anything more. The next spring the steamer *Huron* salvaged the engine, machinery, and *other parts* for the owners and was almost wrecked in the process.

The northern route was just as treacherous for the fastest steamer on the lake. A couple of years earlier, just after midnight Friday, August 20, 1852, the *Atlantic* was hit in the fog by the propeller freighter *Ogdensburgh* near Long Point, Ontario. The two ships pulled apart and went on their way, apparently unaware the *Atlantic* was seriously damaged. Sometime later, the Ogdensburgh *heard the passengers screaming two miles away and hurried to back to the rescue. The* Atlantic *still lies 25 fathoms deep on the Lake Erie floor.*[10]

Although the *Ogdensburgh* circled the *Atlantic* picking up passengers until it sank, reports claim from 131 to 150 people were lost. Salvage efforts were made within a couple of years of her sinking and her safe was recovered in 1856. She is still visible from the surface

An early broadside advertises the MCRR steamship route, c. 1852.

and was reportedly seen as late as 1987. In an effort to protect her, as late as 1996 the Canadian government has successfully sued salvage operators to stop them from disturbing the resting place of this great steamship.

It is likely this tragic event, coupled with the notoriety of holding the Buffalo-to-Detroit speed record, ensured the *Atlantic* of a place in many Great Lake history books. Although the *May Flower* lived two years longer, the absence of a similar speed record and traumatic disaster with loss of life, resulted in the *May Flower* being somewhat ignored by history.

In the 1853 annual report, Forbes announced the coming of two new steamships, which leads us to conclude that the *May Flower* was not the only steamship built by the MCRR. It may, however, be the only one built *entirely* by the company: *The construction of larger Steamboats to run upon Lake Erie . . . has rendered it necessary for this company to improve the character of its North shore line, and they have with reliable associates undertaken the construction of two Steamers.*

The steamer *Buckeye State* was chartered under Captain Jacob Imson, and placed on the route between Buffalo and Detroit in 1855. It replaced the *May Flower* and appears that the steamer was added as an experiment in efficiency. Its engine was a new *compound-cylinder* model constructed at the Allaire Works (formerly owned by Robert Fulton), New York, in 1850. The engine reportedly consumed less than two thirds the fuel required by a similar vessel fitted with the single-cylinder engine and weighed less. We can assume that the engine was a success because the Allaire Works received the contract to build engines for the next two ships on the MCRR line, the *Plymouth Rock* and *Western World*, which would join the *Buckeye State* on the North Shore Line. The *Buckeye State* replaced the *Ocean*, which went on to work the Great Lakes for another 18 years, the last 11 as a barge, finally sinking on October 20, 1873, near Point aux Barques (at the mouth of Saginaw Bay), Michigan. Forbes announced the ships' arrival in the 1854 annual report: *On the 8th and 10th of July, our new boats* Plymouth Rock *and* Western World, *take their places in our line. They are larger than any other boats on those waters, and are believed to be equal in speed, strength and safety, to any steamers in this country.*

In July 1854, the *Plymouth Rock* and the *Western World*, destined to trump the other railroads' new steamboats by becoming the fastest steamers on the Great Lakes, were placed in service at a cost of approximately $200,000 each. Their captains were Geo. F. Willoughby (formerly the *May Flower* captain) and O.C. Stannard, respectively.

They were constructed under the supervision of Captain Isaac Newton of New York, who designed both steamboats after his famous Hudson River ships.[11] These ships were identical and both built at the Buffalo shipyards of Bidwell & Banta by John Englis & Son of Brooklyn. Englis boats were famous for creative stateroom design and fine cabinetwork, and his yard later became famous for building the *Unadilla,* first of the Civil War gunboats in 1861. At 2,000 tons and 363 feet long, they were each 700 tons heavier and 73 feet longer than the *May Flower.* Not only were they larger, they also were called two of the finest ships ever placed on the lakes. In the 1854 annual report, Forbes, in typical understatement, said they *are expected to form attractions to the Lake travel, not before presented.* An 1857 description of the *Plymouth Rock* shows how much of an understatement it was.

> *Her grand cabin extends almost the entire length of the boat, and is furnished without regard to expense, with rosewood furniture; brocatelle, satin, plush silk and embroidered easy chairs, ottomans, divans; the floors are carpeted with the richest tapestry; the painting, wood-work, moulding and gilding are all that art can furnish or admire. The state rooms are not berths, but actual rooms fifteen feet deep, thoroughly lighted and ventilated, with rich carpets, marble-topped washstands and toilets, with water cold or hot, supplied from the engines; and to cap all—the most comfortable thing to a traveler—rosewood French bedsteads, low, wide, and roomy draped with fine muslin printed hangings, and covered with finest Marseilles and linen bedding.[12]*

Within a year the *Plymouth Rock* and *Western World* had trim problems. They were forced into dry dock to have their boilers moved forward 20 feet to add speed. To improve safety, the annual report said airtight fire rooms and blowers were also added *and they may now be considered equal, if not superior in speed, capacity, strength, and safety, to any steamers on the inland waters.*

The MCRR also purchased a steamship that was already built. The 1,830-ton *Mississippi,* built in 1853 by the Morgan Iron Works of New York, was added in 1855, replacing the *Buckeye State.* Forbes stated in the 1855 annual report that the reason for the *Mississippi's* purchase was because the MCRR could not charter another steamship at a reasonable rate. The *Mississippi* was reportedly purchased for $100,000, half of the price of its construction two years before.

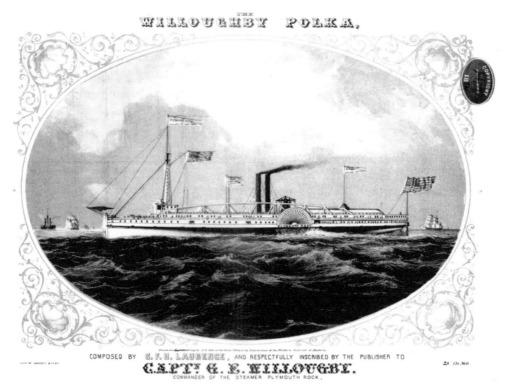

Music score cover sheet and image of the *Plymouth Rock,* 1856. (Courtesy Library of Congress)

The *May Flower* and *Atlantic* were not the only two company steamships involved in marine disasters while on duty. The *Western World* had its share of problems and was apparently difficult to steer and stop. On September 19, 1854, the huge steamer rammed the small schooner *E. G. Williams* into the Buffalo dock, sending her to the bottom in minutes. The *Williams* was raised to sail another day. On June 13, 1855, the *World* ran into the schooner *Cygnet,* at the mouth of Buffalo harbor, sinking her. It appears that the schooner was too damaged for recovery.

But it wasn't just MCRR steamships having problems on Lake Erie. Working for the Michigan Southern Railroad, the *Northern Indiana* caught fire and sank on July 17, 1856. Survivors were picked up by the MCRR's *Mississippi.* Interestingly, the incident took place 5 miles off Point Pelee, apparently within yards of where the *May Flower* went down.

Regardless of the *Western World*'s problems, she and her sister ship *Plymouth Rock,* touched many people in extraordinary ways.

G. F. H. Laurence wrote music in honor of the *Rock*'s captain. The tune is called *Willoughby Polka,* and the sheet music can be found in the American Memory Collection at the Library of Congress.

The *Plymouth Rock, Western World,* and *Mississippi* were the mainstay of the northern route for the MCRR until 1857, when the country's economy took a downturn and passenger traffic finally dwindled to the point the company could no longer justify the expense of steamship operation. At the end of 1857 season, the three ships were moored at the MCRR wharf in Detroit until they were sold to Captain George Sands of Buffalo. He extracted and sold their engines and made the hulls of *Plymouth Rock* and *Western World* into dry-docks and the hull of the *Mississippi* into a coal barge.[13]

No one was surprised at the decline of MCRR's interest in lake passenger traffic. Three years earlier, in 1854, the Great Western Railway completed construction to Detroit, making ship travel on Lake Erie unnecessary. From that point on it was possible to board a passenger car in Buffalo and never leave it until arriving in Chicago. Travel time to Chicago was also cut by another 10 hours. It was the notoriety of the magnificent MCRR steamships alone that kept them running three years past obsolescence.

Other Lake Erie Connecting Lines

In 1849, when the MCRR became involved in moving passengers over water, several other connecting steamship lines on the lake conducted business under contract with the company. The *Hendrick Hudson, Baltic,* and *Empire* worked between Detroit and Buffalo via Cleveland, running daily. The steamer *Arrow* worked the daily Detroit to Sandusky route. The *John Owen* and *John Hollister* were employed on daily trips between Detroit, Monroe, and Toledo. The *Franklin Moore* and *Telegraph* steamers traveled between Detroit and Port Huron every day. Most of these ships and routes were associated with Samuel Ward and later E. B. Ward & Co.

After a couple of years, ship owners, routes, and MCRR contracts changed somewhat. The Detroit & Cleveland Navigation Company of Detroit, owned by Captain Arthur Edwards, ran the line of the same name with the steamers *Baltimore* and *Southerner* from 1850 to 1852. In 1852 John Owen, associated with E. B. Ward & Co., took over and

M. C. R. R. CO.

1856.   1856.

NORTH SHORE LINE OF STEAMBOATS.

DETROIT AND BUFFALO.

THE NEW AND MAGNIFICENT STEAMER, MISSISSIPPI, has been added to this Line, and it will commence running immediately upon the opening of navigation, as follows ;

WESTERN WORLD,
J. H. BARKER, Commander,

Will leave Buffalo Mondays & Thursdays. | Will leave Detroit Wednesdays & Saturdays.

PLYMOUTH ROCK,
P. J. RALPH, Commander,

Will leave Buffalo Tuesdays and Fridays. | Will leave Detroit Mondays and Thursdays.

MISSISSIPPI,
S. G. LANGLEY, Commander.

Will leave Buffalo Wednesdays & Saturdays | Will leave Detroit Tuesdays and Fridays.

These Steamers are all new, of the largest class, being about 2,000 tons each, commanded and officered throughout by men of large experience and capabilities, and fitted up and furnished for the convenience of Passengers, in a style of comfort and luxury entirely unequalled, and are in all respects considered the most desirable Steamers that float upon the waters of the United States.

For the transportation of freight the line will surpass anything ever before offered to the public, having arrangements with parties between Boston and New York, and all points west of Buffalo, to St. Louis, which will enable them to forward goods and merchandize, with greater dispatch *than has ever yet been attained.*

Shippers of Merchandize from the East should mark packages to the care of C. L. SEYMOUR, Buffalo.

Merchandize from the West should be to the care of JOHN HOSMER, Agent, Detroit.

Detroit, January 18, 1856.   **C. B. SWAIN, Agent.**

The compiler would suggest reference to the description of one of the above truly magnificent Steamers, extracted from the Buffalo Republic and New York Citizen found on pages 62, 63 and 64 of this Directory.

J. D. JOHNSTON

Advertisement from *Clark's Detroit City Directory,* 1857.

ran the line with individual ship owners until the line was incorporated under new management and a new name in 1868 (Detroit & Cleveland Steam Navigation Company, then a subsidiary of the MCRR). During the time between 1852 and 1868, nearly a dozen side-wheel steamships worked the Detroit to Cleveland route. The *Forest City, Sam Ward,* and *St. Louis* replaced the *Baltimore* and *Southerner* in 1852. Later the *May Queen, Cleveland,* and *Ocean* (from the northern route), then the *Morning Star, City of Cleveland, R. N. Rice* (named after the then-superintendent of the MCRR), and *Northwest* worked the route until the 1870s. The company continued to operate until 1938.

The 1851 annual report listed lines and the steamships used by the MCRR at that time. On the Dunkirk to Detroit Line, three steamers operated that year: *Keystone State, Niagara,* and *Queen City.* The Sandusky Line continued to operate with just one ship between Detroit and Sandusky, the *Arrow.*

Lake Michigan Connecting Lines

During the time the Central Railroad was still owned by the state, mail and passengers were transported from the western terminus at Kalamazoo to New Buffalo by stage. Captain Samuel Ward secured the state contract to take mail and passengers from New Buffalo to Chicago by ship. The first steamship on the route was the 150-ton *Huron.* Later he built the 250-ton *Champion.* When the MCRR Company took over the route in 1846, Ward still held the contract, opening business relations with the company that would expand steamship operation substantially during the next decade with the development of the Lake Erie MCRR routes.

In 1849 the MCRR connected with two lines operating on Lake Michigan. Between New Buffalo and Chicago, the steamers *Detroit, Pacific,* and *Sam Ward* operated. The steamer *Champion* worked between Milwaukee, Port Washington, and Sheboygan.

As travel west increased and time passed, ships were removed and added and the routes were adjusted on Lake Michigan. By 1851 the MCRR had three connecting lines. One ran to Chicago, Milwaukee, and Sheboygan. This line operated with steamers *Arctic, Pacific,* and *Sam Ward*, with the *Canada* from Lake Erie, frequently substituting. Another company ran one steamship, the *Champion*, between Chicago and Michigan City. The St. Louis and the Sheboygan Line operated with the steamer *Detroit*. The annual report of 1851 gives an overview of the service they provided. (In 1851 two MCRR trains ran each direction from April to December.)

> *Steamers connecting with the night Eastward train, leave Milwaukee in the morning for New Buffalo, via Racine, Kenosha, Waukegan and Chicago, the passengers arriving in Detroit in time to take the Buffalo or Dunkirk Steamers at 11 o'clock A.M. On the 19th of May, a line of first class Steamers commenced running between Detroit and Dunkirk, connecting with the express train of the New York and Erie Railroad. These Steamers, as well as the Cleveland Line, connect at Detroit with our morning train westward and the Buffalo or North Shore line of Steamers connect with the evening train. This arrangement divides the through Westward business (which is much heavier than the Eastward) between the two trains in a satisfactory manner.*

These Lake Michigan ships suffered the same fate as those on Lake Erie, only slightly earlier. The completion of the railroad line to Chicago in 1852 and the Panic of 1857 doomed them. Most of these ships were disposed of to a Chicago group. They became part of the Morton Steamship Lines and operated *for a great many years on Lake Michigan*.[14]

Some appreciation must be given to those who faced dangerous night travel twice a week on the Great Lakes. With hidden shoals and reefs and frequent storms that can match the fury of the ocean, it seems Great Lakes travel was exceedingly perilous 150 years ago. Authorities at the Peachman Lake Erie Shipwreck Research Center say that estimates of shipwrecks on Lake Erie alone *range from 1,400 to 8,000, while confirmed shipwrecks locations number around 270*. All three of the first MCRR steamships to operate the North Shore Line (*May Flower, Atlantic, Ocean*) rest on the bottom of the Great Lakes.

Stage Lines

When the Michigan Central's terminus was Kalamazoo, three men owned the stage route from there to New Buffalo: D. Humphrey, B. F. Haddock and Granville Kimball. *The completion of railroad to New Buffalo destroyed the business of this route as well as others.*[15]

D. Humphrey held the stage mail delivery contract from Kalamazoo to St. Joseph and later merged with Western Stage Company. At the time *fifteen to sixteen stages ran daily to St. Joseph* to catch steamboats leaving for points west. *Later, the stages met the lake boats at Michigan City in the summer, and in winter continued to Chicago. The divisions were broken up as contracts expired and railroad facilities were increased.*[16]

A MCRR document dated October 9, 1896, lists 57 small towns with stage connections to their railroad.[17] These smaller operations were more common and the following example gives us an idea of how these local lines operated. In 1881, J. Devine and Son were running the Dexter & Pinckney & Howell stage line. They would leave the MCRR depot in Dexter at 9:04 A.M., make the loop to Pinckney, then Howell, and return on the same route to Dexter at 4:00 P.M. The seven-hour trip covered 40 miles and hit the Grand Trunk Depot in Pinckney and the Pere Marquette depot in Howell. The run to Pinckney was likely a MCRR contracted route.[18]

Authors of the *Berrien County History* eloquently express their feelings about the demise of the stagecoach: *The Concord coaches-and-four, the gathering of the loitering crowd at the tavern when the horn of the driver was heard in the distance; the alighting, changing of horses, and the crack of the long whip, are all events of the past.*[19]

CHAPTER 9

ROAD TO CHICAGO

While company resources were being poured into the effort to reach Chicago, records indicate Forbes was interested early on in gaining permission from Canadian and Michigan authorities to build the Great Western Railway through Canada. Construction records show that in 1850 the company gave R. Stuart Woods $250 in expenses for his lobbying efforts in *forwarding a road through the province*.[1] Forbes was likely confident permission would be obtained, because the deal would bring tax revenue to Canada and Michigan. With no railroads at all, Canada was instantly agreeable. When no decision was forthcoming from the Michigan legislature, Forbes used the 1851 annual report to encourage stockholders to subscribe individually to the stock of the Great Western Company. The president declared that the connection would only improve the value of the MCRR: *We know of no instance in the history of railroads where so great an advantage could be secured by so small an effort.*

When Forbes finally heard from the Michigan legislature, it was a refusal to alter the MCRR charter to allow company participation outside the country. Lack of direct MCRR involvement in the construction of the line slowed progress considerably. It would take three years for the Great Western to build 228 miles of track from Niagara to Detroit.

The 1851 annual report noted that during the last year the last 16 miles of flat bar track put down by the state between Jackson and Kalamazoo was replaced with heavy 60-pound T rail. Construction records indicate the rail came mostly from the Brady Bend Iron Works in Pennsylvania. Only 50 miles of flat bar remained within the first 80 miles of track and T rail was already ordered and on its way for completion this year. (Names of workers laboring on this section of track are found in Appendix C.) In addition to increasing travel speed, the change from flat strap to T rail allowed the freight cars to carry 25 percent heavier loads, increasing profit accordingly.

Forbes announced in the 1851 annual report that the road to Michigan City had been completed *with its necessary buildings*. One might take from that statement that all stations listed in 1851 timetables had passenger and/or freight depots. Construction records for 1848–1851 confirm a tremendous amount of work on buildings.

In 1851 the company owned 27 locomotives, 28 passenger cars, and 360 freight cars. It was noted that by fall of the year, four first class locomotives would be added from Amoskeag Manufacturing Company, and one freight locomotive would be built at the machine shop in Detroit.

Forbes announced in the 1851 annual report that the total expenses for rebuilding the freight depot, which burned in fall 1850, was $59,175. It cost an additional $328,856 to replace 28 burned

John Jex Bardwell bird's-eye-view photograph of the Detroit depot area, c. 1868. (Courtesy Dave Tinder collection, Clements Library, University of Michigan)

freight cars and pay state taxes of $12,808. Total earnings for the year ending May 31, 1851, were $947,347, which was a 37 percent increase over 1850.

The next big obstacle was getting a charter to construct a track from the Illinois state line to Chicago. J. Berrien was sent to survey the line and a team of lobbyists (J. Burch & Co.; E. Wadsworth; A. Osborn; J. Teammon) was sent to Illinois to work the legislature.[2] Joy also spent time in Springfield lobbying for a charter with the legislature. He hired Abraham Lincoln to help, but as he later said, *I did not succeed in my efforts.*[3]

The next option was for Forbes and company to talk the Illinois Central Railroad (ICRR) into helping. Luckily, original MCRR charter directors George Griswold and David Neal were also original charter directors for the ICRR, and in 1851 Neal was vice president. In addition to needing ICRR help to enter Chicago, Forbes was looking at ways to promote the MCRR through a partnership with the Illinois Central. Having Neal and Griswold on board likely assured that a relationship would develop.

Forbes wanted Neal to extend the ICRR line to the Indiana border to meet the MCRR line that he was building toward Chicago. The MCRR had obtained a perpetual lease of the New Albany & Salem

A John Jex Bardwell photograph showing a ground-level view of the MCRR roundhouse in Detroit, c. 1868. (Courtesy Dave Tinder collection, Clements Library, University of Michigan)

Railroad (NA&SRR) charter for $500,000 and was building a line from Michigan City across Indiana to the Illinois state line. The problem was how to get from the state line over to the ICRR track, which was planned to run southwest out of Chicago. The ICRR wasn't yet built and Forbes tried to get Neal to swing it east to accommodate the MCRR. Neal was likely unable to promise much because the line had no money to add extra mileage, and changing the track's route by putting a dog leg on the ICRR straight line to Springfield would surely bring him political problems. In August 1851, Forbes wrote to Brooks, *it is impossible to say whether he* [Neal] *will change any thing. I wish you would find us an engineer's estimate of the increased distance of going to the Indiana line . . . so that if we have any problem with the Illinois Central in May* [we] *know exactly where we are. . . . If I telegraph you I shall use our arranged letters.*[4]

In the spring of 1852, with an eye to the future, Forbes decided it would be best for the MCRR to ingratiate the ICRR by easing its financial crisis. The Illinois Central was having great difficulty raising the necessary capital to begin building the railroad. None of the typical moneylenders (eastern capitalists, Barings and Rothschild of Europe) would provide construction capital for the prairie railroad.

In the spring of 1852 the Michigan Central Railroad came to the financial assistance of the Illinois Central . . . and agreed to subscribe for . . . $2 million of the Illinois Central paper in exchange for the right to use the Illinois Central line into Chicago upon its completion.[5]

We do know that Neal did not move the ICRR track to the state line, but he did allow the MCRR to provide workers and funding to build into Illinois under the authority of the ICRR charter. The MCRR-built track ran to Kensington, about 14 miles into Illinois, where it met the ICRR line.

Three things highlighted 1852, the fifth full year of operation. All the heavy T iron rail was installed on the Main Line; in 1852 gross receipts for the first time topped $1 million ($1,075,294); and the race with the Michigan Southern to have the first train into Chicago was won by the MCRR.

Some might say the race to Chicago was a two-part affair with the Southern winning the first leg and the Central the second leg. In February 1852, the Northern Indiana track (affiliated with the Southern) connected with the Rock Island main line that ran out Chicago. This connection gave the Southern the title of the first eastern line into the city.

John Jex Bardwell bird's-eye-view photograph of the MCRR Detroit station wharf, c. 1868. The wharf freight house was divided into sections according to destination, which made it easier for ships unloading freight to put all shipments to one location on the same rail car. (Courtesy Dave Tinder collection, Clements Library, University of Michigan)

A little more than a month later, the MCRR connected with the Illinois Central main line at Kensington, giving it access to Chicago on May 22, 1852. The next day the MCRR ran a train into the Chicago to win the title of being the first train from the east into that city.

Contrary to what is reported in many histories, the Southern didn't bring a train in from the east until the day after the Central accomplished the task. Either they thought the race was over, or they couldn't get it done due to finances. It appears to be the latter, as Joy explains: *As we were getting along toward the Lake Michigan terminus, . . . the Southern Company was languishing . . . and we might have bought them out for a small sum. Mr. Brooks and I went to . . . secure the approval of the company. They refused.*[6]

Bringing an actual train into the Chicago apparently was the signal required by residents that a road was completed, not the mere completion of track. The day after the Southern train entered the city, the *New York Times* on May 25, 1852, announced, *The first train of cars through from Toledo completing the Michigan Southern Railroad has arrived; the route is now finished.*

The first MCRR train was received at the new small ICRR depot just outside of Chicago at Hyde Park. Then, with the promise of a financial partnership with the mighty MCRR, the ICRR began work on a grand depot they would share on Randolph Street.

Perhaps the completion of the Main Line to Chicago caused some to think it was time to establish some written rules for engineers. In 1852 the MCRR published a timecard and instructions for conductors and enginemen for running trains on the back of a timetable. These lightly edited instructions appear on the back of the timecard.

1. *The Clock in the Ticket Office at Detroit is the time by which the trains are to run and Conductors and Engineers should daily compare watches.*

2. *Trains are to run under the direction of the Conductor, except when his directions conflict with these rules, or involve any risk or hazard, in either of which cases all participants will be held alike accountable.*

3. *Freight Trains will not be run faster than twelve miles per hour, unless it shall be necessary to get out of the way of Passenger Trains or unless there are special orders to the contrary.*

4. *Engineers will run their train as nearly to the card time as possible, never arriving early or late at a Station, under no circumstances leaving a Station earlier than the card.*

5. *It is not necessary that passenger trains should stop more than three minutes for wood or water at any Station, and when the train is behind its time, the stops should be as few and fast as possible.*

6. *Enginemen should blow their Whistle when within half a mile of every Regular Station and at every signal Station at which the Train is liable to stop to take or leave passengers.*

7. *Passenger Trains will not wait for freight trains. Freight trains will wait at stations or side tracks indefinitely for passenger trains.*

In 1853 the Illinois Central started building its large passenger station at the foot of Randolph Street. *When completed the $250,000 structure would be used jointly by the Illinois Central, the Michigan Central and the Chicago, Burlington & Quincy.*[7] This depot would become the structure through which tens of thousands of emigrants would pass on their way west. The depot was large by 1850 standards, but by 1870 the three railroads operating from the Randolph Street were feeling a pinch for space.

In 1853, Brooks announced that the property along the river near the depot grounds at the Detroit terminus had been filled in and

TIME FOR RUNNING TRAINS.

TRAINS WESTWARD.				TRAINS EASTWARD.		
Freight.	Kalamazoo Passenger.	Through Passenger		Through Passenger.	Kalamazoo Passenger.	Freight.
7. A. M.–Leave..	4.17 P. M.–Leave..	7.30 A.M.–Leave....	Detroit	7.30 P. M.–Arrive.	11.15 A. M.–Arrive.	3.45 P.M.–Arrive.
7.52 Follow Pass...	4.40	7.52 Pass Freight...	Dearborn	7.7	10.52	3.
8.43	5.	8.10	Wayne.......	6.50	10.35	2.25
10.7 Meet Pass....	5.35	8.40	Ypsilanti	6.25	10.7 Meet Freight	1.25
10.55	6.00 Meet Pass..	9.	Ann Arbor....	6. Meet Pass....	9.45	12.40 P.M.
11.50 Meet Freight.	6.25	9.22 Meet Pass....	Dexter........	5.37	9.22 Meet Pass..	11.50 Meet Freight.
12.30 P.M.........	6.43	9.40	Chelsea	5 22	9.2	11.10
1.22	7.7	10 5 Meet Freight.	Grass Lake...	4.55	8.35	10 5 Meet Pass....
2.10	7.35	10.30	Jackson	4.30	8.10	8.55
3.	8.	10.53	Parma	4.5	7.42 Pass Freight.	7.42 Follow Pass..
3.45 Meet Pass ...	8.23	11.17	Albion........	3.45 Meet Freight.	7.20	6.40
{ 4.45 P. M.–Arrive } { 6.50 AM MtPs.Lv. }	9.5 Supper......	12.5 P. M.–Dine....	Marshall.......	3.20 Dine........	6.50 Br'kfst MtFt	{ 5.30 A.M.–Leave } { 5. P.M.-Arrive }
8.50	9.35	12.35	Battle Creek...	2.25	6.	3.45
9.20	10.10	1.5	Galesburg.....	1.55	5.25	2.25
10.10	10.30 P.M.–Arrive.	1.32 Mt Pass&Fr'gt	Kalamazoo	1.32 MtP's & PassFt	5. A. M.–Leave.	1.32 P.M.Mt&Fl'ts
11.55 Meet Freight.		2.7	Paw Paw ...	1.2		11.55 Meet Freight.
12.45 P.M.–Meet Pas.		2.25	Decatur.......	12.45 Meet Freight.		11.10
1.40		2.48	Dowagiac	12.17 P. M.		10.10
2.40		3.11	Niles........	11.52		9.
3.10		3.23	Buchanan	11.37		
3.38 Follow Pass....		3.38 Pass Freight...	Terre Coupee...	11.25		8.
5.		4.11	New Buffalo ...	10.50		6.35
{ 5.50 P. M.–Arrive } { 6. A. M.–Leave. }		4.35	Michigan City..	10.30		{ 5.45 A.M.–Leave } { 6.15 P.M.–Arrive }
7.10		5. Meet Freight..	Porter........	10.		5. Meet Pass....
8.		5.20	Lake.........	9.38		4.5
9.15 Meet Pass..		5.45	Gibson's......	9.15 Meet Freight.		3.
10.		6.5	Junction......	8.55		2.10
11. A. M.–Arrive.		6.30 P.M.–Arrive.	Chicago	8.30 A. M.–Leave.		1. P.M.–Leave.

M. C. R. R. OFFICE, *Detroit, December 3, 1852.*   **J. W. BROOKS,** *Supt.*

This early example of a time card was used by engineers to run a train. The back has "Instructions to Conductors & Enginemen for running Trains." (Courtesy Bentley Historical Library)

John Jex Bardwell photograph of the MCRR Detroit station entrance, guard shack, and attendant, c. 1868. The MCRR's huge grain elevator is in the background. (Courtesy Dave Tinder collection, Clements Library, University of Michigan)

the new wharf in front of it nearly complete. This new property gave the depot a waterfront of 2,202 feet with an average width of 391 feet. The annual report said that *it is probably as well shaped and as conveniently located for a large terminus as that of any Railroad Depot in the country containing 19.77 acres.* In addition to the wharf, a new blacksmith shop was built on the filled in property.

Brooks also informed the stockholders that due to the completion of the road to Chicago, *it is necessary to provide suitable accommodation for the repair and care of the rolling stock at Michigan City. The engine house at this point has accommodations for 16 engines. The blacksmith and machine shop has been constructed here of stone.*

For the first time Brooks outlined his plans in the annual report for splitting up the Main Line into what would eventually be called divisions.

> *When the shops at this place are in readiness for use, it is intended to apportion a part of the locomotives to the line between Detroit and Marshall, a distance of 107 miles, a portion to the line between Marshall and Michigan City, a distance of 120 miles, and a portion between Michigan City and Chicago, a distance of 54 miles.*

The 1852–1853 fiscal year found only two passenger trains operating each way to connect to Detroit and Chicago to the Lake Erie steamers. The Detroit train left in the morning and the Chicago train left in the evening.

Brooks shared his excitement over the future connections the completion of other roads would bring the MCRR. He expected the Great Western to be finished to Windsor by December 1854; the New Albany & Salem Railroad was to be completed to the Ohio River eight months later.

John Jex Bardwell photograph of the approach to the MCRR Detroit station, c. 1868. The MCRR's huge grain elevator is in the background to the left. (Courtesy Dave Tinder collection, Clements Library, University of Michigan)

The number of locomotives did not change over the year, but the number of freight cars increased from 770 to 1,046. Where these cars were built was not indicated, but in addition to the MCRR car shops, Detroit had several rail car manufacturers.

Business continued to grow in the face of the upcoming financial panic. Gross revenue receipts topped $1,149,537.

In 1853, Brooks took a leave of absence to work on another huge project for Michigan—the Locks at Sault Ste. Marie. The experienced Edwin L. Noyes, superintendent of the Androscoggin & Kennebec Railroad in Maine, stood in for Brooks. Under the leadership of Noyes, the A&KRR became the Maine Central Railroad in 1862. In addition to his competence, Noyes may have been chosen to fill in for Brooks because he was a classmate of several MCRR directors having graduated from Brown University and attended Harvard Law School.[8]

Brooks, Forbes, Joy, and another MCRR director, Erastus Corning, were primary financiers of the St. Mary's Falls Ship Canal Company, which won the bid to build the locks. Corning became president of the canal board of directors and, based on high recommendations from other investors, hired Charles Harvey to be canal agent and director of the construction project.

The state contract required that the locks be completed in two years from the date of the contract, April 5, 1853. After nine months on the job and less than halfway complete, it became apparent that Harvey was not experienced enough to get the job done. [W]*ith the entire project in jeopardy, Brooks stepped in to assume full control of the project. Despite a cholera epidemic, a strike, and bad weather, Brooks managed to complete the two 350-foot-long, 70 foot-wide locks on time.*[9]

Michigan offered the St. Mary's Falls Ship Canal Company tracts of land as an inducement and payment to build the locks. Ten years later, the company was still selling that property. In 1865, John Higbee *purchased of John M. Forbes, John W. Brooks 1,700 acres of pine land in Deerfield Township* [Mecosta County], *for ten dollars an acre.*[10]

On January 17, 1854, the long-awaited completion of the Great Western Railway (GWR) of Canada gave the citizens of Detroit a direct route to the eastern seaboard. The occasion was marked with a grand celebration.

> *The first train from London [Ontario], with the principal officers of the Great Western on board, arrived at Windsor about 5 P.M. They were brought across the ferry amid the tooting of steamboat and locomotive whistles and the*

thunder of cannon. A procession was formed consisting of the Great Western offi-
cials, the military and civic societies of Detroit and the mayors of Detroit and
Windsor, which marched through the principal streets to the [MCRR] freight
house at the foot of Third Street, where over 2,000 persons dined sumptuously.[11]

Six weeks later the GWR started car ferry service across to Detroit, which initially was a tug pulling a specially equipped barge.
Within 20 years they were floating more than 120,000 cars across the
river each season.[12]

The GWR owes its existence to the MCRR. It led the group that
included the New York Central Railroad, Canadians living along the
route, and Detroiters in promoting the venture. *By the united strength of*
all, the required life was given to the enterprise, and the road was built, though
with immense difficulty and effort. It was the first railroad in Canada.[13]

Forbes also announced in the 1854 annual report that the New
Albany Road from the Ohio River to Michigan City was completed
and *receipts show a very decided benefit from it.* Detroit to Chicago was an
eight and a half-hour trip and New York to Chicago was *36 hours, in-*
cluding ferries and all stops. Three daily passenger trains ran from Detroit to Chicago and one daily train ran from Michigan City to Chicago
until the close of navigation season reduced the schedule by one. This
Michigan City train linked with New Albany Railroad train coming
from Cincinnati (the Cincinnati Express) before going on to Chicago.

204   THE ILLUSTRATED LONDON NEWS   Aᴜɢᴜsᴛ 22, 1863

CHICAGO, FROM THE MICHIGAN CENTRAL RAILWAY.

This block print of MCRR tracks entering Chicago from *The Illustrated London News,*
August 22, 1863, shows the ICRR/MCRR depot in the distance.

Forbes's message to directors ended with an expression of gratitude to George B. Upton, the company's first treasurer who retired due to *the pressure of private engagements*. Isaac Livermore succeeded Upton. Upton was the first of the initial team running the MCRR to leave the company. Others would follow soon.

Finally in 1854, Joy, MCRR's lawyer extraordinaire, was hired by the ICRR for $5,000 a year to represent its interests.[14] Early in his association with the MCRR, Joy was on retainer and billed the company based on work completed, which gave him the freedom to pursue other interests. By the mid-1800s, Joy was the most qualified and successful railroad lawyer in the country. Thirteen years later he would become the president of the Michigan Central Railroad.

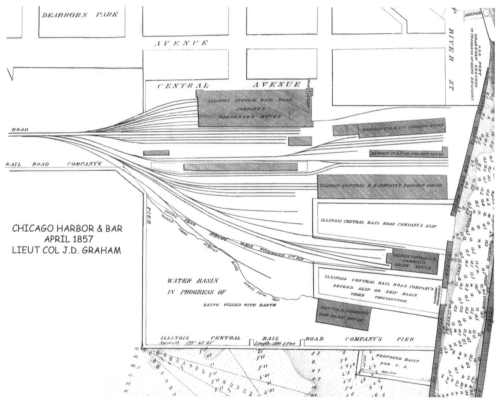

Graham's Chicago Harbor & Bar U.S. Survey Map of the ICRR & MCRR station grounds, 1857 (altered).

CHAPTER 10
THE GREAT RAILROAD CONSPIRACY

No discourse on the MCRR would be complete without some mention of the so-called *Great Railroad Conspiracy*. The infamous event will not be fully recounted here because it would be replowing well-tilled ground. Charles Hirschfield's book, *The Great Railroad Conspiracy: The Social History of a Railroad War,* explains the details surrounding this event. That said, research for this project stumbled upon some interesting points and a new theory developed long after Hirschfeld completed his book in 1953. Covering these points will require a condensed overview of the conspiracy.

The story of the railroad conspiracy actually begins back when the state owned the Central. In the mid-1840s the state was plagued with claims from farmers for cattle accidentally killed by the trains. The state knew many of the bills were inflated or even bogus, but felt it politically prudent to pay in full without question. However, while legislators voiced extreme displeasure with the situation, they had no courage to put a stop to it. It was a problem that was discussed on a national level by railroad men across the country. In February 1846, the editors of the *National Railroad Journal* voiced their opinion on the matter of Michigan lawmakers paying for destroyed cattle.

> *We observe . . . the amount paid for killing animals upon the road has become enormously large. This is all wrong. The road should be, in the first place, well and thoroughly fenced in, with proper preventatives* [for livestock] *from*

going on the track at the crossings, and then the locomotives should have good "cattle catchers" in front, to prevent, as far as possible, any accident; when the companies have done this, they have done all that they can do. Except to have the most careful and sober engineers and conductors—the remainder is for the people along the line, who have cattle to be unruly, and to encroach upon, not only the rights of the company, but also to endanger the lives of passengers, they can, if they will, prevent their cattle from going on the track, as they are, or are supposed to be, in the vicinity of their own premises. And when accidents occur from the intrusion of their cattle on the track, they should not only not be paid for their loss, but the owners of the cattle should be liable for any damage to the property of the company, and also for injury to persons; when this becomes the law, as it must, sooner or later, we shall seldom hear of accidents from cattle on the track—which we are persuaded now sometimes occur from the malicious turning, or salting of them on the track, by some fiend in human shape, who may have some quarrel with, or grudge against the company, and therefore unhesitatingly risks the lives of hundreds of innocent parties, that he may at the same time find a market for his stock, and harass the railroad company. It is quite time that this matter was thoroughly investigated and settled upon [in] *an equitable basis.*[1]

When Forbes and Brooks took over the company seven months later, the problem of farmers *marketing* their stock by placing them between iron rails was not solved. It likely had gotten worse after the state sold the road because it was public knowledge that rich *eastern capitalists* now owned the road. It is not a stretch to believe a farmer might think that if a nearly bankrupt state could pay full or inflated price for dead livestock, a group of wealthy men from out-of-state could do the same.

By some accounts the situation did get worse when a *muskeg* or *dry marsh* was crossed a few miles east of Michigan Center. The railroad built up an earthen berm across the muskeg for the purpose of constructing track up and out of the mire. But was not long before local cattle discovered the track gave them a bridge and shortcut over difficult terrain too. None of this was much of a problem until T rail went in and faster trains could not stop in time to allow cattle to move off the track at the muskeg. It became a point of slaughter.

The MCRR would send out butchers from Detroit to appraise the value of the dead cattle, none of which looked valuable after their mangled carcasses cooked in the sun for several days. Prices offered were insultingly low.

For eight years this practice went on, from the time the state put the initial track across the muskeg until the MCRR reached Chicago.

With finances obligated elsewhere, the area remained unfenced. MCRR records clearly show that fencing was being installed in a large way, but no mention of the work sites are given.

The new president and superintendent evidently tried to resolve the problem by making fencing a top priority. It appears from construction records that they made an attempt to build split rail fences as soon as the superstructure was on the ground. In a three-month period from September to November, 1848, nearly 150,000 split rails were purchased and placed.[2] If an estimate is made that approximately 3,168 rails per mile (if rails were 10 feet long) were used for a three rail fence, then 150,000 rails become 47 miles of fencing or nearly one-third of the distance along existing track (161 miles). Apparently little of the track was fenced by the state.

Not being concerned about political expedience, Brooks attempted to correct the problem in degrees. He announced that the company would no longer pay for livestock killed on the track and would begin charging cattle owners for trespassing. This policy infuriated many farmers along the line. It wasn't long before the farmers near Niles derailed an engine. Rails were torn up near Ann Arbor and at several places along the line farmers would grease the tracks and put debris in the roadway. After considerable uproar in the Marshall newspaper as well some political heat, Brooks backed off his earlier statement and agreed to pay half of the value of killed livestock. It really didn't help much.

The company's attempt to meet the farmers halfway especially inflamed those living between Michigan Center and Leoni in Jackson County. An MCRR engineer (Frisbie) who worked the route at the time and recounted the situation in an 1889 interview:

> About the year 1850 my work called me to run through a region infested with hundreds of desperate conspirators. They would burn timber on the track, and throw stones at engines and trains, and would fire guns at passing engines, so that we sometimes had to lie down behind the driving wheel guards to keep from being shot.[3]

Henry Hall was another MCRR engineer and recalled his experience during an interview in 1887:

> I was on the road during the "great conspiracy," as it was called, when the people used to tear up the track, put on obstructions, uncouple the rails from the

switchbars, block up the frogs and commit all the deviltry that the human mind could invent. This was done between Jackson and Grass Lake.

When I got to Leoni one morning going east, I found a ten-wheeler [had gone] *through the fence into a man's garden, the train staying on the track and running past the engine. We hauled the train back to Grass Lake, and put it on the siding and went on. Someone had blocked the frog some way, and it turned the truck at a right angle, right side up, as level as though she was on the track. A short time* [later] *I was going east and found a passenger engine a little east of Leoni, bottom side up in a little marsh hole. I saw a number of trains off the track at Michigan Center, but they ran so slow after a while that there was not much damage done.*

The road was not chopped out there [brush not cut away next to the track] *and there were tall saplings growing close to the track. On dark nights they would bend one down from each side and fasten the tips together and hang old tin pails loaded with stones and old iron so that they would strike the stack of the front end. At last the company had to run handcars ahead* [to inspect the track] *of night passenger trains between Jackson and Grass Lake.*[4]

A Wayne County farmer took the MCRR to state supreme court over the death of some horses that were struck while crossing the Rouge River over a Michigan Central Railroad bridge just east of Dearbornville (now Dearborn). The opinion was rendered that the railroad was not liable where no negligence was proven. Further, the company's charter stops short of requiring them to fence the route.[5] Brooks probably hoped that court decision would end the problem.

However, the high court's decision appears to have incensed the group and its leaders sought regress from the state legislature. They almost succeeded with a bill to require the MCRR to fence the line, but the members of the House were reluctant to interfere with a railroad company that was paying taxes covering the entire cost of state government.

In the fall of 1850, an editorial in the local Jackson newspaper indicated that the public was against those individuals who break the law and destroy railroad property:

. . . The removing of track from its proper place and fixing it to run a loaded passenger train off a culvert of twenty or twenty-five feet, thus endangering the lives of hundreds of innocent persons, is an act which richly entitles those concerned to ten years' service in the penitentiary house of the state.[6]

Soon the MCRR placed security guards at points along this 20-mile stretch paying them $2 a night to watch track, but it did little good. The company then placed undercover agents in the area to determine the leaders' names and gain evidence for legal action, which they ended up doing. Apparently area residents took exception to the caliber of the men. Over a century ago, *History of Jackson County, Michigan,* cited the following:

> *The railroad company offered a reward of five hundred dollars for the arrest of the parties who tampered with their tracks. A corps of spies was employed, comprising at one period over one hundred men. No less than fifteen of those disreputable scoundrels appeared as witnesses against the very men whose hospitality they enjoyed. This most detestable band of cowards and villains . . . were called from the prison and the brothel, from the counter and the farm, from the sheriff's office, the bar, and even the legislature. For a period of six months did these reptiles carry out a system of espionage, but failing completely to arrest one of the injured settlers in the act, resolved to swear anything and everything that might earn the reward.[7]*

In December 1850, arsonists apparently burned the MCRR freight depot in Detroit. Within months of the depot fire, a group of Michigan Center, Leoni, and Jackson men were arrested. The number of men reported arrested varies from 33 to 50. [Silas Farmer's *The History of Detroit and Michigan* (1890) says 33. Charles V. Deland's *The History of Jackson County, Michigan* (1903) says 37. *The Advertiser and Free Press* (1851) lists 50 names. Charles Hirschfeld's *The Great Railroad Conspiracy* (1953) claims 44 were arrested.] The names of men arrested that appear in the *Advertiser and Free Press* are listed in Appendix D.

Those arrested were transported on an armed MCRR train to Detroit to stand trial. Twelve men were found guilty on September 25, 1851. But the leader, Abel F. Fitch, died while in jail. Sentences given those convicted ranged from 5 to 10 years. A special MCRR train transported the convicted from Detroit to Jackson Prison. They would travel through Leoni and Michigan Center on the way to Jackson.

General public sentiment changed from supporting the railroad to empathy for the convicted. At least one of the defendants was pardoned after serving two years. Another died in prison and one escaped, but within a few years all were pardoned by Governor Kinsley S. Bingham. The guilt or innocence of the defendants is still debated, but the daily vandalism around Leoni stopped. A final chapter on the subject from a Jackson County historian may best describe how looking back over time clarifies events.

> *The fact that the prisoners were all pardoned at the suggestion of the railroad company and their lawyers, that a tender of damages was made to them after being released . . . is of itself vindication enough for all.[8]*

A couple of twists to the story developed after the publication of Hirschfeld's book.[9] Looking back on those days, we are horrified at the thought of derailing locomotives and shooting at trains, but a recent study of the era indicates that a second look might be warranted.

> *Although the actions of the Jackson County farmers might appear astonishing and indefensible to the modern reader . . . contemporaries would not have shared these dismissive views. Indeed observers of the trials expected that . . . the Jackson County farmers would be acquitted on the grounds that they had been defending their established rights.*[10]

Apparently what we fail to see when we look back at this famous battle between the railroad and farmers is the *precapitalist outlook and devotion to tradition as exemplified by the strident defense of the open range that spawned the movement and goaded participants to act.*[11] To many, the tradition and rights of the open range being an important part of farming in Michigan does not come readily to mind. The importance of the open range to the southern and western farmers is much more understood. Yet, just because the importance was minimal to the northern farmer does not mean it had no value to them.

Finally, perhaps the conspiracy leader's (Fitch's) secret relationship with the MCRR influenced his actions. Fitch was an agent for the Underground Railroad at Michigan Center working at some level with the railroad company smuggling runaway slaves (see Chapter 11). This activity was highly illegal, but morally correct. Could Fitch have believed his sharing the work of the *secret service* gave him some expectation of special consideration for his cattle losses?

Ultimately the trial might not have deterred others with a grudge against the Michigan Central Railroad. Just four months after the 12 men were sent to prison, the *Detroit car shops of the company were burned, and in 1854 the passenger depot was consumed by an incendiary fire . . . although there was no direct proof, it was generally believed the they were destroyed in revenge for the actions of the company.*[12]

CHAPTER 11

THE UNDERGROUND RAILROAD AND THE ABOLITIONISTS

The Underground Railroad (URR) was the name given to the loosely organized group of individuals who helped fugitive slaves escape from bondage during pre-Civil War days. The MCRR's role in what was often called *the secret service,* began when the company formed in 1846. These individuals belonged to, or sympathized with, abolitionist organizations. It was during abolitionist meetings that the networks were formed, which laid the track on the Underground Railroad system.

The role of the operator, or conductor, as they were usually called, was to pass fugitive slaves from town to town, often along an existing railway, until they were safely out of southern slave hunters' reach. From 1830 to 1861, safety was found in Canada.

The MCRR's role in transporting slaves was a secret known by Underground Railroad conductors. A URR authority (Siebert, 1963) writes: *Indiana and Michigan were known to have had their steam railway lines in the secret service system . . . the Michigan Central supplied a convenient outlet to Detroit from stations along the way.*[1]

The Fugitive Slave Law of 1837 made it illegal for anyone to interfere with a master's right to his slave property, but the law was weak and contemptible to antislavery sympathizers. Many Michiganders disregarded it completely, running off southern slave hunters who dared to enter the state. The Fugitive Slave Act of 1850 provided special federal marshals to help track down and return runaway slaves, increasing the penalty for assisting in the escape of fugitive slaves.

Erastus Hussey was a Quaker, a mayor of Battle Creek, a Michigan state senator, and the editor of the abolitionist newspaper, the *Michigan Liberty Press*. In an 1885 interview with Charles Barnes, editor of the *Sunday Morning Call*, he let the world know that he was familiar with the inner workings of the secretive Underground Railroad when it operated prior to the Civil War. As the key conductor of the URR at Battle Creek, he was familiar with almost all the operatives from Battle Creek to Detroit. The list of the conductor's locations matched MCRR stations along the line until they reached Ypsilanti. As you can see, the 85-year-old Hussey was unable to remember all the URR agent's names.[2]

URR Station	Conductor
Battle Creek	Erastus Hussey
Marshall	Jabez S. Finch
Albion	Edwin M. Johnson
Parma	Townsend E. Gidley
Jackson	Lonson Wilcox, Norman Allen, one other
Michigan Center	Abel F. Fitch
Leoni	Unknown
Grass Lake	Unknown
Francisco	Henry Francisco
Dexter	Samuel W. Dexter and sons
Scio	Theodore Foster
Ann Arbor	Guy Beckley
Geddes	John Geddes
Ypsilanti	Unknown

Although no record shows these men as being employed by the MCRR (likely to protect the company from legal problems), several were associates through business dealings with the line or connected by geography. For example, the MCRR named an early station after Townsend Gidley, and trains often stopped at Theodore Foster's store and post office in Scio Village instead of the depot because that was where travelers preferred to wait for the train. The depot was just a few hundred feet west of the store. Judge Dexter, as mentioned earlier, was a stockholder and commissioner on the MCRR's predecessor line, the Detroit & St. Joseph Railroad. As postmaster, Henry Francisco handled incoming and outgoing mail from MCRR handlers at Francisco Station.

The Crosswhite Case

One can only speculate how the MCRR became involved in the Underground Railroad and how they stayed out of legal trouble with federal authorities. Perhaps the company had a *do not ask and do not tell* policy of its own—we don't ask how you are using our trains to smuggle slaves and don't you tell anyone if you do.

But the word that the MCRR was antislavery did get out through the actions of one prominent railroad official. In 1848, Joy assisted defense lawyers in Michigan's famous Crosswhite Case. To quickly summarize the story, Adam Crosswhite and his family were runaway slaves owned by Frank Giltner of Carroll County, Kentucky. The Crosswhites fled Kentucky, and the family settled in Marshall, Michigan, in 1843. About 1847 Giltner found their location and sent his son, nephew, and a few other men to arrest Crosswhite and bring him back to Kentucky. It was a legal arrest according to law.

Marshall residents were less concerned about the law and more concerned about the welfare of the neighborhood family. They responded to an alert that the slave hunters were at Crosswhite's home and surrounded the place, refusing to let Giltner's agents take the family. The local sheriff arrested one of the Kentuckians for trespass and *assault and battery for drawing a pistol* on one of the Marshall mob. The trial lasted two days and by the time it was over, the Crosswhites had boarded a MCRR train for Detroit and crossed to Canada and safety. Giltner's agents went home empty-handed.

Eighteen months later Giltner filed federal charges in Detroit against Charles Gorman, one of the Marshall mob leaders and several others. Joy assisted lead lawyer Helmer Emmon in the defense of Gorman and the others. One of the defendants wrote a letter to Brooks asking him to schedule a special train to ferry their friends and family from Marshall to Detroit and back for the trial.

Naturally the trial received national attention, and the first trial resulted in a hung jury. The second trial found for the plaintiff and fined the Marshall mob $1,926 in damages, which was about two-thirds of the lost slave's value. Some historians believe that Kentucky's famous statesman, Henry Clay, was so upset with the low award that he pressed the U.S. Senate to pass the more severe Fugitive Slave Law of 1850.[3]

When former slaves would finally reach Detroit, they would converge on the house of J. C. Reynolds, who was working on the Michigan Central railroad. He lived at the foot of Eighth Street, near where the first MCRR elevator was built. A former URR conductor remembered how slaves crossed the Detroit River.

> We would fetch the fugitives there, shipping them into the house by dark one by one. There they found food and warmth, and when, as frequently happened, they were ragged and thinly clad, we gave them clothing. Our boats were concealed under the docks, and before daylight we would have everyone over. We never lost a man by capture at this point, so careful were we, and we took over as high as 1,600 in one year. When railways began to be built we used to pack them in boxes, and send them by express. We got thirty or forty through in that way, but the danger to their lives by reason of lack of careful handling and fear of suffocation made that means dangerous.[4]

In 1848 anyone reading the newspaper was aware that the MCRR was friendly toward runaway slaves, but few probably realized that many MCRR charter directors were ardent abolitionists. The following cites just a few examples.

The leader of the MCRR, John M. Forbes comments on a related political awakening: *When Daniel Webster made his great speech, on the 7th of March, 1850, supporting the Fugitive Slave Law, and indorsing all the compromises by which we surrendered to the slave-owners, the scales fell from my eyes, and I gave up the Whig party.*[5]

A few years later Forbes was vocal about the practice of slavery and what should be done with those who were in the business. *Can not we at least hang one of the pirates who have sacrificed such hecatombs of Africans? and thus hint to the civilized world that there has been a change of administration since slavers were protected.*[6]

During the Civil War, Forbes *formed a Committee of One Hundred for Promoting the use of Negroes as Soldiers, which raised one hundred thousand dollars* and resulted the development of the now famous black

Fifty-Fourth and Fifty-Fifth Massachusetts regiments and the Fifth Cavalry. Forbes also *drew up an address . . . begging* Lincoln to issue The Emancipation Proclamation.[7]

Several other original MCRR directors were actively supporting abolition. George Griswold, a merchant ship owner, for example, employed runaway slaves and freemen on a regular basis: *. . . the clipper ship George Griswold of New York* [was] *manned by a negro crew.*[8] William Fletcher Weld of William F. Weld & Company, employed freed slaves in his firm. Some became much more than employees: [Forbes] *Freeman was a very faithful, loyal friend, as was Jonathan Harlow, another fine and faithful character to whom all the family were devoted.*[9] Josiah Quincy was the mayor of Boston (1845–1849) when the eastern investment group purchased the Michigan Central. His entire family was outspoken against slavery, and his brother Edmund was a prominent abolitionist.

Long after the initial directors were gone, and the slavery issue settled, the Michigan Central continued to be an equal opportunity employer by hiring blacks. In 1880, the company hired University of Michigan graduate Fred Pelham, who excelled in civil engineering. He became one of the greatest railroad bridge builders in Michigan. His work can be seen at Dexter, Michigan, where his unusual skew arch bridge still stands.

The MCRR also hired Elijah McCoy, an apprenticed mechanical engineer from Ypsilanti and the son of former slaves. It was McCoy who developed and patented a steam pressure lubrication device for locomotives, which was later adapted for use on steamships and ocean liners. Because purchasing agents insisted on buying only real McCoy lubrication devices, as opposed to competitor models, the term *real McCoy* soon entered the lexicon as meaning the real thing.[10]

CHAPTER 12

BROOKS TAKES THE THROTTLE

The MCRR started the 1855–1856 fiscal year with a new treasurer (Livermore), a new superintendent (Rice), and a new vice president (Brooks) sitting in for Forbes. It appears the position of vice president was established at this time. Forbes may have wanted a vacation after Brooks took the previous year off to build the St. Mary's Canal. Or, he may have been testing retirement waters, since we know he left office in 1856. Forbes writes about his last year as head of the MCRR. *I had left the Michigan Central presidency, and though still a director, I considered myself on the retired list and remained quietly . . . all summer, hardly attending at all to the railroad.*[1]

MCRR employees were happy with the promotion of men they held in high regard. *J. W. Brooks, general superintendent; R. N. Rice, assistant superintendent; . . . finer men never lived.*[2]

With Forbes absent from his workstation, Brooks wrote the opening remarks in the 1855 annual report. His opening statement provides some measure of how those involved with the building of the magnificent Main Line felt about its success, and is typically, humbly stated. *This road has assumed a magnitude in length and capacity, cost and earnings not originally anticipated by some of its friends.*

Brooks revealed the total cost of the road from Detroit to Chicago, including the great depot at Chicago, had reached $10,300,147. This total included paying construction costs for the railroad from Michigan

Reuben N. Rice is one of several early officers of the MCRR who had great influence on the character and quality of the company, yet remains largely unrecognized, c. 1860.

City, Indiana, to Kensington, Illinois. In addition, to get across Indiana, the MCRR had to purchase $599,763 in stock of the New Albany and Salem Railroad. To get through Illinois and into Chicago, the MCRR had fronted the ICRR $2 million to help them get started building track and purchased $800,000 in construction bonds to give them long-term support. Although years had passed since the outlay, no return on the money had been realized by 1855. Brooks declared that these roads were valuable feeders, and soon the connections would prove *to have been cheaply purchased*. The Illinois Central's connections to the Mississippi would add 1,500 miles of railroad and steamboat connections to the terminus at Chicago.

The annual report noted that winter of 1854–1855 was so bad, metal on the track and rolling stock became brittle and broken. Winter's length, severity, and *extreme cold caused . . . such a rigidity of track as to prove very disastrous to driving and truck wheels and cranks of engines, as well as to all the rolling stock of the road.*

The winter of 1855 was particularly hard on the northeastern railroads. Many times in January and February, it snowed for days on end, stopping passengers and freight all along the line. One stranded traveler in Chicago wrote a letter to the *New York Times* telling of traveling conditions:

Chicago, Sunday, Feb. 4, 1855

I am this far along, and the prospect of getting from this point is gloomy enough. All the lines from this point [east] are closed, save the Michigan Central, and that is doubtful. The train that takes this letter may get through. Passengers are scattered all along the route and can't get either way. . . . This place is jammed full of passengers, snow-bound. They are afraid to go either East or West. . . . We got within eight miles of Chicago and then froze up. Some of the passengers walked in and got frost bitten. I waited with about two hundred others until sleighs came out for us. There are five trains froze up within 10 miles of Chicago, some going East and some West. It took all night long to bring up the passengers.

. . . Locomotives and tenders looked more like icebergs than anything else—some of them covered entirely up, buried and forsaken. . . . I have met friends here from home who have been waiting here thirteen days to get home.[3]

Superintendent Rice confirmed that all northern railroads *suffered much from the extreme cold weather of last winter and this railroad shared the fate of the others.* A large number of men had to be hired in the spring to get the track back in shape. At least 54 driving wheels, 19 crank axles, and 34 tires were broken due to the hard winter and wrought iron drivers were purchased as replacements. MCRR purchased 30,000 *Wrought Iron Chairs . . . to take the place of the Cast Iron Chairs, considered unfit to remain* [in service].

Even though the winters during the early 1850s were harsh, income was high. Gross receipts increased more than 100 percent from 1852 to 1855 ($2,261,936), providing reason for all to be optimistic about the company's future. Operating expenses climbed as well, and profit stayed below the elusive $1 million level at $938,501.

When the Great Western arrived in Windsor, Ontario, in January 1854, it handled the movement of cars to Detroit by putting them on scows and towing them across the Detroit River. Business increased to the point where this arrangement was unsatisfactory. In June 17, 1856, the *Detroit Free Press* announced that a steamboat was being outfitted by the GWR to ferry cars and freight. It would be years before the MCRR would establish their own carferry between Windsor and Detroit.

The MCRR continued to seek ways to improve the partnership with the Great Western Railway after it was completed in 1854. In November 1856, they linked with their partners across the river. Detroit newspapers announced that the MCRR and GWR added a third partner, the Telegraphic Company, for the purpose of laying *a telegraphic connection with the line which now terminates at Windsor, composed of a series of wires which will cross the river. The wire will be laid to cross the river at Hog Island,* [now called Belle Island] *will be carried across the island on poles in the usual manner, and will then again be sunk in the river, and brought down to Windsor on the other side.*[4]

Reuben N. Rice also made his mark in the 1855 annual report by giving MCRR enthusiasts something that still fuels our interest 150 years later. Rice provided data on all 64 of the company's locomotives, including their unusual names, builder, diameter of drivers, and the number of drivers and cylinders. The list appears in Appendix E. The

MCRR & Great Western Poster. (Courtesy Library of Congress)

Engine *Terrible*, c. 1867. (Courtesy Dave Tinder collection, Clements Library, University of Michigan)

only thing missing is the build date. The report also provided station listings, which is shown in Appendix F.

The year 1856 was good for the MCRR. For the first time net earnings topped $1 million ($1,228,624), but signs of financial crisis loomed the horizon. Brooks noted that although profits were up, *earnings were seriously affected, partially in consequence of the last wheat crop . . . materially damaged from incessant rains at harvest time, thus rendering the bulk of the crop entirely unfit.* An increase in other types of freight filled the void this year.

It was also the year that future president Abraham Lincoln rode a MCRR train from Chicago to Bronson Park in Kalamazoo (August 27, 1856). He came to speak on behalf of John C. Fremont, who was running for the Republican nomination for president. Lincoln spoke against slavery, but was criticized for being too soft on the subject.

The 1856 annual report makes the first mention of the telegraph. The MCRR was building its own telegraph system from Detroit to Chicago (1855–1856), citing that the private company, which was providing the service, was *quite insufficient.* (They don't mention the private company providing insufficient service, but it was probably the Erie & Michigan Telegraph Company, which had an auxiliary

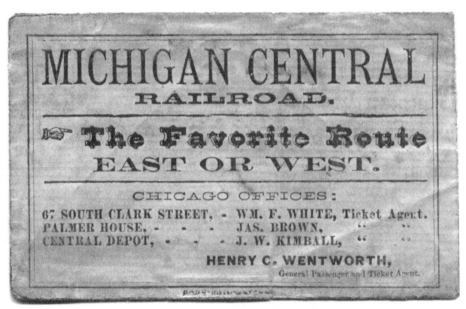

"Favorite Route" ticket envelope, c. 1859.

office in the MCRR freight depot during the early 1850s.) The MCRR-owned telegraph system was finished on June 1, 1856, and would be much more *efficient, reliable, and certain. The line will communicate with every regular Station during the day, and with the most important points during the night, will be of incalculable service in the working of trains. . . . In no way can the desired promptness be attained in so large a business on a single track road without the aid of an efficient Telegraph line.* The 1857 annual report confirmed that it was completed and would allow 50 percent more business by better controlling trains on the single line.

It would be difficult to overstate the impact the telegraph had on the MCRR. Next to the development of the steam locomotive and the invention of the "T" rail, the telegraph was easily the third most important development in railroad history. The MCRR was one of the first railroads in the nation to build its own telegraph line along its right-of-way. The benefits from its use was an immediate increase in safety and efficiency.

Train dispatching did not exist prior to the telegraph's arrival and trains ran as close as possible to time cards indicating when the train should arrive and leave stations. But that method was hazardous because accidents and mechanical problems made it extremely difficult to keep early trains on schedule. Trains ran "wild" as a result and locomotive engineers seldom knew what was in front or behind them. Relative safety was achieved almost immediately when trains were dispatched by telegraph.

At least one other factor related to the telegraph benefited the railroad. The railroad depot with a telegraph became the center of communication for all towns along the road. No longer was the depot only the meeting place of travelers or those shipping and receiving freight. Nearly everyone in town had a reason to visit the depot.

A statement in the 1856 annual report illustrates how fast the area around Chicago was growing. Business on the Joliet & Northern Indiana Railroad was so great in 1855–1856 that the MCRR would not meet the demand for moving freight in a *desirable manner. The want of motive power and cars last year prevented the fair development of the business.* Brooks asserted that adjustments were made to meet the demands for the next year.

The Chicago, Burlington & Quincy and the Galena & Chicago Railroad lines began to operate out of the new MCRR & ICRR depot in Chicago. Brooks believed these lines were feeders to the MCRR and would increase profits.

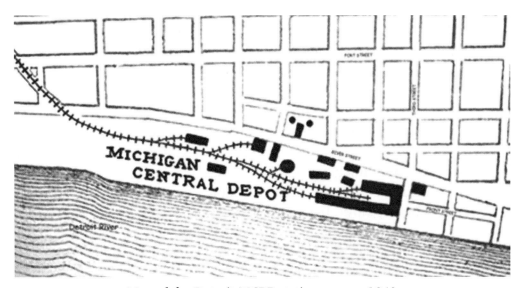

Map of the Detroit MCRR station area, c. 1860.

THE PANIC OF 1857

In 1857 a significant downturn in the country's economy was caused, historians believe, by overspeculation on railroad stocks, overspeculation on land related to railroad line building, low grain prices, and a reluctance of English investors to gamble on American businesses, particularly railroads, because so many had been going bankrupt. European investors had no protection against fraud in America, which caused a temporary mistrust of railroad companies.

In September 1857, only one year after Forbes left the company, he was called out of retirement to help the Michigan Central with finances. The Panic of 1857 was taking a toll on the company, which was used to being flush with money. Although the MCRR was doing better than most, it was still teetering on unfamiliar ground—the possible inability to pay dividends. Forbes's concern is expressed in a letter to a friend about the devalued company stock:

> *We are in such a crisis here as only those who went through 1837 can conceive of. J. K. Mills & Co.* [an original MCRR charter member] *and many stronger houses have gone, and other large ones . . . only exist by sufferance. New York Central Railroad* [stock price] *has run down from 87 to 55, and Michigan Central from 95 to 45, while the weaker concerns are clear out of sight—Erie 10, Southern Michigan 10–15.*[5]

MCRR officials *urgently requested* that Forbes go to London and get a loan from his old friends, the Barings or Rothchilds. They needed $2 million to *prevent the Michigan Central from going bankrupt. Somehow the directors . . . had allowed the company to incur a heavy floating debt instead of selling stock and bonds to meet their outlays.* [Forbes] *could not refuse to go.*[6]

The financial climate was so bad that Forbes started looking internally for ways to save even more operational money. He recommended that another position in the finance department be formed to *inspect in detail the accounts of officers and employees.* The first position of auditor was filled by William Boott.

A tipping point in the Panic happened in October 1857, when the steamer *Central America* was lost in an Atlantic Ocean hurricane taking almost $2 million in gold with her. This loss may have been the event that pushed the country into financial crisis. Railroad work across the country almost stopped until the Civil War. The Lake Erie business was so bad that the North Shore Line steamboats were docked and never redeployed.

The financial situation was hard enough on business, but the company also reported experiencing problems with through shipping due to a massive failure of a key bridge. *In March, the accident at the Desjardins Bridge, on the Great Western Railway, occurred, which stopped the entire through trade over the only connection with the East, and for two weeks, this road was entirely cut off in all freight communication.*

Mother Nature had a hand in disrupting freight and passenger traffic in 1857 as well. The annual report indicates that the problem was not suffered alone.

> *Another unavoidable misfortune, that has had its effect upon the business of the road the last month, has been the late opening of Buffalo Harbor, and the Erie Canal. Constant westward winds during the spring had the effect to keep the harbor at Buffalo filled with running ice, thus closing that harbor for purposes of lake intercourse until the eighteenth of last month; and, up to this date, (fifth of June,) owing to breakages, the canal has not been opened for through business, although it is now daily expected to be ready for use.*

In 1857, the *Johnston Detroit City Directory* listed the current conductors of passenger trains: Levi Carter, Geo. C. Hopper, Samuel Skelding, John Cochran, H. D. Harris, R. W. Hyde, R. W. Post, John Bancroft, Wm. B. Reynolds, George Wandless, C. H. Ingraham, Joseph Harvey, Daniel Wood, N. H. Kimball, and S. T. Moore.

The MCRR's gross earnings dropped more than 20 percent in 1858, prompting the company to develop an agreement with the Michigan Southern to fix prices and divide the profits. Revenue from through passenger traffic was divided equally and through freight profits were divided 58/42 percent with the higher percentage going to the MCRR. The merits of this arrangement were not mentioned, but through passenger and freight business was off by more than 33 percent in 1859. This was the first time the MCRR would participate in a price-fixing partnership. The practice became popular later and was known as a *pool agreement.*

Although money was tight, the MCRR continued to make small improvements in its operation. The first sleeping cars were put in place by the MCRR in 1858. They were of the Woodruff pattern and were day coaches altered by the railroad company.[7] A jointly published

Michigan Central and Great Western timetable indicates by 1860 the MCRR was using Case's Patent Sleeping Cars on night trains. Whether then-superintendent of the car shop, S. C. Case, was connected to the sleepers could not be determined, but it seems likely. Sometime in 1860 the company contracted with George Pullman to remodel two passenger cars into sleeping cars.

Almost from the day the railroad was purchased, politicians began trying to get favors or services for their constituents. A letter written in response to the governor in 1859 illustrates the point and the obvious frustration of Rice.

> *Governor Wisner, Dear Sir,*
>
> *I called upon Mr. R. N. Rice today & presented the letter you so kindly gave me requesting a pass on the M.C.R.R. Mr. Rice declines granting the favor for the reason that he thinks the company now pays more into the State Treasury in taxes than should be required of them & says that they propose to get all they can out of the state in shape of fares on the road.[8]*
>
> *Very Truly Yours, M. Miles*

Apparently the MCRR thought they were doing enough for the state and were not concerned about alienating politicians. It is more probable they responded to those who strongly supported the railroad and ignored the rest.

S. T. Newhall, the competent and respected superintendent of motive power, died on July 1, 1859, after eight years of service. It was Newhall who expanded the repair shops and *had a great talent for construction.* [He] *designed and built for passenger service the locomotive* Challenge, *of which George W. Latimer was the engineer. The* Challenge *was the wonder of railroad men—the biggest, best and most gorgeous engine of her day.[9]*

A. S. Sweet from the Buffalo & State Line Railroad succeeded Newhall, who apparently was a hard act to follow. It appears that the hard-driving Sweet was the main reason for the formation of the Brotherhood of Locomotive Engineers.

> *The death of S. T. Newhall hastened the organization of the Brotherhood of Engineers. The man who took Mr. Newhall's place was an overbearing tyrant. To resist him, and to secure justice, the engineers organized what was then called the Brotherhood of the Foot Board. They hoped to have him removed but failed in this, but out of this society grew that noble institution, the Brotherhood of Engineers.[10]*

The Brotherhood of Locomotive Engineers began with a meeting of MCRR men in Marshall, Michigan, in 1863. The organization was founded a month later in Detroit and is now the oldest labor union in the western hemisphere.

The beginning of the 1860s was filled with events that highlighted the soaring status of the company. On September 21, 1860, the Lord Renfrew, later known as the Prince of Wales, crossed over the Detroit River from Windsor, Ontario, for the purpose of taking the MCRR to Chicago and the Midwest to hunt birds. He was accompanied by a group of other British officials and the local newspaper covered the event.

> [O]*ver this pleasantly graded, and elegantly appointed line to Chicago, having expressed unqualified encomiums on the superior grade, precaution and general police of the Michigan Central. Upon which occasion as a token of his appreciation of the attentions of Mr. Rice, the Prince presented that gentleman with a diamond pin of exquisite workmanship, upon which is inwrought the heraldic crest and motto of the Prince, who, we are informed stated unreservedly his opinion that no English railway line existing could rival in its general details this model road.*[11]

Hopper was the conductor of the train carrying Lord Renfrew; superintendent Rice and MCRR director Farnsworth acted as attendants to the noble passenger. Rice's plush parlor car was used to accommodate the Lord. The train made it to Chicago in 8 hours, 40 minutes, a record time for the day.

Hopper had a busy year in 1860. In addition to working on the train that carried the Lord Renfrew, he was in charge of a MCRR train carrying delegates to Chicago for the purpose of nominating Lincoln for president and the train that carried Stephen A. Douglass on his stumping tour through lower Michigan.[12]

Princes and politicians were not the only ones getting the royal treatment from the MCRR. In 1860 the company made an effort to promote goodwill and increase business by offering to provide transportation to a group of southern dignitaries who were visiting Chicago. Although the purpose of their visit to Chicago was not discovered, a newspaperman captured the event and expounded on the virtues of the MCRR:

> *The excursionists have accepted the invitation of the Michigan Central and Great Western Railroad Companies to an excursion to Niagara Falls. Special*

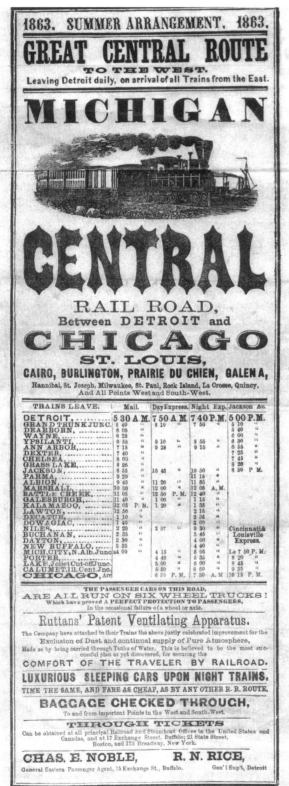

MCRR broadside, 1863.

trains made up as these roads know well and are abundantly able to make up from their splendid equipment, will run over both. The Michigan Central Railroad special train that will leave its great Passenger House at the foot of South Water Street . . . will be in the class and style of its cars, such on one as few roads in the country can command. The Michigan Central has a way and a style in the management of such occasions that makes them memorable. The Director's car, a parlor on wheels, will be a part of this train. H. E. Sargent, Esq. the representative of the road in this city, has been one of the most earnest and indefatigable in attendance and courtesies to these our visitor from the South, and will bear them company to the Falls.[13]

Brooks announced in the 1860 annual report that all the perishable structures, bridges, and culverts, had been *renewed or built of stone . . . 14 pile bridges have been entirely rebuilt, 13 arched and open stone culverts put in place of wooden structures, 40 miles of new fence . . . a carpenter's shop at Niles . . . wood shed at Chicago . . . water-house at Lake station. . . an oil-house at Detroit . . . a windmill at Gibson's for pumping.*

Brooks also was sold on the use of the telegraph, saying that *four year's experience in the use . . . under control of the Company, has settled the question of its importance.* Safety and prompt transmission of correspondence to agents were cited as incalculable services.

The apparent successes of early 1860 indicated that the MCRR was among the few who weathered the financial storm of 1857 without faltering. An early writer credits the MCRR for keeping the company in good stead during the troubled years.

The ownership of railroad shares was considered almost a premonitory symptom of bankruptcy and bankers had learned to fear a connection with railroad enterprises as something fatal to their credit. There are a few exceptions to this general condition. . . . The Michigan Central kept itself in pretty good fame.[14]

By 1860 the presence of the MCRR in Detroit was bringing a manufacturing boom to the city. The Detroit Car and Manufacturing Company (later purchased by George Pullman and Company), the Michigan Car Company, and the Peninsular Car Company all were formed to support railroading activities, as were the Detroit Wheel Company, the Griffin Car Wheel Company, the Russell Wheel and Foundry Company, and the Baugh Forge Company.

In January 1861, movement toward Civil War was eminent. The Confederate Constitution was adopted; Jefferson Davis was elected president of the Confederacy; and the first five of the southern states seceded from the Union. Over the next four years, Michigan would send 90,048 men to war, about 12 percent of its population.[15] Many of these men were employed by the MCRR prior to and after the war. Some left high positions to fight for the Union. One such man was George C. Hopper, passenger conductor on the Detroit to Chicago run.

Hopper resigned as conductor in 1861 and joined the First Michigan Infantry at Ann Arbor as a second lieutenant. Three years later, at the end of the war, he had reached the rank of major. *He was wounded at Gaines Mills and again at the second Bull Run* [where] *he was taken prisoner, but paroled.*[16] He returned to the MCRR and his passenger conductor job after the war and ended his railroad career as the company paymaster. During an 1896 interview with a Detroit newspaper, he talked about his job.

> [T]*hirty years ago the entire system could be paid off in five days. The mileage of the entire road [now] is about 1,600 miles, but to cover it all he has to travel 2,400 miles on each trip. The trip is started from Detroit and occupies fifteen days.*[17]

It is interesting to note that four years after this interview with the paymaster (1896), the MCRR eliminated his position. *The MCRR had abolished the system of paying by car sent out with payroll. Now they will pay with checks. The arrival of the pay car was a major event.*[18]

In 1861 Brooks reported a greater-than 26 percent increase in freight receipts, but passenger revenue was down. The annual report provides a nice overview of types of freight handled and future trends.

> *An important feature of the freighting business is the live stock; the number of cattle moved during the year, reaching 60,857 head . . . small animals and horses, 80,574; the former showing an increase of nearly 100 per cent over the two previous years, the latter a small decrease. The larger proportion of cattle transported are from Chicago, but a considerable percentage of the smaller animals are from local points. There are many important articles transported upon the line, purely local in their nature, such as apples, garden roots, wool, lumber . . . which show a steady gain from year to year, and have an important influence in adding yearly to its local business. The transportation of apples has this year been 100,975 barrels, about 40 per cent more than last, and 150 per cent larger than in 1857. This trade is entirely local, and an increased interest among farmers is manifested from year to year in the introduction of the best varieties of fruit for the supply of western markets, promising at no distant day to become one of the important exports of the State, and furnishing to this company a profitable article of transportation.*

Apparently the increases in freight receipts kept the company in the black as road, bridge, and culvert improvements continued without abatement.

On April 2, 1862, when the transportation of troops to the war in the South was making excessive demands upon the railroads, the Michigan Central engine house was destroyed by fire, and with it nine passenger locomotives valued at $90,000. *The roof and other parts of the square engine-house burned at Detroit in April are being replaced, and the building will again be in use in a few weeks. The damage to engines in the square engine-house in Detroit, at the time of the fire in April, has proved to be less than the estimate made at the time.*

The 1862 annual report showed another increase in freight and a decrease in passenger traffic. Expenditure descriptions were listed to give directors some indication of where all the money was going. Those descriptions now give us insight into the amount of work being conducted in addition to track improvements. The following was purchased and put into place:

> *1,400 cedar telegraph poles; 57 new culverts; 62 cattle guards; 4 highway bridges; 37 miles of new fence; 3,571 feet new side-tracks. Extensive repairs and building were completed: the enlargement of engine-house at Michigan City; a new brick water-house and windmill at Decatur; new small passenger-houses at Pokagon, Chamberlain's, Tolleston and Ceresco; new stationary engine at the Detroit grain-house, and extensive repairs of the building; renewal of the dock in front of same; new stock-yards at Dayton, Pokagon, Dowagiac, Lawton and Kalamazoo; a new roof and general repairs of freight-house at Battle Creek; repainting a large proportion of the station buildings of the line and also the bridges. Finally the following were purchased: 106 new covered eight-wheeled freight cars; 10 new large platform freight cards; and 89 hand, wood and rubble cars.*

The New Albany & Salem Railroad, which had earlier leased its branch from Michigan City to the Illinois state line to the MCRR, was damaged by the Panic of 1857 and had to reorganize in 1859. Its new name became the Louisville, New Albany & Chicago Railway. Still struggling in 1862, it offered to lease a portion of its line from Lafayette, Indiana, to Michigan City. The MCRR accepted the proposal, which opened the door for the company to run through trains to and from Cincinnati, Ohio. It was this section of MCRR-leased road that hosted Abraham Lincoln's funeral train in April 1865.

> *It was in front of that depot* [MCRR at Michigan City] *that the funeral train bearing the body of Abraham Lincoln stopped at 8:25 a.m. on May 1, 1865.*

The train halted under a 35-foot memorial arch, which had been constructed over the tracks. The arch bore sayings in honor of the president and was decorated with flap, evergreen boughs, and choice flowers.[19]

The year 1862 was also the first time the switch from wood to coal-burning locomotives was mentioned. Superintendent of Motive Power A. S. Sweet reported that they had one coal-burning engine and thought they would have one more next year. The MCRR was using Jackson coal produced by mines near Jackson, Michigan. Two of these mines were located on the Main Line, west of Jackson. The Detroit and Jackson Coal Company owned the mine at Woodville and the Jackson Coal Company owned the mine at Sandstone.[20]

The switch to coal would save time spent loading wood into the tender at frequent intervals. In addition, more mileage could be gained from coal than wood. A ton of coal would produce 35.41 miles and a cord of wood 33.62 miles. With the cost just slightly higher on coal, it was economical and efficient to switch.

Passenger revenue had declined every year since 1857, but finally turned around with an increase in 1863 ($2,946,560) and 1864 ($3,434,548). Passenger revenue jumped 18 percent in 1863 and 29 percent in 1864. Freight revenue increased 21 and 4 percent in the same years. Brooks told stockholders,

> *The track, buildings, bridges and rolling stock of the line are in every respect in as good condition as at the commencement of the year, and in no way has the property of the company been allowed to deteriorate in value. Those stockholders who have been over the line during the year can perhaps vouch for the general good condition of the company's track, structures and rolling stock so far as appearances at least go to enable them to form an opinion.*

Some of the items listed as expenses in the 1863 annual report included building track and related items in the past year: *7,920 feet new side track at different points upon line; straightening line near Scio to get rid of bad curves, requiring grading and finishing up of 4,750 feet of new road and fencing; 12 miles rail fence; 19 miles board fence; 75 gates at farm crossings; 30 cattle guards; 14 stone culverts with 324 cords stone; 4 pile bridges with stone abutments with 246 feet aggregate length.* Construction costs of buildings and related improvements were expensive and extensive. Stockyards were built at Lawton and at Michigan City. The stockyard was enlarged at Detroit. New offices were built at the upper end of the brick freight depot in Detroit. Rebuilding 800 feet of dock front entirely from the low-water line was completed as was raising and planking 11,700 square feet of additional platform facilities on the riverfront. Two new elevators went into the wheat-house. A new iron turntable replaced the wooden one at the Detroit engine-house. Three new woodsheds and four new water-houses were built on the line.

On January 23, 1864, the Michigan Central Railroad accomplished something it had not done before; it was featured on the front page of a national magazine. Unfortunately the article did not leave a positive impression of the line. *Harper's Weekly* placed a 12 × 11-inch woodcut image of a MCRR locomotive stuck in the snow on its cover page. The caption beneath read, *Sufferings in a Snowstorm on the Michigan Central.* The story was so good, it was retold in other railroad histories of the day. (See Chapter 14 for information about the incident.)

Brooks reported in 1865 that land was being purchased along the Detroit River, south of the depot, for stockyards. Also, the recurring issue of whether the use of Jackson coal was worth the time and trouble of changing out locomotive iron fireboxes for copper was discussed. Apparently Sweet may have been dragging his feet about making the changes. According to someone who was there, Sweet had issues with using coal.

> About the time coal was discovered on the line of the Michigan Central road near Jackson, Mich. It was pronounced unfit for use by Allen Sweet, master mechanic of that road. It so happened that while I was on a visit to Detroit, I saw Assistant Superintendent C. H. Hurd. . . . I asked him how he got along with his coal burners. He said they were a failure, that the coal was no good. I then told Mr. Hurd, that I had used some of the coal on the Burlington road, and found it superior instead of inferior as Mr. Sweet had stated. There had been a coal miners' strike in Illinois and the Burlington had from necessity got some Michigan coal, so I knew from experience it was good, but Mr. Sweet had agreed to run the road for less money than his predecessor, and he could not do so and change his engines into good coal burners, and he did everything he could to prevent the success. . . . Mr. Sweet, like many other officials, was working for himself more than for the company.[21]

Due to some controversy about when the MCRR changed their locomotives from wood to coal-burning, a considerable portion of Sweet's report from 1865 is quoted.

> During the year we have turned out one copper diaphragm fire-box engine for burning coal. I have also one mongrel engine burning coal and another coal-burning

MICHIGAN
CENTRAL RAILROAD

1864,   1864,

PATENT SLEEPING CARS
—AND—
Ruttan's Warming, Ventilating and Anti-Dusting Apparatus
ARE IN USE ON THIS GREAT THOROUGHFARE.

At the Company's Ticket Office, in the Depot, foot of Third Street,

THROUGH TICKETS
Can be purchased to all the principal Cities and Towns in the United States and Canadas.

The Westward Trains on this old reliable Road connect at Chicago, in the Great Central Depot, with trains of the Illinois Central, and Chicago, Burlington and Quincy Rail Roads, and also with all other trains diverging from that city. At Michigan City with trains of Louisville, New Albany and Chicago Railroad to all parts of Indiana. At Lake Junction with the Joliet Cut-off trains to Matteson and Joliet; connecting at Matteson and Calumet with trains of the Illinois Central Rail Road, and at Joliet with Trains of the St. Louis, Alton and Chicago, and the Chicago and Rock Island Railroads.

All Eastern Trains connect at Detroit with the Great Western and Grand Trunk Railways of Canada, the Detroit & Toledo and Detroit & Milwaukee R. R.'s, and Cleveland Steamers.

The Directors chosen June 22d, 1864, are:

JOHN W. BROOKS, Boston.	ERASTUS CORNING, Albany.
NATHANIEL THAYER, Boston.	D. D. WILLIAMSON, New York.
R. B. FORBES, Boston.	GEORGE F. TALMAN, New York.
H. H. HUNNEWELL, Boston.	J. M. FORBES, Boston.
ELON FARNSWORTH, Detroit.	

OFFICERS:

President—JOHN W. BROOKS.
Vice President—H. H. HUNNEWELL.
Treasurer—ISAAC LIVERMOORE.
Superintendent—R. N. RICE.
Auditor—WILLIAM BOOTT.
Clerk—WILLIAM B FOWLE, JR.
Assistant Superintendent—CHAS. H. HURD.
Local Treasurer—OLIVER MACY.
Local Auditor—JOHN NEWELL.
Cashier—GEO. W. GILBERT.
General Ticket Agent—THOS. FRAZER,
Chief Engineer—JOHN M. BERRIEN.

Master Mechanic—A. S. SWEET, JR.
Master Car Repairs—J. B SUTHERLAND.
Road Master, E. Division, Detroit—C. H. WHITE
Road Master, W. Division, Niles—S. R JOHNSON
Freight Agent, Detroit—L. P. KNIGHT.
Gen'l Freight Agent, Chicago—H. E. SARGENT
C. KNOWLTON, Joliet, Ass't Superintendent Joliet Division, and Northern Division (Lafayette to Michigan City) of the Louisville, New Albany and Chicago Railroad Company, which part is managed by the Michigan Central Railroad Company.

Advertisement from *Clark's Detroit City Directory,* 1864.

passenger engine about ready to come out of the shop. I have just taken another engine in the shop for a new copper fire-box, and also have an engine, which has been blown up; this I shall build into a coal-burner the coming year, with an entire new boiler. I am strongly of the opinion that nothing but copper fire-boxes will stand Jackson coal, and that the diaphragm is essential to the economical use of the same, when considered in connection with the durability of the engines, and shall adopt that plan in fitting up the next coal burners.

The Civil War strained the resources of northern railroad companies by tying up rolling stock for movement of troops and supplies. In 1864 the government had need for rolling stock, so it *requisitioned* it from the MCRR. A half cash, half credit sale was made of 75 freight cars, four second-class passenger cars and one engine. The engine that went to the government was the *Stranger.*

Building expenses for 1864 included: *New grain elevator at Detroit (not finished); new brick passenger depot at Ypsilanti (not finished); engine-house and turntable at Dexter; turntables at Detroit, Michigan City and Battle Creek; extensive repairs of freight and passenger houses at Jackson; and new stock yards at Battle Creek, Augusta, Dowagiac and Chamberlains.*

As mentioned earlier and elsewhere, the officials of the MCRR were staunch backers of the Union and President Lincoln. They continued this support when the war was over. The MCRR sent passenger cars to Indianapolis to pick up discharged soldiers who had traveled from Nashville in cattle cars. *When the Michigan soldiers returned . . . they were all given meals in the Michigan Central depot.*[22]

In October 1865, the huge MCRR Detroit warehouse on Third Street caught fire. Through the bravery of firemen James R. Elliott, *engineers Francis Beaufort and Reilly and Fireman John Kendall, remained at their posts until their coats were burned from their backs.*[23] prevented the fire from spreading, but the warehouse and its contents were destroyed. The November 4, 1865, edition of *Harper's Weekly* described the conflagration.

> *The most destructive conflagration which ever occurred in Detroit took place on the night of October 18. The freight depot and shed of the Michigan Central Railroad, stored with valuable commodities, and representing property in all portions of the country, were totally destroyed, crippling severely one of the most enterprising of Western railroad corporations.*
>
> *The fire broke out in a train of cars, which was being loaded with freight in a section of the depot. A barrel of varnish had been broken and its contents were spreading over one of the cars when a light in the hand of one of the*

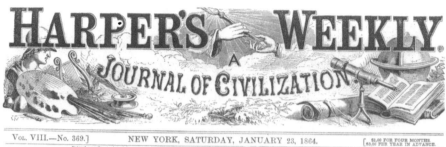

Harper's Weekly Journal, January 23, 1864.

workmen coming in contact with the varnish, the whole car burst into flames. The fire spread rapidly, all efforts to stay its progress proving futile. In the excitement of the moment the burning car, with those ahead of it on the track, was run from where it was being loaded—-near the Third Street end of the depot—to the westerly end of the structure into the open air. The burning material dropped from the car as it passed thus firing the building at numerous points at once. Several trains of cars in the vicinity were also burned. The total loss by the fire is estimated at one million of dollars, the loss in freight alone amounted to one-half that sum. It is feared that three men were burned to death, as they have been missing since the fire.

The 1865 annual report provides some wonderful insight into the planning and development of the MCRR grounds at Third and River Streets. It is difficult to imagine cattle being driven through the streets of Detroit in 1865. Brooks provides the narrative.

Soon after the land for the Detroit terminus was purchased in 1846–47, we made unsuccessful efforts to obtain, in addition, the river front adjoining, and which we had to cross with our tracks to approach our own grounds. The death of the former owner having brought that property into the market, we have purchased it, extinguishing rights to five separate crossing places over our tracks, and giving 3,000 feet of unbroken front upon the river. The increasing density of the population in the vicinity of our terminus, together with our increasing cattle traffic, have lately added very much to the difficulty of driving so large an amount of live-stock through the streets of Detroit to our old place of shipment. To provide a larger and more convenient place of shipment, and one less liable to public objection, we have purchased, at fair prices, several lots upon the river, just below our depot grounds, and accessible to our tracks, which together form a block of about 350 feet deep from street to river channel, with a front upon the river of 358 feet.

Passenger revenue jumped a whopping 30 percent in 1865 and *may be attributed, in a measure, to the movement of troops to places of rendezvous, and thence on their way to the field.* But regular through traffic declined because of a government order requiring all our U.S. through passengers via Canadian lines to have passports.

On another positive note that year, officials announced that the long-awaited grain elevator was finished. It was unsurpassed by any similar structure and *has all the modern appliances for economical working, and will be a source of great convenience, as well as profit, to the Company, in its increased facilities for handling the cereals tributary to the line.* The old elevator remained, but it was in need of repair.

BURNING OF THE MICHIGAN CENTRAL FREIGHT DEPOT AT DETROIT, MICHIGAN, OCTOBER 18, 1865.
[SKETCHED BY L. T. IVES.]

Detroit freight depot fire print from *Harper's Weekly Journal,* November 4, 1865.

Other accomplishments of the year include disposing of the old passenger dining house at Marshall and building a new, larger passenger depot, *with hotel accommodations,* in its place. It was *a credit to the company.* Other improvements at Marshall included: an *Iron turntable,* [with] *stone foundation and curbing, 22 new tubs and 925 feet of iron pipes at the engine-house.*

Other stations along the line saw improvements. A new enginehouse built at Lake accommodated four engines, and new freighthouses at Mattawan and Three Oaks. Salt Creek got a new pile bridge, 100 feet long.

Three through trains were running to Chicago in 1865, as in the previous two years, and using the two through telegraph wires owned by the company. Extra local trains ran to Dexter and Kalamazoo, as business required.

Perhaps the greatest public relations event connected with the MCRR to date occurred on September 5, 1866. President Andrew Johnson arrived in Detroit to start a journey to Chicago. *The Presidential party had a military and Masonic escort to the station of the Michigan Central Railroad, and the President, in leaving, stood on the platform of the rear car, where he was heartily cheered.*[24] The train left Detroit at 10:30 A.M.

and with him were Secretary of State General Grant, Postmaster-General Randall, Admiral Farragut, and others. During the 280-mile trip along the Main Line to Chicago, the President gave speeches at Ypsilanti, Ann Arbor, Albion, Marshall, Battle Creek, Kalamazoo, Niles, and Michigan City before arriving at Lake Street Station at 10:30 P.M.

Gross revenue for 1866 was up again to $4,446,490. A second track was built to connect Grand Trunk Junction to the Detroit station, three miles away. It is believed this track was built to increase access to the GTR ferry system across the St. Clair River at Port Huron as well as to accommodate traffic from other sources in this area. The Port Huron crossing was seldom blocked in the winter. The junction also gave the GTR access to the MCRR stockyards.

MCRR officials took great care in planning the rebuilding of the freight depot that burned down the previous year. The loss was a financial disaster *causing a large extraordinary expenditure for rebuilding, and for payment for property burned for which the Company was liable.* Over $119,000 was paid to claimants who lost property. The 1866 annual report provides a nice description of the new structure.

> *The new building is in a good state of forwardness, and will not only be fire-proof in all respects, but a much more commodious building than the old one. The offices for use of the Freight Department and general offices of the Company, are at the upper end of the main building, 130 feet in length, on Third Street, 36 feet deep, and three stories high, but entirely cut off from the main building by partition wall. Each floor of the office building is provided with ample fireproof vaults, and will be warmed by steam. The offices and main structure will have iron roofs. The walls are now ready for the roofs, which are going on at once, and the buildings will be ready for occupancy at an early day; when completed, it is believed they will be the most perfect buildings of their kind to be found on this continent.*

Not much is ever mentioned about other problems caused by the fire. The docks were also burned and needed extensive repair. Thirteen hundred feet of timber was used to fix the dock on the waterfront. More than 54,000 square feet of floor space covering 750 feet of dock for dock freight sheds had to be built.

Several important developments came to the MCRR in 1867. On January 1, the company joined with five other railroads (Chicago, Burlington & Quincy; Chicago & Alton; Illinois Central; New York Central & Hudson River; Boston & Albany) to form a freight company called the *Blue Line*. The group believed that establishing a line for the sole purpose of forwarding freight between the Atlantic and Pacific coasts without changing cars would be attractive to shippers. Their assumption was correct and the confederation lasted at least 10 years. The Blue Line even printed its shipping documents in blue ink.

Another development recorded in the 1867 annual report seems as if it was a long time coming. Brooks stated that on January 1, 1867, the Great Western Railway finally finished changing the gauge (the distance between the inner sides of the rails of their track) from the Canadian government preferred 5 feet 6 inch width to the 4 feet 8 inch gauge used by the MCRR. But they hadn't actually changed the gauge; they added a gauge and the flexibility for the MCRR to run cars through Canada by adding a third rail.

> *An important feature, however, worthy of notice, is that with the use of the uniform gauge through Canada, one passenger train each way is now running between Chicago and Suspension Bridge daily. The dock, ferry-slip, and tracks fitted for use of cars of both gauges are completed, and property transported by the Great Western Railway, in its own cars, going to local points upon our line, is handled by the Michigan Central at Detroit, under an arrangement made upon the completion of the third rail* [in Canada].

The year 1867 was early in the development of refrigerator cars (more commonly known as reefers), and apparently this experiment didn't take on the first try. Local newspapers indicate that reefers didn't regularly run on the Main Line until 1872.[25] What apparently did take was George Pullman's efforts to get the MCRR to put one of his new Palace Hotel cars on the Main Line. Brooks announced that the Palace Hotel car would run from Chicago to Albany.

Gross revenue for 1867 was $4,325,490 or $121,000 less than the previous year. This 2.72 percent decline was attributed to the lowering of freight rates. Tonnage moved was actually up as business increased.

Brooks left the Michigan Central Railroad presidency in June 1867, after becoming ill over yet another difficult building project. The governor of Massachusetts named Brooks to head a commission with the task of determining how to build a railroad tunnel under the Hoosac Mountains. Brooks took over the project, but technology of the day prevented the project's successful completion. He became very ill over the failure, quit the MCRR and took leave for a short

The approach to the suspension bridge shows the added rail.

time from his other responsibilities, which were many. While still working for the MCRR, he supervised several other MCRR feeder lines. He started as a director on the Chicago, Burlington & Quincy (1857–1876) before leaving the MCRR. He did the same for the Hannibal & St. Joseph Railroad (1857–1870), and was president of the Burlington & Missouri River Railroad and the Omaha & Southwestern Railroad (1872).[26]

Brooks had a falling out with Forbes over a loss of money during the financial Panic of 1873. Forbes felt Brooks led him to believe some railroad investments were sound when he knew they were not. When those companies went bankrupt, Forbes lost thousands of dollars. The friendship formed 27 years earlier was over.

Shortly thereafter, Brooks became ill again and totally retired. He moved home to Boston, and languished with nothing to do for the first time in his life. Sometime later he moved to Heidelberg, Germany, where he died on September 16, 1881.[27] The mastermind that drove the building of Michigan's greatest railroad was dead at the age of 62.

CHAPTER 13

JAMES F. JOY
BUILDS AN EMPIRE

When Joy returned to the MCRR as president, he was also serving as an officer on the Chicago, Burlington & Quincy and the Burlington & Missouri River lines. Such were the job opportunities for a genius in pioneer railroad operations.

In 1868, Joy replaced Brooks and Homer E. Sargent replaced Rice as superintendent. Sargent was formerly a MCRR freight agent in Chicago.

Also, in 1868, the first experiments with three miles of steel rails failed. Because they were more brittle than iron, they subsequently were prone to break more easily. But the previous year's experiment with Pullman's Palace Cars was a success, as Joy announced that the MCRR was extending an interest in the company and would be adding more cars and extending their use to New York and Boston. Company advertisements were calling the Palace Cars something more catchy, *Palatial Sleeping Cars, Pullman's Patent.*[1]

That year the Blue Line was also gaining favor, and the annual report gives us an interesting overview of the specialized freight-handling program.

> *Upwards of one thousand of these [uniformly built freight] cars are now completed and in use, and there has been no instance thus far of a day's delay to freight by reason of detention for repairs incident to running cars of mixed construction to points remote from home. The organization of the Blue Line has so*

far commended itself to the favor of connecting roads that, during the past year, the Providence and Worcester, the Worcester and Nashua, the Housatonic, and the Jackson, Lansing and Saginaw roads have voluntarily subscribed to its articles of agreement, and put in their quota of the new uniform cars. These roads will prove valuable auxiliaries to the line, and share its advantages. The entire business is transacted by the officers and agents of the several roads interested, and its earnings, unlike the generality of other through freight lines, pass entirely to the roads participating in the organization. The following roads, forming an aggregate of 3,020 miles, are now parties to the line, all having put in their quota of new cars, which are being increased from time to time by each: Illinois Central, New York Central, St. Louis, Alton and Chicago, Hudson River, Chicago, Burlington & Quincy, Boston and Albany, Michigan Central, Housatonic, Jackson, Lansing & Saginaw, Providence and Worcester, Great Western, Worcester and Nashua.

The line is thus composed of roads running from the five important Mississippi points, Cairo, St. Louis, Quincy, Burlington and Dunleith to New York, Bridgeport, Conn., Providence, Boston, Nashua, N. H., and all intermediate points, over track of uniform gauge. The cars of this line are also run with through shipments from seaboard cities to St. Paul, Omaha, Kansas City and extreme points of completion of Pacific road, without breaking bulk. Additions have been made to the stock of refrigerator cars, which are in good demand and highly appreciated by shippers of perishable freight in both directions.

Joy was obviously happy with the telegraph system they were using. They were running all trains under direct control of a chief train dispatcher out of Kalamazoo. He reported that during the 12 years the telegraph system has been in service *no accident has ever occurred in the movement of trains under running orders from* [the dispatcher's] *department.*

When James F. Joy became president of the MCRR, he had already been involved with the company for more than 20 years as a lawyer. Through his work with the MCRR and railroad companies in the region, he gained knowledge of railroad operations and the respect of railroad men across the country. During this stage of his career he was known as the best legal mind in the railroad business.

The year 1868 was bad for business. Freight passing through the Huron River valley was delayed. The bridges were damaged or weakened by ice jams stacking up and damaging supports and abutments between Dexter and Ann Arbor, as the water was high that year.

> *The business of the road was seriously interrupted during the first two weeks in March by freshets of unusual severity in the Huron Valley. Several of the bridges were weakened to such extent by passing ice that freight trains were not moved over them for ten days. The passenger trains were all kept running; in some few instances changing passengers and baggage at unsafe points. The loss of traffic thus occasioned by the flood during our busiest season, amounted to upwards of $50,000. All the bridges thus damaged have been thoroughly repaired and are now in better condition than before.*

Another attempt at using steel rail was tried on a portion of the Joliet cut-off. It was relaid in 1868 with three hundred tons of Bessemer-produced English steel rail, manufactured by John Brown & Co. (The "Joliet Cut-off" is the local nickname given to a railroad that extended 44.5 miles from the MCRR Lake Station (later East Gary), Indiana, to Joliet, Illinois. This railroad was built by the Joliet and Northern Indiana Railroad Co., with extensive financial help from the MCRR. Upon it's completion in 1854, the J&NI RR was leased in perpetuity by the MCRR and became it's Joliet Branch. This was the first "feeder" or branch line to be acquired by the MCRR.) Joy liked this steel because it was down at a heavy traffic point during the winter and showed no wear. This success with steel stirred an interest in replacing all the iron rail on the Main Line, but the product needed further testing.

By 1869 the MCRR had 100 locomotives, of which 14 were coal fired; 109 passenger cars; and 1,809 freight cars. Passenger cars were being fitted with Ruttan's Warming, Ventilating & Anti-Dusting Apparatus and the Miller Compression Platform and Canopies, which covered the gaps between cars. The Miller Platforms cost the MCRR $310 each in 1873. It was beginning to be possible to stay warm in a coach and walk between cars and not get wet or covered with cinders and ash.

Four daily passenger trains ran in each direction between Detroit and Dexter. Day and night trains were now running from Chicago to Michigan City to pick up through passengers from Cincinnati, Lafayette, Indianapolis, and Louisville. The 1869 annual report makes the statement

Engine *Barry* helping work on a bridge in Washtenaw County, c. 1869. (Courtesy Dexter Area Historical Society & Museum)

that since opening it had carried more than 10 million people and not one has been injured in a first class passenger coach. No mention was made of the 18 second class passengers killed or the 60 injured at Grand Crossing in 1853. (See Chapter 14 for more information on MCRR train wrecks.)

Building and repairs continued strong in 1869. The highlights were new wooden enginehouses built at Joliet and Niles. A new huge brick freighthouse, 457 feet long by 37 feet wide, with projecting slate roof and offices, was built at Jackson. A new grain and freighthouse went up at Parma, and Ann Arbor's passenger house was enlarged with a dining room and kitchen added.

Also in 1869 the MCRR was operating under the Great Central Route banner, offering four express trains daily (Sunday excepted with only one evening train running) from Detroit to points west. General passenger agents were advertising connections to Milwaukee, St. Paul, St. Louis, Omaha, North Platte, New Orleans, and all points west, northwest, and southwest.[2]

The population along the Main Line was growing and business was booming. For some time the MCRR was running a local freight train between Detroit and Dexter. In 1869 the local was extended to run to Jackson. In September the MCRR tore out the old small turntable that was across the tracks from the Dexter depot and installed one large enough to turn a locomotive and tender.[3]

Passenger cars continued to improve. The 1869 annual report claimed that all 57 first class coaches were in a state of excellence. It also indicated for the first time that a new train brake was in operation (Myer's Brake). All were supplied with the Ruttan plan of ventilation,

> . . . which is successful in the almost entire exclusion of dust and cinders and the production of an abundant supply of pure air. All the twelve-wheeled, first-class coaches are of uniform size and style of build; and in renewing, care is taken to preserve uniformity in the improvements, consisting of raised roofs, and the application of the Miller platform, coupling and buffer, also the Myer's safety train brake. Baggage and second-class cars are added of similar outline and attachments, combining entire uniformity of train, with great strength and resisting power. Several of our trains are now thus made up, and others will be added as the renewals progress.

The price of new freight cars that were obligated by commitments to the Blue Line was $177,888. Land south of the Chicago depot was purchased for $800,000 for the purpose of enabling the MCRR, ICRR, and CB&Q railroads to erect a new, even larger passenger station. After selling the land to the railroads, the city would not allow the station to be built until 1893.

The 1870 annual report listed the companies in which the MCRR had invested through the purchase of bonds. This list illustrates the company's interest in developing feeder lines.

> Chicago, Burlington and Quincy R. R. Co.
> Hannibal and St. Joseph R. R. Co.
> Joliet and N. Indiana R. R. Co.
> Burlington and Missouri River R. R. Co.
> Jackson, Lansing and Saginaw R. R. Co.
> Carthage and Burlington R. R. Co.
> Dixon, Peoria and Hannibal R. R. Co.

In the same year Joy began leasing feeder lines. On January 1, 1870, it leased the Michigan Airline Railroad, which would reduce

GREAT CENTRAL ROUTE.

1868   1869

MICHIGAN CENTRAL R. R.

DETROIT AND CHICAGO.

FOUR EXPRESS TRAINS LEAVE DETROIT DAILY,

SUNDAYS EXCEPTED,

On Arrival of trains on the Great Western and Grand Trunk Railways from the East,

FOR CHICAGO,

MAKING DIRECT CONNECTIONS WITH TRAINS FOR

Milwaukee, St. Paul, St. Louis, Omaha, North Platte, New Orleans

AND ALL POINTS WEST, NORTH-WEST AND SOUTH-WEST.

PULLMAN'S PALACE SLEEPING CARS ON ALL NIGHT TRAINS

The Michigan Central Railroad is acknowledged to be the Model Railroad of the Country, with its Palace Day Cars and Splendid Sleeping Coaches, all of which have six wheel trucks, making this one of the

Safest and Most Pleasant Routes to the West.

Tickets by this Route can be obtained at all Railroad Stations and Ticket Offices in Canada.

JAMES F. JOY, President, Detroit.
H. E. SARGENT, Gen'l Supt., Chicago.
W. K. MUIR, Ass't Gen'l Supt., Detroit.
C. E. NOBLE, Gen'l Eastern Agent, New York.

Advertisement from *Clark's Detroit City Directory,* 1868.

Photograph of MCRR employees and engines 208 & 301 near Marshall, c. 1874.
(Courtesy Dave Tinder collection, Clements Library, University of Michigan)

the route between Detroit and Chicago by 16 miles. The lease included the 11 miles from Niles to South Bend. The Airline acquisition was typical of how the MCRR did business when they believed it benefited the company—they aided it by buying the line's bonds, primarily to ensure it would be properly built, and then they leased it, finishing the building of it themselves.

After the Airline acquisition, the MCRR went on a leasing binge. On April 18, 1870, the Grand River Valley Railroad was brought in; on July 1, 1870, the Kalamazoo & South Haven Railroad joined; on August 31, 1871, the Jackson, Lansing & Saginaw entered the group; and on July 31, 1873, the Detroit & Bay City Railroad was leased.

The addition of the Jackson, Lansing & Saginaw Railroad (JL&SRR) was another first for the MCRR. The JL&SRR was a land grant railroad, meaning the state wanted it built and would pay a land bounty of 500,000 acres to anyone willing to complete the road. Of course the MCRR took the deal, but it provoked animosity on the board, because some believed the land would never be sold and a profit never made from the JL&SRR.

Joy recalled that in addition to leasing, the company was building and buying roads. A few years after the Detroit & Bay City acquisition (1874), *the MCRR purchased the Chicago and Canada Southern and the Canada Southern, which eventually became part of the through line from Chicago to Buffalo.*[4]

The MCRR hadn't added a feeder line since September 7, 1854, when the Joliet & Northern Indiana was leased. The length of time that passed between the first and second leasing gives one an idea of when the company began to feel the effects of competition. Earnings per ton-mile had dropped 48 percent between the end of the Civil War and 1873. Joy's answer to this problem was to carry twice the freight as in previous years. That freight had to come from additional feeder lines.

The 1870 annual report also provided a list of stations and the number of passengers and tons of freight forwarded from each location from May 31, 1869, to May 31, 1870. This list not only is a handy reference to stations operating in those years, it indicates which stations were merely shipping points for freight only. It also shows the difference in levels of activity, giving an idea of why some stations were eliminated over time. These lists appear in Appendix G.

The report also confirms that the road was split into two divisions for repair purposes—from Kalamazoo east and west. C. H. White was the roadmaster from Kalamazoo to Detroit and S. R. Johnson was roadmaster from Kalamazoo to Chicago.

In 1870, James F. Joy was at a high point in his career. Arguably the country's top railroad lawyer, he was also an outstanding president running one of the premier railroads in the nation. The following event reminds us that he had his hand in the operations of a many others. But even the mighty make unwise decisions on occasion, and much like today, the foibles of the rich and famous are covered in the national news. On November 7, 1870, Joy was robbed. He was conducting railroad business with the Farmers' Loan and Trust Company when he left the bank with *a bundle containing fifty bonds of the Chicago and Iowa Railroad Company for $1,000 each.* He first went to the Michigan Central Railroad office, then to his room at the St. Nicholas Hotel (New York City). He left the bundle in his room for a few minutes and on returning he discovered his room had been burglarized and the bonds were stolen.[5] Joy probably did not spend much time worrying about his poor decision as he had a railroad to run and the rails on that road were rapidly deteriorating.

The problem of rapidly wearing rails came to a head in 1870 for three reasons: (1) the single-track railroad was so busy it had reached its capacity to handle more traffic; (2) train speeds had increased because of technological advances in locomotive, rolling stock, and the way in which they were dispatched; and (3) the locomotives and cars had become larger and heavier. Joy said in 1870, *business had assumed its maximum volume with the road in its then condition, and the road was everywhere clogged with it.* The company was forced to again reconsider steel replacements in spite of earlier breakage problems. Apparently improvement in steel production and successes on other railroads boosted confidence in steel.

The job of laying rail on the Air Line was completed in 1871. Joy said it was laid, *all the way, with steel rails from the Scranton Works in Pennsylvania, which are of iron of harder quality than almost any in this country* and was open for traffic on February 1. New Troy Bessemer steel rails were being tested elsewhere.

Finally in 1871 the decision was made to replace all iron rails with steel between Detroit and Jackson. During this replacement, the decision was made to double-track the road between Detroit and Ypsilanti and Niles to Lake Station, approximately 85 miles of the most heavily traveled track. Several years later, in 1873, the company noted that the steel rails *performed with more than ordinary regularity and safety* through a severe winter.

The decision was also made to close company operations at Marshall and move them to Jackson. Jackson had become a hub of several recently acquired branch lines. Also, the change put equal mileage between the yards at Detroit and Michigan City.

The MCRR also began adding Westinghouse air brakes to passenger trains in 1870–1871. A couple of years later, the company noted that it was paying $120 for air brake installation on each car.

The year 1871 was yet another difficult for the MCRR. The Detroit River froze over twice for weeks at a time, stopping freight movements at that point between the U.S. and Canada. Plus, the loss all of its buildings in the Chicago fire left no place to store freight and building materials much needed by the city. At least one freighthouse was made of stone and the walls were still standing, so it was rebuilt. The magnificent passenger house shared by the MCRR, ICRR and CB&QRR was also severely damaged, but it too was rebuilt and used until 1893.

The 1872 annual report provided an overview of how the Chicago fire impacted the property and finances of the MCRR.

> *The large loss in our west-bound freight traffic, both through and local, is chiefly attributable to the great fire at Chicago, on the 9th of October, which destroyed all our freight buildings, and interrupted largely, all business that required depot shelter and accommodation. This interruption continued, in part, until permanent buildings could be restored; our room being insufficient to admit of temporary shelter to any considerable extent, without interfering with the construction of permanent buildings, which were completed with the utmost expedition. The indications of the general spread of the fire, gave opportunity to remove all our trains and cars from its neighborhood, and none were destroyed. A large amount of property in cars at the time of the fire, and such as the limited time would permit loading, was saved; as also were all the books and papers pertaining to the current business of the freight department, from which is obtainable a correct statement of all the freight destroyed. The losses of property in the warehouses are believed to amount to not far from $250,000.*

The same year, Sargent announced a death in the MCRR family.

> *It is quite in place here to make mention of the loss of the valuable services of the late Mr. S. R. Johnson, connected with the road since its ownership by the*

Engine *Falcon*, 1871.

MCRR freight building #70 destroyed by the Chicago Fire.

Company, and for the last eighteen years roadmaster. His judgment in the selection of men, his even justice to all, his rare executive abilities, and fertility of expedients in time of emergency, well entitled him to the respect in which he was uniformly held.

A year later, Sargent also announced that shortly before the 1873 report was presented, the company *met with a severe loss in the death of Mr. S. A. Sweet, for fourteen years at the head of the locomotive department, as its superintendent. During his term of service he has conducted the affairs of this department with great success and fidelity.*

In addition to adding feeder lines to add traffic and fight competition, the MCRR wanted desperately to open a direct connection with the east over the Great Western. But the Canadian managers were very conservative, as evidenced by their reluctance to change track gauge despite 14 years of connecting with the MCRR. Being unable to cross the Detroit River during the winter was an obstacle that had to be overcome. The MCRR sought to construct either a bridge or dig a tunnel under the river. Finally things started to move. On March 8, 1870, the Canadian Parliament introduced a bill to incorporate the Detroit River Transit Company, a company controlled by the Michigan Central and the Great Western Railway. The bill gave the company the authority *to build either a bridge over the Detroit River or to construct a tunnel.*[6]

Some relief was coming into place with the help of a competitor. The Grand Trunk Railroad was building the International Bridge across the Niagara, near Buffalo, New York, which was scheduled for completion late in 1873. They already had a year-around ferry across the St. Clair River *close to the foot of Lake Huron at the point where it is always open. The Board . . . feels that to the extent of the capacity of that road this company will find relief when all other avenues fail, and that probably never again will it suffer so greatly as in the past three winters, and especially in the last.*

Even with the Grand Trunk sending traffic northeast to Port Huron from Detroit across the St. Clair River by ferry and the Niagara River by bridge, the pressure was not off the MCRR to find a way over or under the often-frozen Detroit River. But efforts to build a tunnel failed. Joy announced bad news to stockholders in the 1873 annual report.

> *The Board regrets to state, that the work upon the small tunnel under the Detroit River, undertaken in part as a drainage sewer for the main tunnel, but also to test the nature of the earth under the river, has developed such difficulties, as to compel them reluctantly to abandon that work. The only alternative is a bridge.*

Joy went on to say that Congress had issued a resolution to investigate and determine the feasibility of a bridge across the Detroit River. He was confident because the issue was *so important for all interests in the West, that . . . the report will be favorable.* The commission's December 4, 1873, report was favorable, finding that a high bridge with 150 feet of clearance would not hurt navigation. However, shipping interests successfully lobbied against it and hopes of a MCRR bridge were dashed. The issue would come around again, soon.

It is interesting to note how the increase in feeder lines resulted in the company adding locomotives and workers. The 1870 annual report showed 100 locomotives and 523 men working in the Locomotive Department. The 1874 annual report indicates the MCRR more than doubled its motive power to 209 locomotives and almost doubled its Locomotive Department employees to 1,027. The location of the locomotives in 1874 follows: *Main Line, 152; Jackson, Lansing and Saginaw Division, 20; Grand River Valley Division, 11; Detroit and Bay City Railroad, 11; Joliet Division, 8; Michigan Air Line, Local, 5; Kalamazoo and South Haven Division, 2; Niles and South Bend Division, 1.* A listing of the positions required in the MCRR Locomotive Department in 1870 appears in Appendix H.

The types and numbers of cars were listed in the 1874 report and provide a clear picture of the rolling stock owned by the company.

Type of Car	# of Wheels	Total # Cars
Day coaches	12	74
Day coaches	8	8
Second class cars	12	30
Second class cars	8	4
Railway postal cars	12	3
Baggage & mail cars	12	19
Baggage & mail cars	8	20
Conductors' cars	8	96
Large stock cars	8	164
Double deck cars	8	189
Small stock cars	8	140
Merchandise or box cars	8	1,843
Blue Line cars	8	474
Refrigerator cars	8	21
Platform cars	8	1,332
Derrick cars	8	2
Pile driver cars	8	2
TOTAL		4,421

Gross earnings on freight and passenger traffic in 1872 reached $3,379,625 and $1,687,256, respectively, for a total of $5,066,881. In 1873 the company enjoyed a 13 percent increase overall to $3,852,933 and $1,785,716, for a total of $5,638,649. In 1874 the gross total reached $7,634,081, but the after expenses net was $204,743 less than in 1873. Reasons given for the increase in business, but decrease in profits were *the disturbance and depression in every class of business during three-fourths of the year, resulting from the financial trouble of the country* and the local crop shortage.

The 1874 annual report showed another burst of construction. The Main Line now had 192 miles of steel rails. More than 145 miles of were now double-tracked.

> [S]*idings, including all upon the line and at stations, amount to 114 miles. At Jackson . . . the machine-shops have been completed, . . . also a round-house with 52 stalls . . . a new passenger-house has been built there . . . a new passenger-house at Buchanan . . . a new engine-house at Michigan City, with 22 stalls . . . at Chicago, a freight and office building three stories high . . . at Chicago also a freight house has been built . . . coal sheds and chutes have been erected at Jackson, Michigan City, and Lawton made necessary by the large substitution of coal instead of wood for fuel . . . lands purchased at Chicago for enlarging the station grounds . . . land at Detroit added to station grounds . . . lands at the Junction three miles from Detroit for the erection of car-shops and round-house.*

The year 1875 began with the MCRR in a price war with the Baltimore and Ohio on freight rates. The battle focused on through freight rates from points east to Chicago. The MCRR, Michigan Southern, and Pittsburgh & Fort Wayne railroads banded together to charge a low uniform rate on through freight. Some outsiders watching this fight believed that the group was working against the Baltimore & Ohio for the purpose of striking the B&O *in its vulnerable spot, and compel*[ing] *it to lower rates to Baltimore to a ruinous figure in order to protect business.*[7]

When the government instituted the *Fast Mail* program in 1875, the MCRR wasn't eligible initially because it had no direct line to New York City. Directors quickly remedied that problem by partnering with the New York Central and starting a daily train through to New York.[8]

Facility construction was either limited or not fully reported in 1875. What was reported shows an increase in cooperation between the MCRR and the Grand Trunk.

> *The buildings in progress a year ago at Grand Trunk Junction have been completed, and in addition we have built there a sand-house, with brick walls and stone foundation; coal chutes to hold five hundred tons of coal; platforms and sheds. At Detroit we have built a freight-house and office, with appurtenances for the Grand Trunk Railway.*

Joy took the time to educate the stockholders on company history and his reviews are informative and welcome 130 years later. This time

"The Favorite Route."

1876 **1876**

MICHIGAN CENTRAL R. R.

Four Express Trains Daily between

Detroit and Chicago.

Three Express Trains Daily Between

Detroit, Bay City and Saginaw.

Three Express Trains Daily between

DETROIT AND GRAND RAPIDS.

All Trains upon this Road are equipped in the best possible manner and our patrons can rely upon

Speed, Comfort and Safety,

WAGNER'S PALACE SLEEPING CARS ON ALL NIGHT TRAINS,
And Drawing-Room Cars on Day Trains.

Tickets by this Route can be obtained at all Railroad Stations and Ticket Offices in the United States and Canadas.

JAMES F. JOY, President, Detroit.   H. B. LEDYARD, Gen'l Supt, Detroit.
        H. C. WENTWORTH, General Passenger and Ticket Agent, Chicago.

Favorite Route advertisement from *Clark's Detroit City Directory,* 1876.

he talks about the increases in freight volume over the years in an effort to justify why it is important to double track the entire system and change to steel rails. In 1870 they hauled 823,770 tons of freight and only five years later that had doubled in volume to 1,641,280 tons.

> This shows the steady progress of the business of the road, so far as volume is concerned, even since the panic of 1873, as well as before. When it is considered that from 1858 to and including 1868 there had not been a locomotive added to the power of the road, and but few cars, and but little to the capacity of the track itself, and that even up to 1870 no substantial improvements were made in these various departments, while the country along the line and West had been rapidly developing its wealth and resources and business, and the business of the road had increased more than threefold, until, in 1870, it was wholly unable to meet the demands upon it in any of its capacities of power, cars or track, and that the actual tonnage now moved is again doubled since 1870, all can at least appreciate the necessity of all that has been done, to enable the main line to transact the business which it might be able to obtain. A steel track had become imperative, instead of iron, which could not be maintained with such a volume of traffic. A double track to a very large extent, greatly enlarged power and equipment, enlarged station grounds at all important points, and especially at the termini, as well as entirely new repair shops, both for cars and locomotives, were required.

During the 27 years between 1847 and 1874, passenger traffic increased tremendously but decreases were experienced during the same economic downturns that slowed freight revenue. The 1874 annual report provides a table with the number of passengers and passenger earnings from 1847 to 1874. That table appears in Appendix J.

In 1875, Superintendent Sargent left to run the Northern Pacific Railroad. Sargent also became the president of the Fargo & Southern Railroad. As promoter and builder of railroads in North Dakota, the state honored Sargent by naming a county after him.

Joy brought in William Barstow Strong (1837–1914) as Sargent's replacement. Apparently becoming the superintendent of the mighty Michigan Central Railroad was a golden opportunity to boost your worth in the railroad community. Strong only stayed one year and left to work his way up to president (1881–1889) of the Atchison, Topeka & Santa Fe Railway. Under Strong's eight-year tenure as boss of the AT&SF, the railroad expanded 7,000 miles and he had two towns named after him (Strong City, Kansas, and Barstow, California). Joy filled Strong's position with Henry Ledyard who stayed with the MCRR for the next 40 years.

In 1876 Joy appeared to be defusing stockholder concern by addressing the relocation of company offices. Joy told them . . . *the removal of the treasurer's office from Boston to Detroit . . . was done solely from motives of economy.* While that may have been true, it was also a fact that Boston was no longer the center of company fiscal influence. The MCRR was now 30 years old and almost all the original "eastern capitalists" who brought the railroad to life had died. Brooks was the only original charter member on the board and 1876 was his final year with the railroad. Even Joy, the company lawyer who was involved from the beginning, was only a year away from stepping away from the Favorite Line. It was time for the railroad to have new caretakers to lead it into the next century.

The 1877 annual report should have been the last one from Joy as he left office that year. However, in place of his report, a narrative from new president Samuel Sloan mysteriously appeared. From that point on, the interesting 60-page narratives of the year's major events would turn into 24-page dry reports filled mostly with charts of fiscal information.

Because Joy added so many feeder lines during his tenure, he is remembered as an empire builder. It appears that he may have heard this criticism as he endeavored to describe his philosophy to stockholders through frequent lengthy explanations of his actions. He was frugal to the point of refusing to use a private car when traveling, so he likely did not want anyone to think he spent the company's money recklessly. Many in Michigan held him in high regard and recount his achievements with awe.

> [H]e organized, equipped, and continued the Michigan Central by and through the Chicago, Burlington & Quincy Roads to Burlington in Iowa and Quincy in Illinois; paused to take a breath, crossed these rivers with two beautiful iron bridges, linked up the Hannibal & St. Joseph Road, and finally brought up at Baxter Springs, in the Indian country, on the one hand; then ferried over the Missouri at Plattsmouth, and ended substantially "the Michigan Central Railroad" at Ft. Kearney, in Nebraska, a distance of 200 miles West of Chicago.

CHAPTER 14

WRECKS AND ADVENTURES

Because information about train wrecks and other related incidents generate high interest in enthusiasts, a separate chapter is dedicated to events on the road. This chapter attempts to record bits of information about the most serious wrecks and some of the other interesting events along the Main Line. It begins with first-hand information from an engineer who witnessed many incidents on the road.

Henry Hall was an early engineer on the MCRR, operating during the first dangerous years when track, locomotives and operating procedures were not all they would soon become.

> *I have seen a collision or wreck of some kind on every three miles of road between Ypsilanti and Michigan City. I have seen four bad collisions on one mile of road. Freight cars had but few if any brakes. The telegraph was not used for running trains, and when trains were late they ran feeling for each other, and when running at night had no light except a common tin hand lamp.[1]*

Hall was in a few wrecks himself. Here he recounts a couple of wrecks he was involved in that were typical in the early days—an engine leaving the track and a collision. He paints a vivid picture of life on the road a decade before the Civil War.

I remember of making a very unpleasant trip once on a little Baldwin called the "Ann Arbor." I was fireman, and it had been in the shop to see how she worked. Something was wrong with the centerpin, called the "king" bolt and she ran to one side. We had to back up from Ann Arbor to Ypsilanti where there was a turntable. We left Ann Arbor late in the afternoon and intended to lay overnight at Ypsilanti. When we got to Geddes she went into the ditch; it was almost dark and had commenced to rain. We hunted up two trackmen who lived there and went to work to set her on. You probably have seen strap railroad. There was no ballast or earth above the mudsills, the ties and rails being all above ground, which made it quite a job to get an engine on. We found an iron lever and got some blocks and planks from an old saw mill that was there, and lifted up the drivers, one at a time and blocked them up, put a plank under and got her on. We were wet to the skin. We put her on a sidetrack and went to a house nearby and went to bed. In the morning we slipped on our wet clothes, got breakfast and started again. The track had not been straightened there then and curved around under the hills, following the river on a curve a mile or more long. I went afoot with an oilcan in one hand and a block in the other, and when she would climb the rail I would catch her with the block, oil the rail and try again. When we got to within about fifteen rods of the end of the curve we found a place that we could not pass. We tried every scheme that we could think of, but it was no go. We tried until the train ought to have been there from Detroit, and we were obliged to go to Grass Lake where, there was a turntable, and turn and start for Detroit. We got as far as Ypsilanti that day and staid over night, and went into Detroit the next day. I could name a good many trips not much more pleasant.[2]

Henry's second story is about an actual collision with a freight train. More accurately, a freight hit him.

After another period of time the road reached Michigan City. Business was immense. The road had all it could do. Emigrants were coming by thousands; freight cars were fitted out with benches, and most of the people were hauled by freight trains. They went from New Buffalo to Chicago by steamer. After running to Michigan City for a number of years, the tail of my train was run into at Buchanan. I left Michigan City in the evening and a passenger train followed me later. Buchanan was a flag station; night trains did not stop very often. There were cars to go there and I backed into the siding to get them. I had a new conductor and for some reason he could not couple on. He tried for some time and I guess would have been there yet if I would have stayed with him. I finally told him I would stay no longer and pulled out of the siding and left him swearing. I told him to run back and flag that train if they came and we would get out of the way. He was in no hurry, as the time was not up for them to be there, and I was out to the train before he started back. When I left him in the siding, I pulled the pin behind the tender and left the cars there and he stopped to swear a little before he started back. By the time he got started back, the train came, twelve min-

*utes ahead of time, and smashed up three empty cars on the tail of my train. This
was the only time I was ever run into.*

*And let me here remark, that I always made it a rule to never take any
chances—running on short time or occupying the main track when another
train was due; running by stations to back into sidings where I was to meet a
train, without sending a flag ahead. And many times, for refusing to do so, conductors called me mulish or stubborn but, when I think I am right, I cannot be
driven or persuaded to do anything to the contrary.[3]*

*A few days after the wreck, Mr. Brooks, then superintendent, sent for me to
come to his office; I went and he said to me: "Henry, I have been to Buchanan to
inquire into the cause of the accident and see who was to blame. I do not attach
any blame to you but we are running in competition with the Southern road and
I do not want the public to think our passenger trains run wrong. That freight
train must stand the blame; you go into the shop for a while. In about three
weeks there will be three engines here for the Aurora road in Illinois. I have control of that road. When they get here, I want you to take them over this road one
at a time and, when you take the last, go prepared to stay for a while. If you do
not like it there you can come back; your pay will be twenty-five cents more a day
than we pay here.[4]*

Henry must have liked working on the MCRR for Brooks because after a year, he wrote a letter to Newhall, master mechanic on
the Central asking to let him come back.

*He told me to come and when I arrived in Detroit, he gave me a new Lowell
engine called "Wolf Hound" and a passenger train. I ran her two years. She had
six-foot wheel, inside connection, [with] cylinders 16 × 22, link motion and independent cut-off. She stood so high that she had to have very short stack and she
trailed her smoke so badly that, unless the wind was strong enough to blow it to
one side, I could not see the track when running at night, from one end of the road
to the other, only when standing still at stations. I could not see the fireman in the
cab—this is not a chestnut. The smoke and steam affected my throat and lungs so
badly that I was taken sick and did not do a day's work for more than a year.[5]*

In 1889, another early engineer, Charles H. Frisbie, recorded his
experiences with the engine *May Flower* on the MCRR in the late
1840s and early 1850s:

*I was going over a switch at Dexter, Michigan, when the bar that holds the
rails in place, broke and let the May Flower down on the frozen ground and ice.
She began to slew and started up [the] street, and at about fifty feet from the track
she turned up side down, and where was I? Under her of course, caught by my left
foot with steam blowing on it, But my foot was on the ice and the steam thawed it
loose, when I crawled out with a scalded foot and all my bones unbroken.*

Another time I started with the same May Flower engine, and when three miles out from Marshall, Michigan, I ran over an ox and threw the engine and train, every wheel, from the track. The engine rolled over twice and a half and lay on her back, fifty feet from the track, headed the opposite way. I looked around and found myself, and set up my underpinning, and on taking an inventory, I found one arm disabled, my face and hands scalded, and my shoulder and collar bone were broken. The fireman, poor fellow, fared my much worse, and died in a few days. What did the company do about it? They paid my doctor's bill, [and] they paid my full wages for the full year I was laid up.[6]

There apparently were hundreds of wrecks and incidents on the Michigan Central Main Line during the charter years. The following are the most damaging, in terms of loss of life, injury, or property damage (or most interesting) during the period 1846–1901.

May 12, 1852: Niles, Michigan—*A Westbound MCRR emigrant train left Detroit, followed shortly after by a second Westbound train. The first train was stopped at Niles, when a second train overtook and ran into the emigrant train. The accident killed three persons and severely injured several others. The accident was owing to the carelessness of the engineers.[7]*

April 20, 1852: Leoni, Michigan—*A frightful accident occurred to the Eastern train on the Michigan Central Railroad last week, near Leoni, about sixty miles from Detroit. In turning a curve in the road, a locomotive came sud-*

This 1874 map of the Dexter depot area shows a track set up for a small station.

denly upon the passenger train at full speed, smashing the last car, and injuring a number of passengers, among whom was H. F. Church, Agent of the Ogdensburg Road, who was mortally hurt. Six others were badly injured including the engineer of the following train, Geo. Stanford.[8]

July 5, 1852: Marshall, Michigan—*The passenger train upon the Michigan Central Railroad ran off the track near Marshall on the 5th inst., in consequence of the switch not being properly adjusted after the passage of a gravel train. The fireman leaped from the engine, and fell upon the track in such a manner that the wheels severed his head from his body. The cars were thrown over, and one of them beyond the engine, yet no serious accident occurred to the passengers. Men, women and children were huddled together in one mass, and it is remarkable that such was the result. It is thought some villain changed the switch.*[9]

April 25, 1853: Grand Crossing, Illinois—On a bright moonlit Monday evening, at approximately 9:45 P.M., an Eastbound Michigan Southern Express train seven miles out of Chicago struck a westbound Michigan Central emigrant and freight train in route to that city. The locomotive of the MS train hit the MC train at the passenger-filled sixth car. The ruins of the locomotive, tender, baggage, and a second class car of the express train were mixed together with three passenger cars of the emigrant train in *an immense heap of wheels, iron railings, splinters, doors, etc.* Another first class car filled with passengers was thrown on its side next to the MC track and from this car groans and cries were heard in the darkness. Water covered the ground on both sides of the track and there was no place for the passengers to go for assistance, so the survivors, mostly Germans, huddled on the embankments.

> *The scene which presented itself upon the other side of the Central track cannot be fully described, and time will not efface the memory of that terrible and heart-rending spectacle, from the mind of the unwilling beholder. We saw a heap of runs, from beneath which shrieked out upon the midnight air, cries for help, mingles with the deeper-toned groans of the dying. One by one, those who were able, crawled out from the rubbish, while the uninjured were fully employed in rendering assistance to those unable to extricate themselves. The cause of this collision, rarely if ever equally in its fatal and terrible results, is beyond conjecture. The night was as bright as a nearly full moon and the clearest atmosphere could make it. The two roads cross each other at nearly right angles, and run for a long distance on a straight line. It seems as if it was impossible for both engineers not*

to have seen each other's trains for the distance of at least a half a mile if not a mile, before reaching the crossing.[10]

The locomotive of the MCRR continued on to Chicago, bringing news of the accident. Within two hours two doctors reached the wreck. The initial reports said 18 were killed and 60 injured.

A back-story goes along with this accident. While attempting to build track to Kensington and connect with the Michigan Central, the Illinois Central was blocked by the Northern Indiana Railroad (affiliated with the Michigan Southern) track at Grand Crossing and was denied permission to cross. The ICRR, perhaps having courage by operating in its home state, decided to disregard the wishes of the Northern Indiana company. The ICRR kidnapped a NI night guard placed to protect the location and had a crossing in place by daybreak. Both claimed the right of way. Neither thought it prudent to place signal lights or even to slow down when approaching the crossing.

Believing that the accident could have been avoided, the sheriff arrested the engineers of both trains. Judge Wilson allowed a Mr. Rockham, of the MCRR, and a Mr. Davis, of the MS train, to be released after posting $2,000 for bail. The final disposition of the case was not located. The investigation revealed that negligence and competition caused the accident. The Central train had the right of way, but lingered in the area for the purpose of holding up the rival Michigan Southern train. The Central train also did not have a *regulation headlight*.

The wreck happened in wilderness. The location has been long since swallowed up by the city of Chicago and has been grade-separated for a very long time near the intersection of 75th Street and South Chicago Avenue.

November 10, 1856: Detroit, Michigan—*The express train going east on the MCRR, on Monday evening, was thrown off the track in consequence of a rail placed across it. William Willower, a passenger, was killed, and several others badly injured.*[11]

January 1, 1864: Near Grand Crossing, Illinois—The January 23, 1864, issue of *Harper's Weekly* made this incident the center of conversation across the country, putting a picture of the Michigan Central Railroad on the news magazine's cover for the first time. A previous chapter showed the woodcut of a locomotive with the big stack stuck in the snow, with the caption *Sufferings in a Snow-storm on the Michigan Central.* William Kennedy recounts the incident in 1884.

> *At six o'clock on the morning of New Year's Day, 1864, a train on the Michigan Central railroad, after having got about seven miles out on the prairies from Chicago, plunged into an immense snow-drift lying directly across the track. At first the powerful engine pushed right on, scattering the snow in glittering clouds to the right and the left, and seeming as if it would pull through victoriously. But soon it moved with great difficulty, and at last, after long labor and struggle, stopped short, unable to gain another foot of headway. There were a hundred persons in the train, many of them women and children: they had with them nothing but light lunches, and many had not even a cracker. As the day wore on they tore up the neighboring fences for fuel for the stoves; but the dry wood aided by the gale soon heated stove and pipe red-hot, and set the car-roof on fire. With great difficulty this was extinguished; but the car was now uninhabitable, and the passengers were all huddled together in the remaining car. It was now two o'clock in the afternoon, and the possibility of a terrible death began to haunt the minds of the snow-bound travelers, when (most welcome sight!) a passenger train on the Michigan Southern line appeared at a crossing some four hundred yards off. It was hailed, and the work of transferring passengers began. The drift was ten feet deep, the storm at its height, and the cold so intense that the faces of the women and children were frozen almost as soon as they were in contact with the wind.*[12]

What is not readily known is that the MS train with its double human load soon became stuck as well. Two strong fellows volunteered to trudge back to the city for help and they succeeded. Soon sleighs loaded with blankets and provisions were dispatched to the stalled trains, arriving about 10 p.m. The stranded passengers, thus fortified, spent a tolerable night on the train and took the sleighs back to the city in the morning.

January 26, 1869: Albion, Michigan—About 3:00 in the afternoon a group of passengers at the Albion station were waiting for the approaching train when they were treated to an unusual sight. An old man and his wife (a Mr. & Mrs. Sagon) were racing their wagon to cross the track before the train blocked their way. They didn't make it. The train split the horse from the wagon and wagon with occupants was scooped up by the cowcatcher. *They settled themselves composedly as though nothing had happened. The old lady put her hands in her* *muff, while the old man, with one hand extended, as if grasping the reins, and the whip raised in the other, thus the old couple rode up to the station triumphant, amid the cheers of the bystanders.*[13] When the train stopped the passengers helped them down from the cowcatcher. There was no injury to the horse, wagon, or occupants.

July 20, 1870: Wayne, Michigan—*About 3 o'clock yesterday morning, just after the engineer of the Atlantic express train of the Michigan Central Road had blown his whistle for Wayne Station, and while his train was moving at the rate of thirty miles an hour, he discovered that the switch, which there combines to form a track on each side of the station, was set so that he was running his train right into the rear of a freight train standing on the side track, which was also bound east, but had switched in to give up the main track to the express. [T]he engineer sounded "down brakes" and the brakemen had them on in an instant, but they could only slacken the great speed as the distance was not 300 feet, before the engine went into the caboose . . . tearing it into splinters, destroying the next two freight cars, then overturning itself on the ground with the forward trucks resting in the kitchen of the station agent, which was pretty well torn to pieces. The freight train had been waiting for some time and two brakemen were in the caboose, fast asleep. The body of one, named Joseph Robarge of this city, was fished out of the wreck; but the other named Van Allen, who resides near Wayne Station, lived a few moments after being taken up.*[14]

The fireman of the express jumped free and dislocated his shoulder. Isaac Kimball, the engineer, also jumped free, but hit the water tower and appeared to have internal injuries. The baggage master was in the middle of his car and was untouched after both ends of the car were smashed. Passengers were knocked from their seats, but unharmed. Some who were sleeping were barely awakened.

As one might have guessed, the accident was caused by a negligence of the switchman. He forgot to close the sidetrack switch after the freight pulled off the Main Line.

The real story of this accident was not about participants in the wreck, but about the widow of Joseph Robarge, likely fast asleep in her Detroit home, not knowing of the terrible accident.

Many will remember that a year or two ago a fireman named Moses Robarge (who was a cousin to Joseph Robarge) was killed at Huron Station, by the explosion of a locomotive boiler. Moses left a widow, whom Joseph, the latest vic-

It might have been a Manchester (1870) like this one that was involved in the Wayne accident. This photo of the engine *Cassopolis* was taken at Jackson in 1885.

tim, subsequently married. Now the poor woman is a second time widowed by nearly the same terrible agency, which deprived her of her first husband.[15]

October 10, 1879: Jackson, Michigan—*A serious accident occurred on the Michigan Central Railroad, a short distance east of Jackson, about 1 o'clock this morning. The Pacific express train, bound west, which left Detroit 40 minutes late, came in collision with a switch engine on the main track at that place, telescoping the baggage and express cars, and piling the remaining coaches, 11 in number, on top of each other. The first coach was filled with emigrants, most of whom were killed or seriously injured. It is supposed that there were about 20 or 25 passengers killed and 20 to 30 wounded. The train was made up of seven Wagner sleepers, four passenger coaches, and mail and baggage cars.[16]*

As is often the case, fate played a part in selecting who was hurt or killed. The tender of the express engine was telescoped into the baggage car, which was forced into the mail car. The mail car knocked the first passenger car off the track onto an embankment and the passengers inside were unhurt. The second and third coaches continued straight into the mail car and there injured and killed the inhabitants. Passengers in the fourth car and the following Wagner coaches were unhurt. The engineer and fireman of the express train (Milton Gilbert and C. B. Smith) were literally torn to pieces, but the engineer and fireman of the switch engine escaped injury by jumping from the engine. Early reports had nine killed and 28 injured.

A preliminary investigation found that Yardmaster Evander Colwell, who had worked for the company three years, asked the telegraph operator how late the Pacific Express was. The reply was that it was 45 minutes late out of Detroit. Colwell then directed Robert R. Jones to get on the track and move cars, indicating it would only take 20 minutes. Jones objected, saying he knew the train was due, but was essentially overruled. He had just gotten his switch engine out on the main track when he saw the light of the express. The Pacific Express had made up the time.

Jackson artist Marcus H. Kerr, a well-known local painter, captured the wreck in a drawing and sold prints on 4 (6-inch cards. Also, the accident so caught the public's awareness that *Harper's Weekly* ran a block print illustration of the wreck in its November 1, 1879, edition titled *The Accident on the Michigan Central Railroad Near Jackson.*

THE ACCIDENT ON THE MICHIGAN CENTRAL RAILROAD, NEAR JACKSON, MICHIGAN.—From a Sketch by W. A. Paris.—[See Page 867.]

This *Harper's Weekly Journal* print shows the October 10, 1879, wreck at Jackson.

August 24, 1886: Battle Creek, Michigan—*On August 24, 1886, just outside Battle Creek, a Chicago bound freight rear-ended a passenger train. Two people were injured and defective brakes were cited as the reason for the wreck.*[17]

March 27, 1888: Burnside, Illinois—The fast night express on the MCRR that left Chicago at 9:00 P.M. wrecked just south of the crossing at Burnside. Conductor Grosvenor tells about the accident:

> All there is to it is that we were crossing the Belt Line 11 miles this side of Chicago. Just as we crossed, the Wabash freight, coming along on the belt, plunged into our rear sleeper. It did not cut it in two because the Wabash train was not running more than six miles an hour. I guess those fellows did not know the road and the heavy train pushed them into us before they knew it. No one was killed, and all the injured people were able to walk and went on to their destination.[18]

October 13, 1893: Jackson, Michigan—October was a bad month for accidents in Jackson and Friday the 13th was a bad day for visitors to the Chicago World's Fair. At least a dozen died on the spot and another 30 were badly injured, of few of which were not expected to survive.

> A terrible railroad wreck occurred in this city at 9:30 o'clock this morning, in which many persons either lost their lives or were badly injured. The accident was to two Delaware, Lackawanna & Western World's Fair excursion trains, one closely following the other. They were loaded with passengers from the towns along the line of the road in New York State.
>
> At Jackson the Michigan Central Railroad maintains a lunch counter, and the passengers of the train in advance were taking breakfast when the rear train, coming in and becoming unmanageable, ran past the semaphore signal and crashed into the rear of the first section.
>
> The rear train is said to have been running on a headway of twenty-six minutes at the rate of about forty miles an hour. The engineer was powerless to stop for the reason that the airbrakes refused to work. When the crash came the rear cars of the first section were thrown in all directions, and the wreck contained nine coaches and a badly broken locomotive. A trainman says that the second special came rushing into the yard at full speed. He heard the engineer whistle for brakes and then for hand brakes. The hand brakes were applied, but it was too late. Two cars had been thrown crosswise of the track, one had been driven completely through another, while the others were derailed and some had been toppled entirely over.
>
> The wreck is the first one of consequence that has occurred on the Michigan Central Road in fourteen years. It is a singular coincidence that both these disasters occurred in the yards of the road in this city, and in the same month, and on the same day of the week, Friday.[19]

CHAPTER 15

SLOAN AND VANDERBILT BATTLE FOR CONTROL

The historical record is much confused about the takeover of the MCRR by New York interests from Boston interests. How it happened, when it actually transpired and who was involved provide an interesting story.

At 9:00 in the morning of June 25, 1877, a battle was waged at the MCRR freight office in Detroit during the annual director's meeting. Only a dozen people were present, and no blood was shed, not even an argument made. It was big time, New York–style business being conducted by three of the richest men in America in a small, dusty office on the Detroit River waterfront.

The participants in this battle came to Detroit with their entourage by special train. One of them was already a director of the MCRR—millionaire New York banker Moses Taylor. The others were Jay Gould and William H. Vanderbilt, two of the country's greatest railroad venture capitalists and developers. (It could not be determined if Gould and Vanderbilt were present or if they sent representatives, but arriving via special train gives the impression very special passengers were on board.)

The MCRR management had failed to make dividend payments in 1874 and 1875, which was highly unusual. As a result, some stockholders wanted a change in management of the company. With stock prices down, all three men saw an opportunity to gain control of the

Midwest's premier railroad. The weapons of choice and by law were stockholder's votes called proxy votes, which could be given to a representative to form large voting blocks, and these men carried bundles of proxies.

Three impartial *inspectors of the election* were hired to count the votes. Those gentlemen retired to another room to count the bulky rolls of proxies while Joy conducted meeting business. It was Joy's last meeting as president and he recommended that the end of the MCRR fiscal year be changed from May 31 to December 31 to coincide with the rival Lake Shore & Michigan Southern to *compare simultaneously the doings* of the MCRR with the LS&MS.[1]

Other business included reporting that all but five miles of iron on the Main Line had been replaced by steel. Gross revenue increased to $6,850,964. Net earnings increased by $1,160,000, which would result in a 6 percent dividend for stockholders. Announcing a dividend after going two years without one on the heels of this takeover attempt must have been some affirmation for President Joy.

When the votes were counted and reported, 187,382 votes were cast. Moses Taylor, who wanted the current management to remain the same, controlled about 80,000 votes. Gould controlled about 45,000 and Vanderbilt only about 30,000. There was no indication of what happened to the other 32,000 votes. Voting resulted in only two changes to the board: Fredrick Billings of Vermont and August Belmont of New York were replaced by J. V. Barron of Concord, New Hampshire, and Edward Austin of Boston, Massachusetts. The Boston contingent had gained one seat and the current management was saved: . . . *the effort to displace the existing management was an utter failure and . . . the victory being thus clearly with the friends of the present management, Mr. Vanderbilt placed his proxies in Mr. Taylor's hand and gave up the contest. Somewhat later Mr. Gould took the same course.*[2]

Taylor supported the current management, but President Joy and Treasurer Livermore stepped down after the takeover attempt. The presidency passed to MCRR Vice President Samuel Sloan and Benjamin Dunning succeeded Livermore. It was the first time a vice president had succeeded since the selection of Brooks 20 years earlier. Taylor was likely comfortable with Sloan, having already picked him 10 years earlier as president of a railroad he owned back east (the Delaware, Lackawanna & Western Railroad). Some histories claim that William H. Vanderbilt selected Sloan in some sort of political compromise. But when Sloan came on board, Vanderbilt had finished a distant third in proxy voting with no leverage to press for anyone's employment at the MCRR.

Something about Joy's departure during this power play is suspect, however. Close review of the June 1877 annual report finds Sloan reporting as president on August 31. Why was Joy's last report as president replaced by Sloan's report prepared two months later than customary? Superintendent Ledyard's report was dated May 31, as customary, but addressed to Sloan instead of Joy. Perhaps Joy did not prepare a report for the 1877 report out of frustration or lack of interest based on the knowledge that he was moving on.

Samuel Sloan was only president of the MCRR for one year, but he was a national icon in railroad administration with a town named after him in Iowa and a statue in New Jersey.

If Joy was fired instead of willingly stepping down from the presidency, his reputation was not harmed in any case. For at least a year, he continued to participate in MCRR board of director meetings. After some time off of work, Joy picked up another job as president of the *Detroit Post & Tribune* (1881) and as a director and president of the Wabash, St. Louis & Pacific Railroad (1884).[3] He died in Detroit on September 24, 1896, at his house on West Fort Street and is buried in Detroit's prestigious Elmwood Cemetery. The *Detroit Free Press* ran an obituary the next day that was several pages long. Joy was easily Michigan's greatest, and one of the nation's greatest, nineteenth-century railroad builders.

Sloan joined the MCRR in 1876 as a director and vice president. He was a former New York state senator, president of the Hudson River Railroad until Vanderbilt and the New York Central took it over, and the long-time president of the Delaware, Lackawanna & Western Railroad (the DL&WRR was owned by MCRR director Moses Taylor). Sloan was to continue as president of the DL&WRR while running the MCRR.

Perhaps it was the thought losing another presidency to Vanderbilt that made Sloan sick just days after accepting the MCRR top post. At least twice during the opening days of June 1877, newspapers reported that he was ill. *Mr. Samuel Sloan was at his office yesterday until noon, having recovered from his recent illness. Mr. Sloan telegraphed to his Superintendent, Mr. Ledyard, at Detroit not to . . .* increase the speed of the MCRR fast train to match the speed of a new LS&MS train. Sloan cited the danger of more speed and the expense of operating faster as his reasoning.[4]

Perhaps Sloan's illness lingered on due to stress. The Panic of 1873 slowed the economy and it had not fully recovered. Reduced profits as a result of rate wars put the railroads at risk of failure. The *New York Times* (January 7, 1878) reported that 54 railroad companies were sold under fore closure in 1877 and 60 more cases were pending. By the time Sloan took over the MCRR in summer of 1877, railroads in the east (the NYCRR, the PRR, and the B&O) were trying to survive by cutting employee pay by 10 to 15 percent. In protest, railroad workers were striking freight service, burning buildings and rolling stock. Violence reached a point where U.S. President Rutherford B. Hayes had to call in federal troops to stop the property damage. It was a tough time to be running a railroad, but Sloan had good help. It appears that he handed off the looming strike issue to his superintendent, Henry B. Ledyard. More about how the strike effected the MCRR is covered in the next chapter.

When Sloan's reign ended the next year, the company was earning two-thirds of its income from freight. The gross revenue was $6,498,126, down $352,837 from 1876. The company owned 219 locomotives, of which 135 burned coal and 84 burned wood.

After leaving the MCRR, Sloan continued as president of the DL&WRR until 1899. Even though he didn't leave much of a mark on the MCRR, he was an American dynamo who touched thousands with his leadership. Sloan, Iowa, is named after him, and he was one of several men to start a banking business known today as Citibank. He died in Garrison, New York, in 1907.

Vanderbilt Triumphs

The setting of the 1878 board of directors meeting was similar to the previous year's annual election. It was held in Detroit at the MCRR offices at 10 o'clock in the morning on June 24, 1878. Dignitaries again arrived in town on special trains. William H. Vanderbilt, his sons, Cornelius, William K., and a host of others were in the party. Augustus Schell presided and on the motion of Joy, who must have been attending as a stockholder, called for the counting of the votes.

The same three men as last year were inspectors of the election. Ex-governor Henry P. Baldwin, Christian H. Buhl, and S. McCutcheon, the U.S. district attorney, all of Detroit, were selected as proxy vote and ballot counters.

It took until 2:30 that afternoon to complete the counting. This time Vanderbilt brought 80,000 votes owned by him and his sons and 20,000 proxy votes that others signed off to him. A total of 838 share-holders voted their 55,000 shares for the current management. Nearly 100,000 voted for Vanderbilt and a change in management. *It will thus be seen that owners of shares valued at $3,000,000 did not vote at all, and that a vast majority in number of the shareholders were hostile to a change.*[5]

The new directors were William H. Vanderbilt, Augustus Schell, Cornelius Vanderbilt, Samuel F. Barger, William K. Vanderbilt, Anson Stager, William L. Scott, and Edwin D. Worcester, all from New York, and Ashley Pond from Detroit. Vanderbilt selected himself as president, Ledyard remained as superintendent, Cornelius Vanderbilt bumped Dunning as treasurer and Edwin D. Worcester took the place of Rolston as secretary. Another big change was the loss of Nathaniel Thayer of Boston, who had been on the board of directors for 20 years. The new board had to operate without a single director who had historic knowledge of company operations. It didn't seem to matter much.

One of the first things Vanderbilt did was tour the facilities. *No action was taken respecting the working official of the road . . . the general expectation being that sweeping changes will follow. Mr. Vanderbilt and party passed the remainder of the day inspecting the different departments of the Central in this city . . . and tomorrow morning will depart for Chicago.*[6]

The previous year Joy had enacted a policy requiring that financial reports be published at year's end to make them

The Vanderbilts were company benefactors spending more than $100 million renovating and upgrading the MCRR from 1878 to 1901. They controlled the old MCRR line as part of the NYCRR system until 1954 when Robert Ralph Young took power.

comparable to other railroads. That meant Vanderbilt had to prepare an annual report just six months into the job. He was likely pleased to announce gross revenues were up to $6,872,094 in 1878, or $373,968 over 1877. Also, quite a bit of work on the railroad had been completed in 1878.

An iron truss, double track pivot (later called a swing) bridge was built over the Calumet River on the Main Line. Twenty-six wooden bridges were rebuilt, and 2,617 feet of bridge through cuts were filled. The number of locomotives remained at 219, but 167 were coal burners, while only 52 were still wood burners. Twenty-two new locomotives were . . . *built at the company's shops during the past year to take the place of those condemned for service. The Freight Car equipment has been increased by purchase of 100 box-cars; 247 freight cars of various classes have been built in place of cars condemned for service, and 91 cars of various classes rebuilt. A new Freight House of brick, 182 x 36 feet, has been built at Ypsilanti. New frost-proof tanks, with steam pumps, etc., have been built at Kensington, Kalamazoo and Vandalia, cost of same being included in working expenses.*

It was a tough time for Vanderbilt to be running a railroad too. Just eight months after he took over the presidency, a major rate war was starting. An old eastbound freight pool was in place and the pool was split between the NYCRR, Erie, PRR, and B&O. Each faction argued the other was cheating by selling below rates. By summer 1878 representatives of 20 railroads met in Buffalo and ironed out their differences to end the impending rate war. A new eastbound pool from Chicago was formed with new divisions of tonnage that was agreeable to all.

The annual election of officers was held in Detroit in 1879 and 1880, as required by the MCRR Charter, but the company meetings were now held in New York at the Grand Central Depot built by the Vanderbilt family. For several years running, Vanderbilt and the entire board of directors were reelected.

Gross earnings increased for the first two years of Vanderbilt's presidency. Total revenue after adjustments for 1878 was $6,991,758; for 1879, $7,415,428.

During 1878 and 1879 bridges were a major focus of company improvements.

Construction and repairs listed in reports included the following: Wooden Pile Bridge over Trail Creek, at Michigan City (Main Line), 178 feet in length, replaced with Through Iron Truss, Double Track, Pivot Bridge, Stone Abutments and Centre Pier; Wooden Pile Bridge over Huron River, two miles west of Ypsilanti (Main Line), 161 feet 2 inches in length, replaced with a

Through Iron Truss Bridge, Stone Abutments; Wooden Pile Bridge over Huron River, west of Fosters (Main Line), 165 feet 4 inches in length, replaced with a Through Iron Truss Bridge, Stone Abutments; Wooden Pile Bridge over the Huron River, east of Delhi (Main Line), 100 feet span, replaced with a Through Iron Truss Bridge, Stone Abutments; In addition to the above, 31 wooden bridges of various lengths have been rebuilt, and 883 feet of bridges filled, requiring 40,844 cubic yards of earthwork.

The issue of building a bridge over the Detroit River was also revisited in 1879. A second commission made a report on November 21, finding that a "low" bridge with 60 feet of headway would not injure the shipping industry. They stated that less than one half of all the vessels passing under the bridge would be of the sailing type that can lower their masts. They recommended approval, but again the effort was blocked by the shipping industry.

The number of locomotives (219) did not increase, but now included 184 coal burners, and 35 wood burners. The carshops built 173 cars in 1879, which comes out to about three per week. Even then they couldn't keep up with the need as the company had to purchase 140 more freight cars from other sources.

The engine *Captain* at the Michigan City, Indiana, roundhouse, c. 1880.

The last annual report of the decade announced the first serious accident with a high death rate since the 1850s. The company would end up paying more than $70,000 in damages to families of those injured and killed. More about this accident is found in Chapter 14.

> *On the 10th day of October 1879, a serious accident occurred at Jackson Junction by the collision of the Pacific Express train with a yard engine, which was occupying the main track in direct violation of well-known rules. In this accident 15 persons were killed (including two employees), and 36 passengers injured.*

In 1879, the financial statement of the Land Commissioner of the Jackson, Lansing & Saginaw Railroad Company was included in the MCRR annual report for the first time. The JL&SRR was the only line controlled by the MCRR to receive a land grant. The lease of this line 1871 was modified in 1876 to include the purchase and cancellation of bonds through the proceeds of land sales. The value of the outstanding bonds equaled the estimated value of the land grant assets ($3,740,000 versus $3,715,000). *The opinion has prevailed, that the lease of the Jackson, Lansing & Saginaw Road . . . was an onerous one, the information thus furnished by the Commissioner becomes of importance. It is reasonable to anticipate the slight difference will readily be met by the now constantly increasing valuation of the lands.*

In 1880 gross revenue made a fantastic jump to $9,085,748, an increase of $1,670,320 over 1879, or nearly 23 percent. That profit helped fulfill an ambitious rebuilding plan that included constructing some of the greatest passenger depots in the country (Ann Arbor, Battle Creek, Kalamazoo, Niles, Grass Lake, Albion, Lawton, Michigan City).

With all the passenger and freight buildings in place, bridge repair and replacement continued to be a major priority in 1880. Apparently wooden piles soaked in linseed oil prior to placement were finally deteriorating after 30 years of being submerged in Michigan's rivers. The heavier engines then coming into use was also a major factor in the decision to replace these structures. It appears that the company started replacing wood with steel. Those repairs included the following:

> *Repairs are the following replacements of Wooden Pile Bridges, over Huron River, with Iron Truss Bridges, Stone Abutments: One and one half miles west of Ann Arbor, 127 feet in length; 1 mile west of Fosters, 120 feet in length; 1 mile east of Delhi, 160 feet in length; mile west of Delhi, 160 feet in length; 1 mile west*

of Scio, 120 feet in length. In addition to the above, an Iron Bridge 632 feet in length, with Stone Abutments and Piers, has been built over the St. Joseph River, at Niles, for the second track.

The number of locomotives remained the same at 219, but the number of coal burners continued to increase (192) and the number of wood burners decreased to 27. Thirteen locomotives were built at the company shops to replace those too worn out to repair. The first mention of building postal cars (3) appeared, and ownership of freight cars increased by 900 cars. That brings the total to 6,067, which is an increase of 5,000 cars over the previous 10 years. Where these cars came from was not indicated.

In 1880 the railroad was a highly developed operation. However small villages with flag stations did not always receive the railroad's full measure of sophistication. A 1937 interview with a former White Oak resident gives us insight into flag station tribulations during the 1880s.

> *Especially in bad weather it was considered quite the thing to take the train to town at Lawton or Decatur and we young fellows would make many unnecessary trips just for the ride. This was a source of irritation to the train men when trying to make time and they would express their displeasure at having to stop the train for some of us country bumpkins in strong, vigorous, profane language.*
>
> *During the presidential campaign of 1880 there was a big mass meeting in Decatur and a cousin and I decided to attend. The train went through White Oak about 5 A.M., so we arose early and walked the three miles to the depot, arriving a full hour before train time, and there in the chill grey dawn of a frosty September morning we shivered and shook until the train arrived.*
>
> *Trains only stopped at White Oak on signal, which signal being a board on a tall post pulled into horizontal position by means of a wire and held by hooking the wire over a spike. We set the signal and awaited results. In the half darkness the train ran past the depot a good quarter of a mile where it waited for us to catch up by active running. There was the usual exchange of red hot compliments and all was well.[7]*

Earnings decreased in 1881 to $8,936,000. Passenger revenues were up in 1881, but freight revenue was down $500,000 in spite of total tonnage going up almost 5 percent. Low rates and higher labor costs were given as the reason.

Henry C. Wentworth, general passenger agent for 25 years, passed away on December 28, 1881, in Chicago. He was the first to begin heavily promoting the MCRR through advertisements. He may have initiated the line's attempts at a nickname, *The Favorite Line* (c. 1856–1880) or the short-lived second effort, *The Dining Car Line* (c. 1880–1883), before the company settled on the *Niagara Falls Route.*

Some expenditures for construction on the road were cited in 1881. Bridges continued to be a major focus and wood was being replaced with iron truss and stone abutments. *Huron River, one mile west of Ann Arbor, 120 feet in length; Huron River, two and one-half miles west of Ypsilanti, 120 feet in length; Creek, west of Dexter, 54 feet in length; Coffee Creek, one-half mile east of Porter, 108 feet in length; Arch Culvert, 24 feet opening at Salt Creek, three and one-half miles west of Porter.*

Building repairs were slowing to a trickle. New passenger houses were completed at Lawton (made of stone) and Albion (made of brick). A new office and trainmen's house (dormitory) was built at Michigan City, and a four-stall brick engine house constructed at Kalamazoo.

Apparently the need to purchase 900 new freight cars in 1880 opened the eyes of officials that room had to be made for all this rolling stock. Forty-seven acres of land was purchased outside of Detroit, near the company's car shops for the purpose of building a new yard for *the handling of freight trains, and delivery of cars to connecting lines. Some 14 miles of track have already been laid. It is expected to add to this yard from year to year as the requirements of the traffic may demand. In connection therewith, a freight transfer house, car repair shop, and train master's office have been built.* [This was the beginning of what would become the Junction Yard.]

Locomotives now numbered 254, with 241 coal burners and only 13 wood burners. The MCRR continued to push for the change from wood use to coal in locomotives because it saved labor and refueling time.

Improvements in telegraphing on the MCRR continued to develop into the 1880s. Newspapers announced the most recent upgrade in 1882.

> *For a long time . . . the Michigan Central Railroad company* [has] *been in the habit of obtaining the time to regulate their clocks from the observatory at Ann Arbor. Twice a week the regulating was done, an operator going from Jackson to Ann Arbor. But telegraphing by hand was likely to result in slight errors . . . M. A. Hill . . . has invented . . . a device for telegraphing to any given point the precise time. A large clock . . . will be placed in the observatory at Ann Arbor and astronomically regulated. Connected with this is a secondary clock, which will run two minutes each day, beginning at 11:59 A.M. and stopping at 12:01 P.M. When it begins to run it automatically operates a telegraphic sounder, which for the first minute strikes once a second and at precisely noon begins a pe-*

culiar and unmistakable double clock-click continuing for one minute. All watches can be pulled out and set at 12 o'clock and when the double stroke begins the owners of the time-pieces know that it is 12 o'clock.[8]

The results of a wrongful death settlement made by the MCRR leaked out in 1882, giving the public a peek into an area of business seldom seen by the public. Early in 1881, John C. Joss was killed by a train east of Niles. His widow sued and settled for $12,000, an extraordinary amount for the time. Her case was likely helped by the fact that her lawyer was an ex-congressman and current auditor of the treasury.

The 1882 annual election was held in Detroit on May 4. As happened in the prior three years, the previous year's president and board were reelected. Half-year statements for 1882 showed a significant decrease in gross revenue compared to 1881 ($4,177,500 against $4,340,000). Crop failures in Michigan, low freight volume, and low rates were cited as the reasons.

At the close of 1882, Vanderbilt was successful in getting a 21-year lease agreement with the Canada Southern Railway. The agreement would go into effect January 1, 1883, and would result in the lines being operated as one single unit. From this point on, the CSR was considered part of the Main Line for annual report purposes.

Bridge repairs and building construction continued at a slow but steady pace. A second-track bridge over St. Joseph River at Niles, 632 feet in length, and a new bridge over St. Joseph River at Three Rivers, 210 feet in length, were built. A new passenger house was constructed at Michigan City and new stockyards were built near the Detroit car shops.

The big surprise of 1882 was the report from the car supervisor. He announced that *the freight equipment has been increased by the addition of one thousand and ninety-four cars of various classes,* pushing the total number of MCRR cars beyond 7,000.

When an increase in combined earnings ($14,009,766) was announced in June 1883, the three-year slide in MCRR revenues under Vanderbilt leadership was broken. Vanderbilt evidently knew the revenues would show an increase and perhaps took the opportunity to leave the company on a high note. A month before the financial report was given to the newspapers, he stepped down from active management of the MCRR, LS&MS, and the NYCRR. He wanted to remain a director for a while and established the position of chairman of the board of directors for his sons to ensure the roads would remain under Vanderbilt control.

Before leaving the presidency, Vanderbilt wanted to make another impact on MCRR operations by changing an old tradition. Just months before, his move to form a partnership with the Canada Southern set the stage for a stunning announcement on June 5, 1883.

> *For 25 years trains running east on this road have been designated by odd numbers, and those west by even numbers. This order on this road has been run on Chicago time, and those on the Canada Southern by Detroit time. On and after Sunday the trains of the entire system will be run on Detroit time . . . the MCRR will be withdrawing all through sleepers and coaches from the Great Western Division of the Grand Trunk and the entire through passenger service of the Michigan Central will be over the Canada Southern.[9]*

Newspapers announced that when the new $6 million cantilever bridge over the Niagara River was complete, *all Michigan Central through trains will run into Buffalo by way of Niagara Falls. This move of Vanderbilt in severing long existing relations between the Great Western and the Michigan Central will surprise railroad men throughout the country.*[10]

Several things were happening at the same time when this decision was announced. The Canadian government had just allowed the Grand Trunk Railway to acquire the Great Western Railway. The MCRR had a long-running traffic agreement with the GWR that was assumed by the GTR. Right in the middle of that happening, Vanderbilt was building a double track from Welland to Niagara for the sole purpose of providing service to Buffalo over the new GTR bridge (built in 1873). During the GTR acquisition of the GWR, officials decided to raise the use fees of the bridge, infuriating Vanderbilt. Instead of paying the excessive fees, Vanderbilt decided to build his own bridge—the Michigan Central Railroad Cantilever Bridge, just 10 minutes walk south of the Grand Trunk Lower Arch Bridge and which would block a full view of the falls from the GTR bridge. The new bridge opened on December 20, 1883, to a great celebration with 10,000 onlookers and 20 locomotives testing bridge strength by pulling loaded gravel cars across it.[11]

From that point until well into the next century, MCRR trains passing through Ontario stopped 10 minutes at the Falls View Station to view the magnificent Niagara Falls. The MCRR commissioned several artists, such as Charles Graham, to paint this view over the years. Prints were made of the paintings for use in advertisements, and postcard souvenirs, and were framed for hanging in all MCRR depots as the company adopted the motto, *The Niagara Falls Route.*

MICHIGAN CENTRAL R. R.

DOUBLE TRACK.   **STEEL RAILS.**

WITH ITS CONNECTIONS, FORMS

THE DIRECT ROUTE
——FROM——

MICHIGAN

TO ALL POINTS IN

ILLINOIS, IOWA,
KANSAS, NEBRASKA,
COLORADO, DAKOTA,
MANITOBA, ARIZONA,
TEXAS, NEVADA,
MONTANA, OREGON,
AND CALIFORNIA.

LOWEST RATES.

To obtain Safe and Quick Transportation, buy your Tickets over the MICHIGAN CENTRAL. For sale at all offices in Michigan ; at General Office, 154 Jefferson Avenue, and Depot, foot of Third Street, Detroit, where Sleeping Car accommodations may be secured by letter or telegram.

Passengers by this Old and Favorite Route will find it provided with every essential to make Railway travel Safe, Speedy and Luxurious.

For any information relative to this Route not obtainable from your Home Agent, apply to

O. W. RUGGLES,

C. A. WARREN,   Gen'l Pass. and Ticket Agent,

Pass. and Ticket Agent,   CHICAGO.

154 Jefferson Ave., DETROIT.

Advertisement from *Week's Detroit Directory,* 1883.

More bridge work on the Huron River was completed in Vanderbilt's last year as president. Four iron bridges between Ypsilanti and Ann Arbor replaced wooden structures. The locomotive equipment increased by the addition of 51 engines, *four of which were acquired with the Saginaw Bay & Northwestern Railroad; one was built at the company's shops, and forty-six were purchased. The latter are first class engines, nine of them being especially designed for fast passenger train service.*

Some significant work in improving the yards and terminal facilities at Detroit was completed in 1883. In addition to work on the new passenger station, more than 1,000 feet of new dock was built, the *Twentieth Street Yard (old Stock Yards) has been filled and graded . . . to admit the laying of over two miles of freight tracks. New tracks have been built, including one main track from Detroit to Springwells. Ten thousand tons of new steel rails have been laid in the main track between Kensington and Detroit, replacing partially worn rails, which have been transferred to and laid on branches;* worn rails next went to side tracks before being scrapped.

William H. Vanderbilt stepped down as president in 1883 and only stayed two more years as a director of the MCRR. He died on December 8, 1885. Although his goal of full control of the MCRR didn't come in his lifetime, it was eventually achieved when the NYCRR purchased enough stock to become majority owners in 1898.[12] During the short time Vanderbilt was running the MCRR, he left a permanent mark on the company. One of his best decisions was the selection of his successor as president—Henry Brockholst Ledyard.

Frequently used logo prior to 1900.

CHAPTER 16

LEDYARD MAKES HIS MARK

In August 1877, in his third year on the job as superintendent, Ledyard was put in a situation that would endear him to the company's employees. The country was in the fourth year of a depression and many railroads were trying to keep from going bankrupt through means such as cutting wages. Railroad construction had almost stopped, many industries and businesses were going under, and many previously employed men became tramps roaming the country looking for work.

The Great Railroad Strike of 1877 began on July 16 in Martinsburg, West Virginia, over a 10 percent wage cut instituted by the B&O Railroad. The strike rippled across the country through rail centers in Philadelphia, Pittsburgh, Louisville, Cincinnati, and Chicago, with more than 100 strikers killed, thousands injured by state militias, and millions of dollars in damages to railroad property sustained. Detroit waited and worried.

Ledyard told newspapers that the MCRR would not resist strikers and if trains were stopped the crews would be

Henry B. Ledyard would lead the company for the next 43 years and would be associated with the railroad longer than Forbes, Brooks, and Joy combined.

discharged. He went on to say that because the road was not making any money at the moment, it didn't particularly matter to him whether the trains ran or not. The only people hurt would be the employees and the public who could not get transportation or goods. His approach worked as newspapers articles attest: *Detroit, Mich, July 25— On the Michigan Central Road matters at this end of the line are going on as usual, except that no through freight is being handled, but way freight is very freely sent and received at stations in this State.*[1]

At the western terminus things were not as peaceful. On July 25, mobs of Chicago hoodlums, mostly non-railroad men, roamed the rail yards and forced the temporary shutdown of the most of the railroads there. The state militia was called to quell the enraged mobs and 18 died in the battle. No Michigan Central men were involved in the action.

A couple of days later, on July 27, 1877, the *Ann Arbor Courier* announced that Ann Arbor's militia was ordered to protect MCRR interests.

> On Tuesday evening, Captain Revenaugh received orders from the Adjutant General to report at Jackson, Wednesday, forenoon. Accordingly the drum was heard at their armory calling a meeting, when the orders were read to the company. Wednesday morning they started for Jackson on the Day express fifty strong. It is the intention of the Michigan Central to concentrate their rolling stock there in case of a strike on the railroad, and to have the State militia protect it. Another case for ordering them up was that a large number of coal miners had struck for larger wages, and fears are entertained that they may endeavor to repeat the Pittsburgh horror on a small scale.

The strike peaked on July 28 and within days almost everything was back to normal. Detroit was essentially untouched by the strike, which is a testament to the regard MCRR workers held for the company. Within a month Ledyard rewarded MCRR employees for their company loyalty by addressing one of their long-standing complaints about an increase and equalization of wages. The superintendent traveled to Chicago to announce to the MCRR's 200 men working there (switchmen, yardmen, and warehouse laborers) that their payroll schedule was being *graduated according to a scale, which had previously been approved by the employees themselves. In a very few instances a small percentage was taken from the salaries paid at present and heretofore, but, as a rule, the pay was increased . . . from 4 to 12 percent. The advance will probably average 6 percent.*[2] This new scale found beginning levels starting at the following pay: freight house labor, $1.15 per day; engineers at $2.50 per day. It appears that the new scale was comprised of three grade levels for each job.

Ledyard's fair but firm handling of the MCRR during the strike and how he personally handled the equalization of wages issue after the greatest labor dispute in U.S. history would foreshadow how he would run the company over the next four decades.

Ledyard graduated from West Point in 1865 and served in the West during the Indian Wars. He was developed as a railroad man in what amounted to an MCRR farm club system. He interned at the Chicago, Burlington & Quincy, a product of the Forbes, Brooks, and Joy collaboration. Joy hired William B. Strong as MCRR superintendent in 1874, and Strong brought in Ledyard in as his assistant. Ledyard took the presidency

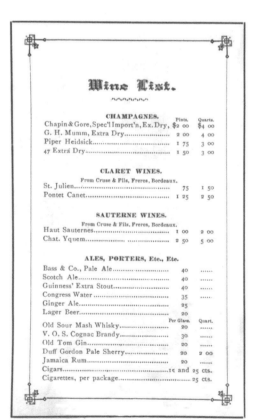

MCRR dining car menu, c. 1880.

of the MCRR in 1883 when Vanderbilt stepped down. Henry had been in the "system" for 14 years.

In 1883, after Vanderbilt left the company in the black again for the first time in a couple of years, Ledyard acted on ideas about using some of that profit to improve the railroad. In Ledyard's first annual report in 1884 (which utilized charts in place of the rich narratives of earlier years), he noted the improvement of the yards at Detroit by saying 1,000 feet of new dock had been built and a new passenger station constructed. *Seven bridges have been rebuilt. Fifty-one engines and 934 cars have been added to the rolling stock.* Ten thousand tons of new steel rail were laid between Kensington and Detroit.

Among improvements to the Canada Southern: the completion of the cantilever bridge, the 14-mile loop to Niagara Falls and the completion of an iron transfer boat that would carry 21 railroad cars across the Detroit River were highlighted.

The completion of the cantilever, or thereafter known as the Michigan Central Bridge, changed the company forever. More will be said about that later. But the addition of a transfer boat for use across the Detroit River brings up one of those issues that remains a little muddy due to previously written conflicting or incomplete information.

The Great Western Railway was the first to operate carferries between Windsor and Detroit in the 1850s. The Canada Southern Railway began operation of two car ferries (the *Transport* and the *Transfer*) between Gordon, Ontario, and Stony Island, Michigan, in the 1870s. CSR track ran from Stony Island across a bridge to Grosse Isle and across another bridge to Slocum Junction, Michigan, which is just south of Trenton, Michigan. These bridges were built and operated by the Canada Southern Bridge Company and one of them crossed the west channel of the Detroit River. The carferries ran from a slip on Stony Island crossed the large east channel of the Detroit River to the slip at Gordon, Ontario.

When the MCRR cut ties with the Great Western (which had become part of the Grand Trunk) and leased the CSR, it immediately wanted the terminus of the CSR to be closer to Detroit, rather than 20 miles or so south of the city. In 1882 the CSR built track from Windsor to Essex Centre, Ontario to redirect the main line of the CSR to Detroit. After the Windsor to Essex Centre connection was finished, the Essex Center to Gordon, (and to Gross Isle) portion of the rack was relegated to that of a secondary route.

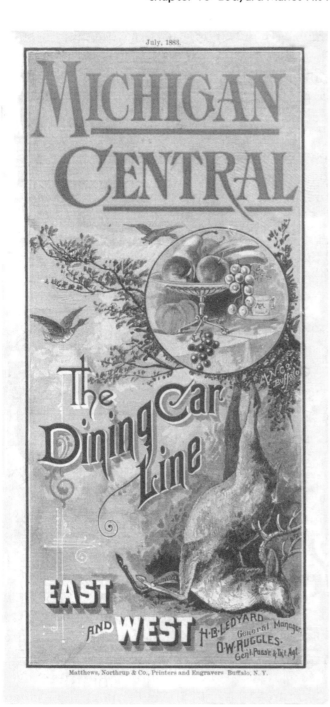

July, 1883.

MICHIGAN CENTRAL

The Dining Car Line

EAST AND WEST

H.B. LEDYARD General Manager.
O.W. RUGGLES. Gen'l. Pass'r & Tkt. Agt.

Matthews, Northrup & Co., Printers and Engravers Buffalo, N. Y.

This 1883 timetable shows the use of another nickname.

With the CSR now in Windsor, the Michigan Central started a carferry operation between Windsor and Detroit (1883). The first MCRR ferry between Windsor and Detroit was the iron-hulled *Michigan Central,* which is mentioned in the 1884 annual report. Within four years the MCRR was ferrying more than 285,000 railcars a year across the river.

Traffic across the river became so heavy a steel ferry called the *Transfer II* was added on January 13, 1889. The Transfer II was a 280-foot long steamer built by the Cleveland Ship Building Company in Cleveland, Ohio. It was powered by both paddle wheels and screw and traveled at 12 miles an hour on open water and 10 miles per hour in ice.[3] By 1895 the number of cars being carried across the river hit 322,828—the result of 21,121 trips made by the ferries that year.

> *The time of actual ferriage in summer from shore to shore, not counting the great loss of time in breaking up trains, is 12 minutes east-bound and 10 minutes west-bound. In the winter, including nearly four months of the year, about 30 minutes are required for each trip each way.[4]*

Ledyard noted that all 396 locomotives (CSR owned 125) on the line were coal burners except one. Freight cars now outnumbered passenger cars on the MCRR by 72 to 1 with 8,771 and 121 respectively. If freight cars averaged 40 feet in length in the late 1880s and if all were parked on the westbound track from Detroit, the line of cars would have reached almost to Jackson.

Financial reporting changed somewhat in 1884 with the previous year's figures from the MCRR and CSR being combined. Perhaps the figures were aggregated because the lease agreement with the Canadian road required the MCRR to share one-third of the net profit of the combined systems with the CSR. Together the gross revenue for 1883 was $14,009,766. In comparison, the total for 1882 was $12,330.040. The increase from 1882 to 1883 was therefore a nice 13.62 percent and a great first year report for the new president.

Year two was not so great. The 1884 report showed gross revenue down 16.75 percent to $11,659,077. Net earnings were down 36 percent. No reason for the decline in earnings was given, but there was a mild economic recession in 1883.

The election of directors was held on May 7, 1884, and it now consisted of the following members: From New York were W. H. Vanderbilt, Cornelius Vanderbilt, W. K. Vanderbilt, E. D. Worcester, S. F.

Barger, and Chauncey M. Depew. Henry Ledyard and Ashley Pond, both from Detroit, and W. L. Scott of Erie, Pennsylvania, rounded out the board. Pond replaced Anson Stager who died.

MCRR management continued to be dogged by freight pooling and rate problems in 1884. The Toledo, Cincinnati & St. Louis sued the MCRR because it refused to accept a train of cotton. Unofficial sources say Ledyard ordered agents not to accept freight from companies not in the pool. The Toledo, Cincinnati & St. Louis officials claim they offered to pay the published rates for through freight. The federal court ordered the MCRR to accept the freight.[5]

In the fall of 1885 and spring of 1886, the MCRR was dealing with dishonest freight agents. On the Buffalo end of the line, MCRR agent Joseph Wilkins stole several thousand dollars and fled to Canada. He eluded capture for a couple of years, but when caught received a five-year prison sentence. At Jackson, agent W. L. Richardson, who worked for the company for eight years, stole more than $6,000. The money was apparently spent on extravagant living. The disposition of his case is not known.[6]

The MCRR is known for several firsts in railroad operations. In what might have been one of the first efforts in company health care, in October 1885, the MCRR sent out a special car to vaccinate all employees for smallpox.[7]

Annual elections for 1886 were held on May 8 in Detroit. The same board was elected with the exception of John V. Farwell who replaced William H. Vanderbilt, who had died in December 1885.

The 1886 financial report showed declines again. Gross revenue in 1885 was down to $10,707,394, a reduction of $950,000. The reason cited for the loss was low freight rates. An example was provided to assist in understanding how rate fluctuations affect revenue. Despite a 95,000-ton increase in total tonnage shipped, a rate reduction of .086 of one cent per ton per mile meant a *very small reduction has resulted in a loss of revenue amounting to over $1,050,000.*[8] A reduction in passenger rates per mile was compounded by a reduction in passengers carried. No dividend was offered that year, but the NYCRR, with its combined railroads, grossed $30,500,000 in 1886.

Construction in 1886 was highlighted by purchasing land for additional yard room at West Detroit (Junction Yard) and land at Ann Arbor for a new passenger station. No new locomotives were added in 1886.

At the close of 1886, Ledyard made a decision that was deemed innovative by some. To stop the decline of freight revenues, he published a notice to agents that all arrangements to split through rates with other railroads would be accepted only if a minimum proportion was received by the MCRR. It was a surcharge added to amounts charged on distance traveled on MCRR lines if the regular rate failed to meet a minimum fee. Apparently other roads, including the Wabash, were starting to do the same thing.

All these troubles with shipping pools and rate cutting resulted in the U.S. Congress passing the Interstate Commerce Act in 1887. The intent of the Interstate Commerce Act was to force railroads to charge fair rates to their customers and make those rates known to the public. It also outlawed freight pools. The 1887 act created the Interstate Commerce Commission (ICC), which was the regulatory and enforcement arm of the law.

Shippers and railroad men differed on their thoughts about the law. Shippers thought it was a railroad law and the western business would suffer while the east benefited. Railroad officials thought they would be overregulated, lose control of rate fixing, and lose revenue. Ledyard said railroad officials would know in two months whether the law would hurt or help.

One thing was certain: The fear of the law touched the MCRR long before the law took effect. Shippers anticipating a law being not favorable to them shipped everything they could to beat the deadline. In March, the month before the law took effect, the MCRR had the biggest business surge in its history. In an interview with the *New York Times*, Ledyard gave his opinion about the new Interstate Commerce Commission and its immediate future.

> They complain at Washington, of a scarcity of room for the silver dollars that are piling up there. Why, the room needed for the silver dollars is hardly worth mentioning in comparison with the space the Inter-State Commerce Commission will need. The commission is young yet, and it is pushed. Where will it get clerks to handle the documents as well as room for storing them? The Michigan Central will send the commission 2,000 documents a year. We must send them copies of all documents issued. If we send so many, how many will roads like the New York Central and the Pennsylvania send? Why, the commission will be buried under paper before it's a year old.[9]

Partially due to the boost in shipping during April, the May's combined 1886 earnings jumped nearly 15 percent to $12,295,827.

Officials said the increase was due solely to an increase in rates per ton from .0560 to .0686, because the tonnage shipped actually decreased. Passenger revenues increased as well (16.08 percent) with an increase in passenger numbers and an increase in the rate per mile from 2.033 to 2.143. Expenses that year included 8,500 tons of new steel rails, 375,000 new cross ties, 35 miles of new side track, and 158 miles of new fence.

The vice president of the Canadian Pacific Railway was at the May 4, 1887, annual meeting of MCRR directors, and newspapers speculated about the reasons. Chauncey M. Depew was thought to be considering a partnership with the CPR, which was seeking a connection with Detroit. Newspapers mention a tactic used by the Canadian company that was key to many railroad problems, which Ledyard outlined during an interview a couple of years later.

In responding to criticism of the integrity of railroad presidents and managers by an entity not identified by Ledyard, the president of the MCRR consented to a long interview to set the record straight on who is to blame for most of railroads' problems.

> *I affirm that the railroad managers of this country are as honest, as hard working, and as careful of the interests of the stockholders they represent . . . as the president of any bank in this country. . . . One of the primary causes of all this trouble may be traced directly to the policy of the banks. It is a notorious fact that nay five men in this state may organize a corporation for the building of a railroad, and with no money of their own issue bonds of the basis of $20,000 a mile, negotiate the bonds with the banks in New York on a basis of 90 per cent, which yields $18,000 a mile in cash. The road is built for $15,000 per mile, and the incorporators pocket $3,000 per mile out of the project, while the banker floats the bonds at probably not less than 95 cents and so clears a handsome profit on the deal. The interest on the bonds, which cover not only the cost of construction, but the profits of the projectors and those bankers, must now be paid. The public must pay this and if the road were simply built to blackmail an established line into buying it out of competition, and was not a necessity, the loss falls heavily on the investors.*[10]

Ledyard provided an example of the problem, which he described as *guerilla methods*. He cited the situation that faced the New York Central. The West Shore Railroad was building parallel to the NYCRR and the line wasn't needed; and it couldn't get funding or business. It was built for the purpose of blackmailing the NYCRR into buying out the competitor. Vanderbilt didn't need or want the line, but felt pressure from stockholders who were worried that competition would hurt their dividends. Finally, as stockholders for the WSRR were about to go under, Vanderbilt offered half the value of the road. The other half was a total loss to stockholders and *a greater blow to the prosperity of New York State than a panic could have been.*

In 1886, the Michigan Central Railroad, Grand Rapids & Indiana Railroad, and Detroit & Cleveland Steamship Navigation Company formed the Mackinac Island Hotel Company to build a luxury hotel on the increasingly popular summer vacation spot. Although not on the Main Line, the opening of the Grand Hotel on Mackinac Island warrants a mention as an event of note because it lifted the status of the railroad to a national level. On July 10, 1887, the fabulous hotel opened and has since been visited by at least five U.S. presidents: Harry Truman, John Kennedy, Gerald Ford, George H. W. Bush, and Bill Clinton.

Total trackage continued to increase on the MCRR. In 1887–1888 there were 1,221.49 miles of road operated by the company with an additional 472.93 miles on the CSR and 624 miles of sidetrack between the two roads. Revenue jumped by 15.20 percent in 1887 over 1886, with freight at 17.27 percent and passenger at 13.97 percent increases. Figures show gross revenue at $14,164,490.

Gross earnings were down to $13,770,522 in 1888 due partly to the low rates prevailing on eastbound through traffic for most of the year, and partly to the falling off in westbound through traffic.

In 1888 locomotives owned by the company totaled 279: 128 were owned by the Canada Southern. All 407 were coal burners.

Another vintage correspondence from the era illustrates how political pressures were recurrently applied in an attempt to procure special favors from the MCRR and how Ledyard handled them. In 1888 Michigan Governor C. G. Luce sent Ledyard a letter asking him to see whether he could help a lady who had petitioned him for assistance. The women's son was killed while working as a brakeman on the MCRR, 13 years prior.

Hon. C. G. Luce, Governor, Lansing   *Dec. 9, 1888*

Dear Sir

I have your letter of Dec. 8ᵗʰ enclosing a letter from Mrs. Sweet, which I herewith return.

The circumstances connected with the death of her son while an employee of this company . . . showed conclusively that there was not the slightest liability on *the part of this company. On account of their financial situation, the company contributed some $200 to the family. This was very much in excess of any expenditure needed for the funeral purposes, and was practically a donation. We have since then constantly given Mrs. Sweet passes . . . as often as once a week. Others in like situation—and I regret to say that there are many—whose relatives have been injured or killed in the service of the company . . . have made application for similar favors.*

There is really no reason why Mrs. Sweet should be granted favors, which are denied others. I am willing, however, at your request, to send her a trip pass, and I will do so today . . . but I must ask that this be the last. You can readily see that, in the position I occupy, having to deal with thousands of persons, my action must be consistent with all.[11]

Yours truly, H. B. Ledyard, Pres.

It is surprising that the Michigan Central didn't have more trouble shipping freight and passengers into or out of Canada. The first bump in usually smooth transition across country boundaries came during the Civil War when through passengers started needing passports. The travelers and MCRR experienced some inconvenience, but it was relatively minor. It wasn't until 1889 that a freight issue surfaced with a competitor. The MCRR filed a grievance with the Interstate Commerce Commission against the Grand Trunk. It seems the GTR set special lowered freight rates for coal coming into Canada. The issue apparently was mild compared to the greater concern raised by the case. Were Canadian railroads in any way under the jurisdiction of the ICC? The fact that Canada railroads were shipping much more to U.S. ports than U.S. railroads were shipping to Canada made Grand Trunk officials acquiesce. Joseph Hickson, general manager of the GTR said the company felt authorized to make special rates and *thought it was in the best interest of United States coal companies and of our customers. Now the Michigan Central does not know how it is hurt by this traffic, nor does anybody else apparently.[12]*

Town prosperity and MCRR success was so closely connected that railroad activities were of high interest. Newspapers along the Main Line kept track of railroad activities and proudly announced improvements in the company's operations. In May 1889, it was reported that MC began lighting passenger coaches with incandescent electric lights. *Many of the coaches also now have steam heat.[13]* Around this time steam heating of passenger cars was still being perfected. The biggest problem was relieving locomotives of the power-reducing steam-heating drain.

In 1889 gross earnings from traffic was up only $10,000, but an improvement in motive power continued. The number of locomotives jumped to 284 owned by the MCRR and 135 owned by the CSR.

The MCRR did not give up on building a bridge across the Detroit River. It petitioned Congress for another commission to review the request. Another commission was formed and presented its report on July 19, 1889, again supporting the request to build a bridge. They found that a high bridge with 140 feet of clearance would be no problem to shipping interests. For the third time the commission's findings were ignored and permission to build was not given. No reasons were given for the "no" vote.

The ICC continued to be a thorn in the side of the MCRR in the 1890s, as it was for many other railroads. In a case that had taken over a year to come to trial, MCRR Chicago general freight agent A. McKay, Blue Line agent E. L. Sommer, and a Mr. Nichols, local MCRR freight agent, were charged with giving a customer a two cent discount on shipping 100 pounds of grain. The crime was discovered when the shipper sold the grain cheaper than anyone else for several weeks. The shipper claimed he didn't know the rate as it changed frequently, and the chief freight agent was livid that anyone would claim he was giving anyone an illegal deal on shipping. Nichols and

An advertisement for Martin's Steam passenger car heaters claimed MCRR patronage in 1888.

Sommer were found not guilty. A third party, a Mr. Street (affiliation not provided), was given a $3,000 fine.

Several months later the ICC ruled against the MCRR in a suit brought by shipper John P. Squire & Co. The MCRR had charged him a rate for shipping cattle that Squire thought was inappropriate. So did the ICC. The fine was not announced.

Perhaps the spate of cases and suites against the company were due to the MCRR's publicized financial success. By 1890 gross revenue climbed slowly to $14,340,000 and additional yard space, station grounds and right of way was purchased for work at Detroit, Kalamazoo, Ann Arbor, Jackson, and Battle Creek and also for building a second track between Dexter and Grass Lake.

In 1891 profit reached an all time high at $16,178,030. Newspapers called the increase in profits *extraordinary prosperity*. Perhaps the prosperity moved the Vanderbilt-controlled company to announce that they too would build the long-sought tunnel under the Detroit River. The Grand Trunk Railway had just opened a single track St. Clair Tunnel at Port Huron near where their ferries formerly crossed the river. One can imagine the turmoil in the MCRR boardroom when the GTR gained the huge competitive edge.

The MCRR had held permission from Michigan and Canadian authorities to build a tunnel for years, but they could find no reliable company to do it for a contracted price. Experienced contractors wanted to take the job and be paid as they progressed. Estimates for this type of work ranged from $5 million to $15 million, with no guarantee that costs would stop at $15 million. If the price was not enough to make management wince, it was also well documented that passenger traffic suffers when a tunnel is on the line. But in 1891 it seems that after waiting nearly 20 years for a bridge that apparently would never be permitted to be built, plans were being made for a tunnel.

Work on the new railroad tunnel under the river at this point is to begin at once on the Canadian side, about a mile back from the river. The tunnel will cross the river a short distance below the present Michigan Central transfer ferry and will open on the main line on the Detroit side of the river. . . . [T]ubes of steel plates will be constructed. These will be reinforced with heavy angle iron and this again with five rings of brick and concrete. A cross section of the big tube is a perfect circle as this shape resists any pressure. The diameter is 31 feet outside and 27 feet inside measurement. The bottom will be filled with concrete for a depth of about 5 feet and on this the stone ballast and tracks will be laid. The tracks will be 75 feet below the surface of the water. Several months will be consumed in pre-liminary work and the actual labor of excavation will probably not begin until early in the autumn. The projectors hope to have this important work fully com-pleted inside of three years.[14]

But as we now know, the announcement was either a ruse, or just a bad snap decision that resulted from the shock of being beaten by the GTR. Or perhaps the financial panic of 1893 was being felt in spite of record profits. Construction on the tunnel did not start until 1906 and it took four years to finish.

After 12 years of bickering between railroad companies under Vanderbilt control, the chairman of the board brought the managers of the companies together to form an advisory council for the pur-pose of *preserving harmony* between these trunk lines and their con-nections. How well this plan achieved its goal was not reported.

The lines might not have gotten on well, but they were on a finan-cial upswing. In 1891 the MCRR bumped a semiannual 2 percent divi-dend up 1 percent as net income doubled due to a reduction in operating expenses. As mentioned earlier, earnings in 1891 were up again and although dividends didn't reach previous year's levels, stock prices closed the year high at 106. To give an idea how that compared to other lines, the ever-stable Chicago, Burlington & Quincy was at 97; the Illinois Central was posted at 98; and the New York Central was at 109. For an idea how railroad stock compared to affiliated businesses, the Western Union was at 94 and American Express was at 118.

On February 22, 1892, ex-U.S. president Grover Cleveland vis-ited Ann Arbor by special train over the MCRR. His party arrived at the new MCRR station at 11:45 a.m. and was met by 5,000 citizens.

In September 1892, long time MCRR treasurer Henry Platt died in New York. He became an assistant to the treasurer in 1878 and treasurer in 1883.

To those working on the railroad, the financial Panic of 1893 was hitting Michigan harder than previous financial depressions. MCRR crews were reporting more bums and tramps along the line then ever before.[15] Railroad crime increased on the nearby LS&MS, to the point of major concern. On September 12, 1893, robbers stopped a LS&MS train at Kessler, Indiana, shot the engineer and blasted the US Express Company's safe with dynamite. On July 24, 1895, robbers ambushed a train at Reese's Siding near Toledo (also on the LS&MS) and at-tempted to blow up the safe but failed. Three months later in Erie,

Pennsylvania, a LS&MS freight conductor was shot in the head in an attempted robbery. The MCRR was lucky never to have had such an event on the Main Line to date. But as a preventative measure, the MCRR let it be known that they were taking extra precautions against robbers by having the following notice printed in the newspaper.

The Michigan Central Railroad Company has equipped all its express trains throughout with riot guns for the reception of train robbers. They will discharge six cartridges containing seventy-two buckshot in three seconds and tear an eight-inch hole through anything. We hope we will not have to use the riot guns, but if we do our men will shoot to kill . . . if any train robbers give our men a chance there will be some without any heads at all.[16]

The announcement worked for more than a decade to dissuade thieves. It appears the first armed robbery of a Main Line train didn't happen until September 27, 1916. At least two robbers hid onboard an east-bound train at Ypsilanti, stopped the train at gunpoint near Dearborn, and took registered mail from the baggage car. They were never apprehended.

In the midst of the 1893 financial downturn, the MCRR reported record earnings. Another all time high was reached in gross revenue—$16,075,000. Net earnings also increased $12,576, and semiannual dividends remained at 2 percent. The locomotive count stood at 310 for the MCRR and 151 for the CSR.

In 1894, for the first time, the financial downturn began to impact revenue. Gross earnings were reported at $12,700,000, a decrease of $3,527,000. The decrease was blamed on the financial condition of the country and officials claimed revenue would have been worse if not for increased passenger traffic due to the Columbian Exposition. Company fliers show that the MCRR shipped advertisements written in several languages to Europe to promote the exposition. The 1894 semi-annual dividend remained at 2 percent. Total mileage of main track for the combined system stood at 1,619.52 with 243.95 of second track and 864.87 miles of sidetrack.

It is fortunate to have an illustration about the level of freight traffic passing a single point on the Main Line in 1895. Someone in Dexter spent one cold night in February counting trains and found that in one 24-hour period between February 20 and 21, no fewer than 29 freight trains with 717 cars passed through Dexter, Michigan.[17]

In 1895, the MCRR was not only increasing its volume of traffic on the Main Line, it was increasing speed significantly. On October 1

Advertising in Europe hoped to bring business to the MCRR during the Colombian Exposition.

a train made an astoundingly fast trip from Buffalo to Chicago covering 511 miles in 9 hours and 45 minutes. The average rate of speed was a little over 52 miles an hour. The train in question was the *J. Pierpont Morgan Special* consisting of a baggage car and two sleeping cars. *The best burst of speed made on this run was between Fargo and Charing Cross* [over Canada Southern track], *the distance being covered at the rate of 72½ miles an hour.*[18]

In 1895 gross revenue rebounded to $13,651,420. In 1896 it was up a little more to $13,821,614. Freight tonnage was down, but the rate per ton was up from 0.617 to 0.636. A local newspaper along the Main Line reported that in 1895 the MCRR abolished the system of paying by car sent out with payroll. One wonders how the workers first felt about checks replacing cash for their labor.[19]

Yet another joint traffic agreement for the MCRR was in the works in 1895. All of the Vanderbilt-controlled railroads and eight other systems (Chesapeake & Ohio; Pennsylvania; Grand Trunk; Baltimore & Ohio; Erie; Lackawanna; Lehigh Valley; and Wabash) formed a committee with a board of directors to ensure the agreement would hold.[20]

In 1896 the annual report indicated that the MCRR acquired *terminals and belt line facilities at Chicago and East Chicago, under which it will have its own direct connection with the Stock Yards at Chicago, and with the belt line around the city, intersecting all lines entering Chicago.*

Gross revenue in 1897 decreased slightly to $13,697,239, while gross freight tonnage was up. The reason, of course, was that the rates for freight and passenger traffic were again reduced below levels from 1895.

In 1898 the total gross revenue moved up to $14,046,148, which was an increase of $349,000 over 1897. Both freight and passenger earnings increased although rate per ton-mile on freight decreased a half-cent. The second track between Ypsilanti and Dexter was still under construction.

Also in 1898 the MCRR adopted a new symbol to represent the railroad. Many railroads across the country had emblems or insignia that were immediately recognizable, while the MCRR had none. As mentioned earlier, in the 1850s it began using the nickname the *Favorite Line* and used it off and on until the 1880s, but it didn't strike the imagination of the traveling public. *The Great Central Route* was used for 20 years as a general heading until ties with the Great

Western were cut in 1882. The company tried the *Dining Car Line* and it lasted just about a year until the *Niagara Falls Route* became a permanent fixture in 1883. But even then it lacked a visual representation because illustrating the falls for use as a logo was difficult. For several years, they tried using two conductors holding up a Niagara Route sign, but that was not memorable. Maybe that is why they ran so long with the phrase, *The Only Route to Niagara*, as a subtext under *The Great Central Route*, so they would not have to develop an accompanying logo.

The lack of a memorable logo may have been the impetus to try something with a visual impact. So in 1898 it designed a *winged female indicating speed, bearing above her a shield with a view of a MCRR train at Niagara Falls. On a tablet below appears the names of the principal cities touched by the line.*[21] The design was used for the cover of this history. It only lasted a few years until replaced by the New York Central System oval.

The next year, 1899, showed a tremendous $1,457,914 increase over the previous year. Both freight and passenger revenues were up. But the last year of the century was costly in other ways to the company. Three key officials died while in office. The annual report made the announcement.

> *Your Directors have to record, with regret, the loss, by death, during the year, of two efficient and faithful officers: D. A. Waterman, who had served as Auditor of the Company from December 1st, 1875, until November 1st, 1892, and as Treasurer from November 1st, 1892, until the date of his death, April 2d, 1899. O. M. Barnes, Land Commissioner of the Jackson, Lansing & Saginaw Railroad Company, who had served the Company in that capacity from September 1876, until the date of his death, November 11th, 1899.*

In the page following that announcement, the long tribute to Cornelius Vanderbilt appears. His death required an emergency joint meeting of following roads:

> *Boards of Directors of the New York Central and Hudson River Railroad Company, the Chicago and Northwestern Railway Company, the New York and Harlem Railroad Company, the Lake Shore and Michigan Southern Railway Company, the Michigan Central Railroad Company, the Canada Southern Railway Company, the New York, Chicago and St. Louis Railroad Company, the Cleveland, Cincinnati, Chicago and St. Louis Railway Company, and the Chicago, St. Paul, Minneapolis and Omaha Railway Company, held at the Grand Central Depot on Thursday, September 14, 1899, at 10:30 A.M., to take action . . .*

The MCRR closed the century with a total gross revenue for 1900 that made company history. The jump to $16,730,131 from $15,504,062 the previous year showed an increase of $1,226,000. The increase, however, was not just based on a jump in freight tonnage (55,455,453) and passenger traffic (12,273,560). As seen previously, the real reason for the increase was that *rate per ton per mile* increased .028 cents and the *rate per passenger per mile* increased .013 cents. The semiannual dividends were 2 percent, paid July 28, 1900, and 2 percent paid January 28, 1901.

Miles operated in 1900 were 1,621.48 of main track, 262.21 miles of second track and 969.26 miles of sidetrack, for a total of 2,852.95 miles. All but 128 miles were laid with steel rails. The MCRR owned 310 locomotives and the Canada Southern owned 151. The average distance traveled by these locomotives in a year was 41,028 miles and their average yearly repair bill was $2,960.

Gross revenue in 1901 was another huge record for the MCRR at $18,490,273. It was an increase of $1,760,000 over the previous year. The freight traffic jumped *in tons moved one mile* of 73,550,830. That increase generated almost one million dollars alone. Even passenger traffic showed an increase of 50,962,836 in passengers moved one mile and over three quarter million dollars increase in revenue. This increase was accomplished in spite of a decrease in the rate per passenger per mile from 2.194 to 2.034 cents.

By the end of the century, early concerns about the profitability of leasing the land grant Jackson Lansing & Saginaw Railroad were proven to be unfounded. Since the land commissioner's report became a fixture in the company's annual report, 342,248 acres were sold. During that time acreage and timber sales on that land were totaled together, but the total revenue generated was $4,319,938. The total was $700,000 over the anticipated figure, and 157,752 acres, having the estimated value of $1 million, were still left to sell.

All through the 1890s, the state wanted to revoke the MCRR's original charter and place the railroad under the general railroad law of the state. For nearly a decade the company was against this and fought it through political channels, then threatened lawsuits. But eventually MCRR officials changed their minds. Perhaps the tremendous profits that the generated in the 1900 and 1901 allowed them to not worry about the state's action. The last year the MCRR operated under its original Michigan charter was 1901. The battle for the mighty Central's charter is outlined in Chapter 18.

Many historical accounts credit Ledyard with taking a broken-down country railroad and making it a jewel. To be clear, the road did make wonderful strides over his tenure. He was known as someone who *kept his railroad in the front rank by instinctively doing in advance what necessity would compel later on.*[22] One example of this amazing foresight and business sense was he frequently ordered side tracks to be built where no businesses existed. Of course businesses came to these pre-developed locations and the road made record profits with him at the top. Yet the fact is, the MCRR was one of the most outstanding railroads in America before Ledyard's leadership. Long before Ledyard, the line was operating the fastest trains in the nation over the best track in the country. He understood how to make it better and did it with strength and resolve.

Battle Creek Depot

Niles Depot

CHAPTER 17

DEPOTS, FACILITIES AND BRIDGES

It is difficult to locate and verify pre-1901 information about station locations along the Main Line. The three primary sources of information are county histories, the MCRR Construction Distribution Ledger B 1848–1851 and MCRR annual reports, 1847–1901. Huge information gaps plague these resources, even the annual reports. The earliest have little to say about depot construction; the main focus was track building and the procurement of rolling stock. During the years surrounding financial downturns (1857, 1873, 1893), building construction slowed on the Main Line. During other blocks of time, the extra revenue was dedicated to adding freight cars and feeder lines. In later years, the annual report format changed and building information was omitted altogether.

With the surfacing of MCRR Construction Distribution Ledger B 1848–1851, a small window of time is provided to pinpoint some information about early construction at station sites. Many entries give builder names and dates not commonly known.

Some information about post-World War I building property exists. The collection of 1920–era MCRR property valuation photograph negatives, currently housed at the Allen County Museum in Lima, Ohio, had companion informational files to those properties. It is not clear what type of information is contained in the files, but some believe floor plans and date of construction are given. For reasons known only to the donor, the property information files did not come to Lima with the negatives. They are currently in private hands and access was not attained after several attempts. It is believed that these records, and the copies of property valuation documents held by the U.S. government, only cover structures in existence at the time of the property assessment (1919–1920), which is out of the time frame of this history.

In general terms, many of the first depots on the MCRR were long, narrow, rectangular structures often described as having Gothic (with scalloped or spiked fascia boards) or Italianate (with bracketed cornices) influenced design, sitting parallel to the track. They served a duel role as passenger and freight buildings. The earliest depots had no bay windows, but did have oversized front window casements. Bay windows were later added to many of these buildings after the mid-1850s. These structures, in general, were split into three rooms: a waiting room, a freight room, and an office for the agent. Later freight rooms became baggage rooms when separate freight houses were added.

As towns grew and needs changed, the depots developed into a more standard design, sometimes called modified Queen Anne (having gabled and broad eaves). Several along the Main Line had a second floor or attic space designed to house the agent and his family. The Dexter depot, for example, had only enough additional room for the agent to sleep. Local carpenters built the early depots following simple plans, but most of the Main Line depots built after the Civil War were unique, designed by different firms giving each town something different.

Surprisingly, annual reports from the 1880s omit the efforts to upgrade depots on the Detroit to Chicago Main Line. It was during this time that the magnificent Romanesque (rounded arches, towers, stone or brick) depots were built at Ann Arbor, Grass Lake, Battle Creek, Kalamazoo, and Niles for the purpose of impressing passengers enroute to the Chicago Exposition in 1893.

Station development began when the state owned the road. Brooks made one of the first comments about structures on the MCRR Main Line in his review of the route for eastern capitalists. In 1845 he said that four stations houses built by the state existed on the road. Those stations were not listed but are believed to have been at Detroit, Ypsilanti, Dexter, and Grass Lake. Within a year after Brooks made his trip on the line, but before the formation of the MCRR

Company, the state built stations at Ann Arbor, Davidson, Jackson, Marshall, Battle Creek, and Kalamazoo.

With the MCRR Company in control after 1846, station building was pressed hard and soon the stations west of Kalamazoo had company depots with some room for handling freight. Many were likely single structures that served as both passenger and freight depots. In 1848 the annual report stated that *the depot buildings at Niles and between that place and Kalamazoo are in a forward state soon to be ready for business. The locations for depot buildings west of Kalamazoo have been determined to be: Paw Paw, Decatur, Dowagiac, Niles, and New Buffalo. There may be need for two stations between Niles and New Buffalo. Between all these stations there may be placed signal* [flag] *stations.*

By 1850 most stations on the Main Line had depots of some sort in place. In the 1850 annual report, Brooks states *a few of the stations upon the old line between Detroit and Kalamazoo have not been provided with the longer turnouts* [siding tracks to load and unload freight] *and full depot accommodations. These it is desirable to complete at no distant day . . . and to get rid of the local charges upon freight by the private warehouses.*

In 1851 Forbes announced in the annual report that the road was completed to Michigan City and *all the necessary buildings were in place.* One might take from that statement that all stations listed in 1851–1852 timetables had passenger and/or freight depots. Construction records confirm that a tremendous amount of work on buildings was happening between 1848 and 1851. Surprisingly, some of those MCRR buildings listed in construction records were in places along the Main Line not recorded anywhere else (such as Sylvan in Washtenaw County). Also, some stops on the Main Line had no depots at all and were just freight transfer points, usually near a mill (for instance Kellogg in Washtenaw County).

It was not until 1858 that all station buildings were completed to their satisfaction. In 1858 the annual report stated *and all the interior stations, with the completion of the freight depot at Galesburgh last fall, are amply accommodated with the proper buildings for the transaction of business with the public and doing the work of the Company, it not being probable that further expenditures for buildings of any kind will be necessary upon any part of the line for many years to come.*

In 1861 the annual report referred to all stations when discussing improvements to Battle Creek depot. *It will be necessary to expend something in the renewal of passenger-house at Battle Creek, and for extensive repairs of the freight depot at same place. This passenger house being the only one upon the line that was not constructed entirely new from foundation upon the transfer of the road by the State in 1846.*

Based on that comment, readers are led to assume that all depots built before MCRR took over were either sold and moved off site, or torn down and rebuilt. Primary source information confirms that not all the buildings erected by the state were torn down. The construction ledger lists entries that indicate people were paid to move earlier depots away (Jackson and others) in 1849. The state-built Dexter depot (1841), apparently rebuilt by the MCRR, existed until the 1960s. Sold in the 1880s, the building was hauled away by a farmer for use as a barn.

Michigan is fortunate that so many MCRR Main Line depots still exist. At last count at least 21 are still standing (all or part), although some have been moved away from the track. Those are Detroit, Ypsilanti (2), Ann Arbor (2), Dexter, Chelsea, Grass Lake, Jackson, Albion, Niles, Kalamazoo, Battle Creek, Augusta, Decatur, Dowagiac, Galien (2), Lawton, Three Oaks, and Michigan City. In the last several years, MCRR stations built after the turn of the century in Hammond, Indiana, and New Buffalo were destroyed by arsonists.

The following station information gives an overview of early station facility development. It was pulled primarily from annual reports and is italicized but not footnoted. Some of the milepost distances from Detroit to the discontinued stations are estimated and appear in brackets [MP 57.5] with mileage rounded to the tenth. All other milepost distances were taken from MCRR mileage books. Over time many of the milepost distances changed slightly as stations moved or track was straightened. Only stations listed on timetables or in annual reports between 1850 and 1896 are covered here, although some of the accompanying photos are of depots built a little later. A chart related to mileposts, stations (1850–1896), and agents working in 1896 appear in Appendix M.

Detroit

The beginning of the MCRR Main Line was at the bumping post (end of track) at the Third Street station from which all distances to stations, junctions, bridges, and culverts on the line were measured. This bumping post (MP 0.0) was just a few feet west of Third Street at the old depot and remained there for at least 130 years.

The first Detroit station house was built or purchased by the state prior to 1838. It was a one-story, wooden structure that served both passenger and freight business and was located at the intersection of Woodward and Fort Streets in Detroit at Campus Martius. It was torn down to build the city hall. In 1848 the MCRR shifted the Main Line toward the river and built a new depot on Third Street between River Street (later known as Woodbridge Street and later Jefferson Avenue.) This is now roughly the present location of Joe Louis Arena and the Detroit River. It remained in service as a warehouse for years after a newer depot was built in 1883. The last depot at this location was built in 1896 at the corner of Third and Woodbridge streets, and operated until the upper story and clock tower burned in 1913. It was replaced by the great Michigan Central Station on Vernor Ave. and 16th St. near Michigan Ave.

<u>1848:</u> *The works at the Detroit terminus are nearly completed. The new passenger depot is finished and is 325 feet long by 75 feet wide. The principal wharf, upon which the freight depot is constructed, is 1,090 feet long. The water there is from 12 to 20 feet deep. The surface of this area was filled in and raised from 8 feet to 25 feet. The brick freight depot is 800 by 100 feet, is completed, and has machinery for hoisting and elevating freight to the second floor. The machine shop for the repair of locomotive and the iron work of cars is completed of brick and in operation. This is a three section, two-story. The main body is 64 by 90 feet. The right wing is 40 by 63 feet, the left wing 40 by 48 feet. The lower stories of the wings have blacksmith and boiler shops. Adjoining this main building is a circular engine house, 130 feet in diameter with a turntable in the center and tracks for sixteen locomotives. The car shop is not yet started.* This strip of riverfront land, which was originally part of the Lewis Cass farm, was sold to the MCRR by Admiral Oliver Newberry for $35,000.[1]

<u>1851:</u> *The freight depot in Detroit, which was destroyed by fire in November last, has been rebuilt in a very substantial manner. The new structure has four brick partition walls cutting the chamber rooms into five parts, the more effectually to secure it against a like accident in future. The grain depot with machinery was finished.*

<u>1853:</u> *The piece of waterfront at the Detroit depot ground that was purchased in 1851 has been filled up and the wharf in front nearly completed.*

This brings all the land at this terminus into one body and with a front upon the river of 2,202 feet and an average width of 391 feet and probably is as well shaped and as conveniently located for a large terminus as that of any Railroad Depot in the county containing 19.77 acres. Upon a portion of this ground a new blacksmith shop has been constructed 180 feet by 55 feet and . . . renders their shop . . . for the manufacture of 25 double freight cars per month.

<u>1854:</u> *The buildings at Detroit are in good repair; a new fire proof building at Detroit, connecting the passenger with the freight house, has been built.*

<u>1860:</u> *Reconstruction of* [the] *oil-house* [was completed], *including the iron tanks holding 12,000 gallons.*

<u>1861:</u> *Considerable modifications have been made in the company's machine shop at Detroit; extensive repairs to the building being necessary, it was deemed judicious to transfer some branches of work from the second story, concentrating all work practicable upon the first floor, and* [placed] *under the more immediate supervision of the Superintendent of Repairs. To accomplish this, it was necessary to erect a one-story brick addition upon the vacant ground between the machine shop and the blacksmith shop, requiring two side walls only and roof. This improvement has been completed, and is now occupied; the size of the shop, now containing nearly all the machinery and tools, and in which the greater part of the work connected with the locomotive department is done, being 190 by 92 feet; adjoining it and connected by tracks through doorways, is the blacksmith and boiler shops, 180 by 52 feet. Steam pipes, for warming, have been put in both engine houses and machine shops in Detroit this year. The passenger-house, at Detroit, has been repaired and painted on the outside.*

<u>1862:</u> *A new stationary engine at the Detroit grain-house, and extensive repairs of the building were completed.*

<u>1864:</u> *New grain elevator at Detroit started (not finished); new turntable at Detroit.*

<u>1865:</u> *Paving with Nicholson pavement, 365 feet in length, in front of premises at Detroit was finished. An additional 350 feet of 20-foot sidewalk*

was completed. A building 40 feet in width, and 590 feet in length was constructed to the pile bridge approach to Detroit station to get more freight facilities, and for the accommodation of new elevator.

<u>1866:</u> *650 feet of 10 foot fence was constructed in Detroit.*

<u>1867:</u> *The Freight Depot at Detroit, 800 feet in length and 150 in width, (including the docks in front,) with iron roof over the whole, has been completed during the year and is in use. This building, with office building attached, three stories high, is fireproof in all respects, and is a most substantial structure.*

<u>1875:</u> *At Detroit we have built a freight-house and office, with appurtenances for the Grand Trunk Railway. The construction of new shops, elsewhere, left the buildings formerly used for shops, and standing in the yard fronting on Woodbridge Street, in Detroit, to be made useful for other purposes. They had become both inadequate and of no use for the former purpose for which they had been used. All except those immediately on the street have been removed, and the space occupied added to the station yards. Those fronting upon that street have been remodeled and repaired, and converted into a freight-house, which is used by the Grand Trunk Company.*

<u>1883:</u> *The important work of extending and improving the yards and terminal facilities at Detroit has progressed in a very satisfactory manner. Over one thousand feet of new and substantial dock has been built, and three and one-half acres of earthwork filled, thus affording to that extent additional yard room. The construction of the new Passenger Station at Detroit has also progressed very favorably, and it will probably be completed about May 1 next.*

Detroit Stock Yards (MP 1.7)

The MCRR stockyards, prior to 1882, were at 20th Street, MP 1.7. As the railroad's business was growing in Detroit, along with the city, they decided to convert this location into an area of team tracks, and move their stockyards to an area along the southwest side of the developing Junction Yard area, near the new carshops and along Dix

Avenue. This location also provided better access to inbound and out-bound stock traffic between Detroit and Toledo via the newly-acquired Toledo, Canada Southern, and Detroit Railway, via a lead at Waterman Ave. The Stockyard handled livestock cars for the livestock yards be-side it. Many meatpacking and rendering plants eventually located along Dix Avenue, as a result. The MC Stockyards were abandoned in the late 1940s.[2]

1882: *Stockyards have been built near the company's car shops at Detroit.*

1883: *The Twentieth Street Yard (old Stock Yards) has also been filled and graded sufficiently to admit the laying of over two miles of team freight tracks.*

Bay City Junction (MP 2.2)

This junction was took its name from the Detroit and Bay City Rail-road Co., which opened its line from Bay City Junction to Oxford in 1873. The MCRR helped build the line, and then in 1881 took it over as their Bay City Division. It was later protected with an interlocking switch and signal system operated from a tower.[3]

West Detroit (MP 2.9)

First called "Springwells", and later "Chicago and Canada Grand Trunk Junction" (shortened to "Grand Trunk Junction"), this station was first established when the Chicago and Canada Grand Trunk Junction RR terminated here, and a predecessor company of the Lake Shore and Michigan Southern RR crossed the MCRR at this location in 1854. It later became the intersection of the Wabash Railway and a termination point for the Pere Marquette Railway as well as the Toledo, Canada Southern and Detroit Railway, which later became part of the MCRR. This vicinity became a major, busy interchange point for railroad traffic in the Detroit area, and for the MCRR. It was later protected by variously updated interlocking switch and signal systems operated from a tower.[4]

1883: *New and additional tracks have been built, including one main track from Detroit to Springwells.*

Junction Yard (MP 3.9)

Earlier called the Grand Trunk Junction Yard, this location appears on station listings in the 1870s. After the turn of the century, this location became a yard system comprising many different smaller yards in this huge area, each serving a different purpose. Livernois Yard (1920s–1930s) became the largest yard. West of this was the Trainyard, developed after 1900, which became the main classification yard, and was eventually extended west into present-day Dearborn.[5]

1873: *Lands have also been bought at the Junction three miles from Detroit, for the erection of car-shops and roundhouse. The lands purchased comprise nearly 100 acres. The construction of shops for repairing cars is now in progress upon these grounds, and by the close of this season it is hoped they may be in readiness, and all shops removed from the station grounds* [at Third Street], *which are all needed for station purposes.*

1874: *Repair shops for cars and engine-house were constructed.*

The car barn built in 1873 at Grand Trunk Junction Yard. (Courtesy Jim Harlow)

1875: *The buildings in progress a year ago at Grand Trunk Junction have been completed, and in addition we have built there a sand-house, with brick walls and stone foundation; coal chutes to hold five hundred tons of coal; platforms and sheds for surplus coal for emergencies.*

1880: *Brick Engine and Boiler House at Car Shops, Detroit, with new Corliss 87-horse power Engine and Boilers were constructed.*

1881: *The rapid increase from year to year of the freight traffic of the Company has rendered increased terminal facilities an absolute necessity. With this in view, there were purchased during the last year, outside of Detroit, near the Company's Car Shops, 47 acres of land. On this land there has been commenced the construction of a yard for the handling of freight trains, and delivery of cars to connecting lines. Some 14 miles of track have already been laid. It is expected to add to this yard from year to year as the requirements of the traffic may demand. In connection therewith, a freight transfer house, car repair shop, and train master's office have been built.*

Town Line depot was used well into the 1960s, c. 1920. (Courtesy Charles Conn)

Town Line (MP 7.3)

"This station did not appear on station listings before the 1890s. Later the location of a junction of a cut-off line to River Rouge, it became a telegraphic

clearance point for freight trains entering and leaving Detroit. It was so named because its location was on the township line between Springwells and Dearborn townships."[6]

Dearborn depot. (Courtesy Charles Conn)

Dearborn (MP 10.2)

The first depot at this location was the tavern owned by Conrad Ten Eyck (c. 1837). It was located just west of the Rouge River.

<u>1857:</u> *The completion of the Passenger and Freight House (combined in one) at Dearborn.*

<u>1869:</u> *Eighty-two feet of new woodshed built.*

<u>1870:</u> *Woodsheds 1,276 feet long and 32 feet wide, with 14 feet posts and a shingle roof were built.*

<u>1878:</u> Depot burns (October 21).

Inkster depot. (Courtesy Jim Harlow)

Inkster (MP 13.6)

This was a telegraph station that appeared in 1870 station listings.

Eloise depot. (Courtesy Charles Conn)

County House (Eloise) (MP 15.2)

This location appears on 1850 station listings and was a county house infirmary serving as a "poor house." When it also started a treatment program for tubercular patients, it became known as *Eloise Sanatorium*. By the late 1890s the station name was changed to Eloise. It was later renamed *Wayne County General Hospital*.

Wayne (MP 17.5)

This station appears on station listings in 1850. The depot here was burned prior to 1919 and was replaced with a temporary shelter.

    <u>1868</u>: *New baggage room* [was added]; *two wood sheds were erected each 1,500 feet long.*

    <u>1870</u>: *An addition to the passenger house, 18x12 feet, for telegraph office erected.*

    <u>1871</u>: *Passenger-house was repaired.*

Wayne depot.

The Wayne Junction tower is on the left (looking west). The photo was taken by Hickok & Corlett, women photographers working in Wayne, Michigan, in 1892–1893. (Courtesy Wayne Historical Museum)

Wayne Junction (MP 18.0)

Established in 1871 on the southwest side of the city of Wayne when a predecessor of the Pere Marquette Railway built through here, this location included a railroad hotel, the PM switch and signal system operated from a tower after 1893.

Secord [MP 21.0]

This station appears on the 1870 station listing, and is gone by 1890.

Sheldon (MP 22.2)

This station appears off and on station listings from 1850 to 1896.

Denton depot is on the right.

Denton (MP 24.8)

This station appeared on station listings in 1855.

Wiard's (MP 26.7)

This telegraph station was another that appeared on station listings late in the century (1896).

Wiard's Siding. (Courtesy Charles Conn)

Ypsilanti (MP 29.4)

The state built the first small wooden depot at this place in 1837. When a magnificent three-story brick depot was built in 1864, the wooden depot was cut in half and one part was attached to a house on the corner of River and Babbitt Streets, which still exists.

1849: MCRR paid S. W. Walker for work on the passenger, freight, and waterhouse.[7]

1864: *New brick passenger depot at Ypsilanti (not finished); Repaired engine pump and freight houses, also telegraph office; put in new a pit and turn-table, also* [installed a] *foundation for scales.*

1869: *Put in flume and turbine wheel, with 2,000 feet water-pipe, for the better* [water] *supply of engines.*

1871: *Addition of three new stalls to engine-house completed.*

1878: *A new Freight House of brick, 182x36 feet, has been built.*

1910: The third-story of Ypsilanti's magnificent depot burned in May. That portion of the depot was removed, and the remaining lower section remodeled. In 1939, after a huge wreck of a freight train that destroyed the front of the station, it was once again remodeled. This portion still exists.

The lower section of this second Ypsilanti depot is still in place.
(Courtesy Bentley Historical Library)

Lowell [MP 32.1]

This station not appear on 1850 station listings, and it appears that it was abandoned as a station just after the MCRR took over. In the 1830s it was a promising community with a flourmill and a wildcat bank (the Bank of Superior). The MCRR maintained a siding there for decades.

Geddes (MP 33.3)

This station was located on the west side of the Huron River Parkway.

A rare photo of the Geddes Mill depot.
(Courtesy Bentley Historical Library)

Ann Arbor (MP 37.3)

The original station was located about one-tenth mile west and across the tracks of the existing depot.

1845: In the afternoon of June 4, 1845, the depot, *which had recently been completed at a cost of $5,000,* burned to the ground.[8]

A portion of the second Ann Arbor depot exists as a home.
(Courtesy Bentley Historical Library)

1849: MCRR paid S. W. Walker for work on the passenger, freight, and water house.[9]

1863: *Extensive repairs of freight house at Ann Arbor completed.*

1866: *1 wood shed at Ann Arbor built.*

1867: *1,446 feet 6-foot sidewalk & Platform at Ann Arbor* [was added].

1869: *Passenger house enlarged and dining-room and kitchen added.*

1870: *New blacksmith's shop, 35x30 feet, for repair of rails erected.*

1871: *Freight-house repaired, with new office added. New large frost-proof water-tank, with stone foundation erected.*

1887: A new stone depot designed by Spier & Rohns was built east and across the tracks of the old depot location. (This depot now serves as a restaurant.) A portion of the old depot was later moved a few blocks away and is now a residence at Beakes and Fifth Streets.

Kellogg's [MP 38.8]

This freight-only station was at Kellogg's Mills on the Huron River and was listed in 1870–1872 station listings.

Foster's (MP 40.5)

Another mill location, this station appears on 1850–1896 station listings. It was located on the south side of the Huron River and just east of the bridge. The depot was removed during the double tracking around 1900. A shelter was put in its place on the north side of the track, near the foot of the old wrought-iron bridge.

In this Paul Richmond photograph of Foster's Station, note in the foreground to the right, is one of the first types of Automatic Block Signals the MC had on their main line, c. 1920. At this time, a shelter house replaced the depot, which is barely visible at the left of the tracks next to a ruined mill warehouse.

Farmer's Mills (MP 41.9)

This station appears on the 1850 station listing. It was taken off listings in the mid-1850s and returned in the mid-1870s, only to be removed in the late 1890s when the Osborn Mill closed. No indication that a passenger house was built here along the Huron River could be found.

Delhi (MP 42.6)

This station built in 1866 was removed during the construction of the double track around 1900. From 1900 to about 1940, this station's passengers used small shelters to keep out of the rain. Delhi freight houses were destroyed by a tornado in 1917.

In this rare photo of the 1866 Delhi depot taken c. 1880, a few of the features in this image tell a lot about MCRR operations at Delhi during this time. First, the short, white-painted pole with the bracket and rope attached is for hanging mailbags to be caught by nonstop trains. The small building to the left of the depot is probably a coal shed and/or section house. The pole with the cable drop leading to it would be a telegraph line, assuming that this building hasn't been wired for electrical service yet at the date photographed. Next, the tall, white-painted pole with the dark bottom and attached ladder, one can see toward the top of the image, a pole upon which, at the very top, would be mounted the train-order and manual block signals. These signals would be lower-quadrant (blades down at 180 degrees indicating "no orders" or "clear block" for trains traveling against the current of traffic on a double track) semaphores, if one could see them. The ladder was for the agent-telegrapher to fill the kerosene lamps mounted behind the blade's glass roundels to light the lamps when necessary and clean the glass when necessary. On the building in front, mounted above head-height, is a V-shaped "train indicator box." In the upper set of windows in this box would be displayed the number of the train that passed most recently ahead. In the lower set of windows would be displayed the time the train passed. The reason this information was displayed to trains was that the rules of operation called for trains to space themselves for a certain time interval apart from each other, before the advent of Automatic Block Signals, such as are on this Main Line now. It was strictly up to a following train's crew to keep their trains spaced apart, so as to avoid disastrous rear-end collisions. The display of the preceding train's passing time in this box eliminated the need for the next train to stop at the station and determine that information from the agent/telegrapher. The agent-telegrapher on duty was required to keep that information displayed in the box undated as trains passed the station. (Information from Jim Harlow)

<u>1866:</u> *A new passenger house was built.*

The depot was removed at Delhi in 1901 when the double-track was built. It was replaced by this shelter, which eventually ended up as a chicken coop in the author's grandfather's back yard.

Scio (MP 44.2)

This location had a mill siding, freight house, passenger house and agent.

Dexter (MP 46.9)

<u>1841:</u> *The iron horse . . . thundered up to the depot.*[10]

<u>1849:</u> The MCRR paid S. W. Walker for work on the passenger, freight, and water house.[11]

<u>1850:</u> The MCRR paid R. Schuyler for building a passenger house.[12]

<u>1851:</u> The MCRR paid R. Schuyler for work on a freight house.[13] MCRR paid Lewis Wilson to put locks on Dexter depot privy.[14]

The first MCRR depot in Dexter. (Courtesy Dexter Historical Society and Museum)

1864: *Engine-house and turntable was built.*

1869: *Addition to the freight house, 26 feet by 40 feet,* [was built] *and new floor to passenger house* [added].

1870: *Built a new turntable with track under walled and sides walled.*

1887: A new wooden depot was completed. It was designed by Spier & Rohns. (It still exists.)

Chelsea (MP 54.2)

1850: A passenger house was built.[15] MCRR paid for labor on a passenger house.[16]

1868: *New baggage room built, repaired wheat and water houses, and laid 100 feet sidewalk.*

1869: *New wood house, 60 feet by 30 erected.*

1870: *Addition to grain house, 38 x 20 feet for grain car and track built, also timber bridge* [was purchased] *for approach to same, 260 feet in length.*

1871: *New well, 26 feet depth, 25 feet diameter, for supply of trains* [was dug]; *new wind-mill and* tower, *with 1,800 feet of water logs, conveying abundant supply of water from spring constructed.*

The first Chelsea depot, damaged by vandals. (Courtesy Chelsea Historical Society)

<u>1880:</u> *Improvements in Passenger House made.* (This depot was designed by Mason and Rice of Detroit and completely rebuilt as new. It still exists as a museum.)

Davidson [MP 58.0]

The depot and eating house built by the state burned down in 1848. The station was then moved to Chelsea and new depot was built in 1850.[17]

Sylvan Center [MP 57.9]

This station was built by the MCRR, but never appeared on station listings. Perhaps track straightening in the early 1850s moved the line north of the village and the station was abandoned at that time.

<u>1849</u>: The MCRR constructed a sidetrack at new station at Sylvan.[18]

Francisco (MP 61.2)

This station appears on the early 1850 station listings. The passenger house remained until the 1930s.

The second Francisco depot was torn down in the mid-1930s.

Grass Lake (MP 65.3)

<u>1842</u>: The state built a depot at this location.[19]

<u>1868</u>: *Two hundred feet new sidewalk laid; wheat house and cattle yards* [were repaired].

<u>1870</u>: *Graded for and built new stock yards, also repairs to grain house made.*

<u>1887</u>: *New passenger house built.* (It was designed by Spier & Rohns and still exists as a community center.)

<u>1889:</u> The old wooden depot remained next to the new stone depot until November 3, when it was torn down.

The stone depot was renovated and is now a community center.

Leoni (MP 68.3)

This station appeared on 1850 station listings and remained at least until 1905.

Michigan Centre (MP 71.7)

This station appeared on station listings from 1850 to 1890.

Jackson Junction (MP 74.5)

Established in 1871 as the eastern termination point of the Michigan Air Line Railroad Co., this station was also the west endpoint of a huge yard built by the MC after moving the locomotive and car shops from Marshall. Railroad traffic was directed at this junction well into the 20th century by non-interlocked target signals operated by trainmen and a telegraph operator.

Jackson Junction, c. 1920. (Courtesy Charles Conn)

Jackson (MP 75.6)

<u>1841:</u> Henry C. Orendorff had the contract for building the first station erected for the Michigan Central in Jackson when it was owned by the state.[20]

<u>1850:</u> The MCRR paid A. E. Lyon to remove the Jackson Depot.[21]

<u>1850:</u> The MCRR paid for labor to build a new passenger house.[22]

<u>1851:</u> The MCRR paid $1,200[23] for labor to build a fourth-class passenger room attached to the eating-house.

<u>1863:</u> *New brick engine-house at Jackson erected. Extensive repairs of freight-houses at Jackson completed.*

<u>1864:</u> *Extensive repairs of freight and passenger houses at Jackson* [made].

<u>1867:</u> *Platform at Jackson, 100′ by 18′ built.*

<u>1868</u>: *Repaired freight house and wood house; built new refreshment room and new telegraph and baggage rooms.*

<u>1869</u>: *A substantial brick freight house, 457 feet long by 37 feet wide, with projecting slate roof, and offices, has been completed by this company at Jackson, at a cost of $25,377. This is required to accommodate our own business at that point, as also in connection with the joint business of the Jackson, Lansing and Saginaw, and the Grand River Valley Roads connecting there.*

<u>1870</u>: *Temporary engine house, at cost of about $800; removed and repaired coach house, repaired old freight house.*

<u>1871</u>: *New engine-house (wood), with stalls for ten engines erected. New turn-table, 80 feet of coal shed, with cranes* [were constructed as was a] *temporary blacksmith shop and New telegraph office.*

<u>1873</u>: *At Jackson, where so many divisions of the road center, the machine-shops have been completed, and are now just put into use. Also a roundhouse with 52 stalls, the whole on a scale adequate to the present and probable future demands of the road. A new passenger-house has been built there, suitable to the wants at that place. Coal sheds and shutes have been erected made necessary by the large substitution of coal instead of wood for fuel.*

<u>1874</u>: *Repair shops for engines at Jackson, engine-house at Jackson complete.*

<u>1876</u>: A new brick depot was built by prolific architect, Henry A. Gardner. This is one of the oldest original train stations in the country that is still in use as a depot.

Jackson's second depot. Original photo comes from the *1929 Jackson Centennial.*
(Courtesy James Damaron)

Woodville (MP 78.8)

Apparently this siding was established after the MCRR began the switch from wood to coal for locomotive fuel in the 1870s. The Detroit and Jackson Coal Company had a mine at Woodville.

Sandstone (Trumbull) (MP 81.8)

This location appears on the 1850 station listing. The Jackson City Coal Company owned the Sandstone Mine located here. Around 1890 its name was changed to Trumbull and moved about a mile west (MP 81.6).

Gidley's (Parma) (MP 85.4)

This location appears on the 1850 station listing, but in the 1855 listing its name was changed to Parma and moved a mile west (MP 86.4). The last depot existed into the early 1970s.

<u>1868:</u> *Built new baggage room and cattle yards.*

<u>1869:</u> *A new grain and freight house has also been located at Parma, with bins of 40,000 bushels capacity.*

<u>1871:</u> *New grain house bridge erected.*

Louis Pesha photograph of Parma depot. (Courtesy David Tinder collection, Clements Library, University of Michigan)

Concord (MP 89.2)

This location appears on the 1850 station listing, but by 1873, its name was changed to North Concord.

<u>1881:</u> *New Water Works have been constructed.*

Bath Mills (MP 92.3)

This location appears on the 1850 station listing and remained on listings at least until 1905.

Newburg Mills (MP 94.2)

This location appears on 1850 station listings, but is absent from 1855 to 1874 as a passenger station, yet continued to handle freight. Then it returned to the passenger station listing in 1896 and was gone again by 1905.

Albion (MP 95.9)

<u>1850:</u> The MCRR paid labor to building a passenger house.[24]

<u>1866:</u> *New cattle yards constructed.*

<u>1868:</u> *One hundred feet new sidewalk laid; repaired wheat house; shingled freight house, 200 by 50 feet; repaired cattle yards and water houses, and put in two new tubs.*

<u>1881:</u> *New brick passenger house at Albion erected.* (It still exists as a train and bus depot.)

The second Albion depot was built in 1882.
It was recently restored and serves as a bus station and train depot.

Marengo (MP 101.2)

<u>1868:</u> *One hundred feet new sidewalk laid.*

Marengo depot. (Courtesy Jim Harlow)

Marshall (MP 107.7)

The location of the first locomotive and car repair shops on the Main Line outside of Detroit. Also the location of the first "eating house" to serve passengers traveling to points west. The repair shops were moved to Jackson in the early 1870s.

1849: The MCRR paid Nash & Clark $1,000 for building a depot and eating house.[25]

1849: The MCRR paid Jacobs & Garrison for working on the depot and eating house.[26]

1849: *Completing buildings and machinery at Marshall.*

1849: *Eating House at Marshall.—In a few days the building at Marshall intended for the Eating House, will be finished and sufficient time will be given the passengers on both the trains going east and west, to take dinner at this place.—The building is fitted up in good style and arranged in such a manner that persons can enjoy the luxury of a good dinner as comfortable as at the best Public House. The House is to be kept by G. W. Lester, who is more familiarly known as the chicken pie man from the delicious dish of this article that he always furnished his guests, when he resided at the Refreshment house at Davisons.*[27]

1851: *Ira Nash of Marshall . . . had the contract for preparing the roadbed and filling the marsh where the depot grounds now are. He also constructed most of the original telegraph line of the MCRR.*[28]

1863: *Extensive repairs on engine-house, rebuilt freight house.*

1864: *Shops are under supervision of A. J. Scoville and will require new boilers this year.*

1865: *Passenger-house, Iron turn-table, stone foundation and curbing finished. 22 new tubs and 925 feet of iron pipes* [were placed in] *engine-house. Within the past year, the old passenger dining-house at Marshall has been disposed of, and a new and spacious Passenger Depot, with hotel accommodations, has been erected in its place. The building is an elegant and*

Marshall station area map, 1868. A. Ruger, Chicago Lith. Co.
(Courtesy Library of Congress)

*substantial structure, provided with all the latest improvements, and can seat
in its dining hall at least three hundred persons. An establishment of this kind
has long been needed, and instead of repairing the old building at a heavy expense, it was deemed better economy, even at the high cost of labor and materials, to erect a building that should be a credit to the Company; and it is
believed that all that was aimed at has been accomplished.*

    <u>1869</u>: *Repairs to machine shop and engine house floors and repairs of
station house; etc.*

    <u>1870</u>: *Built new wood house, 350 x 40 feet, 14 feet posts, with shingle
roof; freight and grain houses shingled; repairs to machine and blacksmith's
shops* [completed]; *new coal sheds erected.*

    <u>1871</u>: *Engine-house repaired, with new floors and partially new roof.*

    <u>1885</u>: *New water tank, with pump erected, etc.*

Emerald Mills (MP 109.7)

This early mill site location appears on the 1850 station listing, but
was never listed again. The mills were built in 1848 and were located
on the Kalamazoo River about two miles from Marshall.

Ceresco depot, c. 1920. (Courtesy Allen County Historical Society)

Ceresco (MP 112.9)

<u>1862</u>: *New passenger station finished.*

<u>1868</u>: *One hundred feet new sidewalk laid.*

Whites (Wheatfield) (MP 114.5)

This location appears in station listings for 1873; in 1896, it is listed as Wheatfield.

Nichols (MP 119.9)

This was the location of a joint depot at the intersection of a prede-cessor railroad that later became the Grand Trunk Western Railroad, owned by the GTR of Canada, by 1878. Later the western endpoint of a huge yard and locomotive facility of the GTW, this station took

Nichols depot.
(Courtesy Willard Library)

its name from a large manufacturer of farm implements having its factory located here. The railroad intersection was later protected with an interlocking switch and signal system, operated from a tower.

Battle Creek (MP 120.8)

<u>1861</u>: *It will be necessary to expend something in the renewal of passenger-house at Battle Creek, and for extensive repairs of the freight depot at same place. This passenger house being the only one upon the line that was not constructed entirely new from foundation upon the transfer of the road by the State in 1846.*

<u>1862</u>: *A new roof and general repairs of freight-house at Battle Creek.*

<u>1863</u>: *Rebuilding freight-houses. New brick passenger-house (not quite completed).*

<u>1864</u>: *Labor paid for new turntable and new stock yards work.*

<u>1866</u>: *New turntables finished.*

Battle Creek depot area map, 1869. Note the "witch-hat" tower-type buildings at both ends of the station grounds, which were trackside "water-houses" enclosed over wells to help keep the water for locomotives from freezing in the winter. A water tank inside was heated by a stove in the winter to keep the water warm. Early maps and photographs show these water-houses were present at many MCRR Main Line stations prior to 1870. (Courtesy Library of Congress)

The first Battle Creek depot.
(Courtesy Willard Library)

<u>1867:</u> *Freight house, addition of 200 feet by 10 feet* [constructed].

<u>1868:</u> *Ticket office altered and repaired; wheat house repaired; barn repaired; one new baggage room altered and repaired; built new reservoir and laid 120 feet iron supply pipes across river.*

<u>1869:</u> *New water house, two new pumps, 100 feet 10 inch iron water pipe, and 200 feet supply pipe* [completed].

<u>1888:</u> The new station was constructed of red sandstone. It was designed by Spier & Rohns and still exists as a restaurant.

Bedford (MP 126.3)

The small Calhoun County station appears in 1873 through 1890 station listings.

Augusta (MP 130.4)

<u>1863:</u> *New small passenger-house at Augusta erected.*

<u>1864:</u> *New stockyard at Augusta* [constructed].

<u>1866:</u> *New passenger house at Augusta erected.* (It still exists as a local museum.)

Louis Pesha photo of the Augusta depot. It now serves as a local history museum. (Courtesy McKay-Dole Library, Augusta, Michigan)

1868: *One hundred feet new sidewalk laid.*

Galesburgh (Galesburg) (MP 134.8)

The spelling of the station house name changed after World War I.

1854: *New passenger station and a brick water station erected.*

1857: *The erection of the Freight Depot at Galesburgh.*

1867: *Freight house thoroughly repaired.*

1868: *One new baggage room; old one repaired; wheat house repaired; 400 feet sidewalk laid.*

Galesburgh depot, c. 1910. Note the early spelling.

Comstock (MP 139.7)

This station appears on 1850 through 1905 station listings.

Comstock depot, c. 1920. (Courtesy Charles Conn)

Kalamazoo Junction (MP 143.4)

Originally located at the intersection of a railroad that became a branch of the LS&MS (1869), two other railroads - the Grand Rapids and Indiana, and the Chicago, Kalamazoo and Saginaw (which was eventually controlled by the MC), it later intersected the MCRR here. All crossings were later protected with interlocking switch and signals systems, each of which briefly had their own tower. Currently the site of one of Michigan's last interlocking towers.

Kalamazoo (MP 143.6)

<u>1846:</u> The new depot is . . . *the best in the state.* [29]

<u>1854:</u> *An elegant and commodious passenger house of wood and two large water stations of brick were constructed to replace those destroyed by fire a year and more ago.*

<u>1862:</u> *New stock yards at Kalamazoo completed.*

<u>1866:</u> *New turntable, new telegraph offices and battery rooms* [built] *at Kalamazoo.*

<u>1868:</u> *General repairs of freight house; new platforms at passenger house erected.*

<u>1869:</u> *Repaired roofs and dock; new and permanent foundations for new turn-table.*

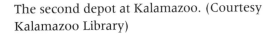

The second depot at Kalamazoo. (Courtesy Kalamazoo Library)

<u>1870:</u> *Addition to passenger house, 24x20 feet, and enlarged ticket office.*

<u>1871:</u> *New freight office erected.*

<u>1878:</u> *New frost-proof tanks, with steam pumps, etc., have been built.*

<u>1881:</u> *A four-stall brick Engine House at Kalamazoo completed.*

<u>1886:</u> A new depot was built at Kalamazoo. It still exists as a train and bus station.

Oshtemo (MP 149.4)

This station, first appearing in 1870 listings, was eliminated circa 1901, when the MCRR relocated their Main Line between Kalamazoo and Mattawan. It later became a station on the Kalamazoo, Lake Shore and Chicago Railway when the MCRR sold the original line to this company. (Meintz: *Michigan Railroad Lines*, 2005)

Oshtemo depot.
(Courtesy David Tinder collection, Clements Library, University of Michigan)

Mattawan (MP 155.9)

This first station upon entering Van Buren County appears on 1855 through 1899 station listings.

1865: *New freight-house erected.*

1868: *Repaired platform.*

Mattawan depot.
(Courtesy David Tinder collection, Clements Library, University of Michigan)

Paw Paw (Lawton) (MP 159.9)

This station appears on the 1850 station listings. By 1870 the name was changed to Lawton.

1848: W. Mason built an engine shed.[30]

1862: *New stockyards finished.*

1861: *All the station buildings were repainted.*

1866: *2 wood sheds at Lawton erected.*

1867: *Passenger station thoroughly repaired, with addition of new ticket and telegraph office.*

1868: *New coal house, 200 feet by 16, with crane and buckets for coaling engines was built.*

1870: *Repaired passenger station.*

1873: *Coal sheds and shutes have been erected.*

1881: *New Passenger House at Lawton.* (It still exists as a VFW hall.)

The Lawton depot built in 1881 is currently standing vacant.

White Oak [MP 161.9]

This location first appears in the 1870 station listing but is not in the 1890 listing. This long siding saw *heavy shipments of logs, lumber, stave and heading bolts, railroad ties, tan bark, to say nothing of large quantities of wood for the locomotives.*[31]

Decatur (MP 167.6)

<u>1848:</u> The MCRR paid T. H. Thomas for building a passenger house.[32]

<u>1861:</u> *All station buildings have been repainted.*

<u>1862:</u> *A new brick water-house and windmill at Decatur erected.*

<u>1866:</u> *2 wood sheds at Decatur erected.*

<u>1867:</u> *Passenger house similarly improved, and new brick water house, 22 feet in diameter, and 40 feet well, 10 feet diameter.*

<u>1868:</u> *Two new baggage rooms; also repairs of platforms.*

<u>1870:</u> *Repaired passenger station; raised floors, etc.*

The third MCRR depot at Decatur is still standing and being used for storage. The original freight house is attached to the Decatur Elevator Company's structure.

Glenwood depot.

Tietsorts (Glenwood) (MP 172.9)

This Cass County station appears in the 1870 station listings, but by 1890 its name changed to Glenwood.

Dowagiac (MP 178.8)

This station appears on the 1850 through 1899 station listings.

1861: *All the station buildings were repainted.*

1862: *New stock yards finished.*

1868: *Repairs to passenger, freight and grain houses.*

1898: A new stone and brick depot was built; It still exists as a train depot.

The Dowagiac depot is still used as a train depot.

Pokagon (MP 184.9)

This station appears on 1855 through 1905 station listings.

Pokagon depot, c. 1920. (Courtesy Charles Conn)

<u>1862:</u> *New small passenger houses at Pokagon, and New stockyards finished.*

<u>1868:</u> *New freight house and wood shed erected.*

Niles (MP 191.6)

<u>1848:</u> The MCRR paid John Orr for building a passenger house.[33]

<u>1849:</u> The MCRR paid Jacobs & Garrison for working on a depot and eating house.[34]

<u>1860:</u> *Carpenter shop 24x48 feet erected.*

<u>1866:</u> *Niles passenger house enlarged.*

<u>1867:</u> *Passenger house improved by an additional room for refreshment purposes, 30 by 22 feet.*

<u>1868:</u> *New water house erected.*

The first Niles depot. (Courtesy Fort St. Joseph Museum collection)

1869: *Repaired roofs and dock; new and permanent foundations for, and new turntables. New wooden engine house has been built at Niles, to replace that destroyed by fire a year since.*

1870: *Enlarged dining-room, and put additional sleeping rooms over kitchen.*

1891: New sandstone depot designed by Spier & Rohns was completed. It still exists as a train depot.

West Niles (MP 192.8)

This location appears on 1896 to 1899 station listings as a prepaid station (not regularly attended by an agent).

Buchanan (MP 197.8)

1848: The MCRR paid John Orr for building a passenger house.[35]

The third Buchanan depot.

1866: *Passenger house enlarged.*

1868: *Moved and repaired freight house.*

1869: *Built new freight and grain house, with bins of 10,000 bushels capacity.*

1873: *A new passenger-house at Buchanan erected.*

Terra Coupee (Dayton) (MP 202.4)

This location appears on 1850 station listings, but by 1870 the name was changed to Dayton.

1849: The MCRR paid Ferson & Orr for building passenger and freight houses.[36]

1862: *New stock yards finished.*

1867: *Passenger station improved by adding a room for ladies.*

Dayton depot, c. 1920. (Courtesy Allen County Historical Society)

Wilson's [MP 204.0]

This location appears in 1870 as a freight station listing only, but it was actually in operation since 1855. Known as Wilson's Siding, it connected with Wilson's sawmill on Mill Creek and was a lumber and wood fuel loading point for the MCRR.

Galien (MP 205.4)

This location appears in 1870 through 1905 station listings.

<u>1863:</u> *New small passenger-house at Galien erected.*

<u>1969:</u> *Built small grain and freight house.*

<u>1870:</u> *Repaired and painted station buildings.*

<u>1881:</u> *New Water Works have been constructed at Galien.*

This Galien depot (1870s) exists, but has nearly collapsed. Across the street is the newer brick depot (1913) and it too is deteriorating. (Courtesy David Tinder collection, Clements Library, University of Michigan)

Barnett's Siding (MP 209.2)

This location appears in an 1896 station listing and remains until at least 1905.

Avery's (MP 210.0)

This location appears in an 1870 schedule listing as a siding to Avery's sawmill and remains until at least 1905.

Chamberlain's (Three Oaks) (MP 211.2)

This station appears in an 1855 schedule listing. By 1865 the name was changed to Three Oaks.

<u>1862:</u> *New small passenger house erected.*

<u>1864:</u> *New stock yards Chamberlains finished.*

<u>1865:</u> *New freight-house erected.*

<u>1881:</u> *New Water Works have been constructed at Three Oaks.*

<u>1898:</u> New brick station was built at Three Oaks. It still exists.

Three Oaks depot now houses a bicycle museum.
(Courtesy David Tinder collection, Clements Library, University of Michigan)

New Buffalo (MP 218.3)

This location appears on the 1850 station listing. The second and last depot was brick and sold to private owners. It was gutted by fire in the early 1970s and was torn down.

1848: *Dock at New Buffalo started.*

1849: *Dock at New Buffalo completed.*

1854: *New woodshed, 300 feet long to replace one destroyed by fire.*

1869: *Raised and repaired passenger house.*

1870: *New, frost-proof Burnham water tank, of increased capacity, in place of old water house and tank.*

The second MCRR depot in New Buffalo was recently damaged from fire after sitting vacant for years. (Courtesy Bob Rosenbaum)

Corymbo, Indiana (MP 222.9)

Located just across the Indiana State line, it first appeared on station listings in 1870. When the village died out (sometime after 1905), the original Corymbo depot was moved by flatcar to Grand Beach, Michigan (a depot established after 1905). That depot soon was deemed too small for the passenger traffic presented and was replaced.

The former Corymbo depot was moved by flatcar here to Grand Beach station, but was soon replaced by a larger building. (Courtesy Art Lamport)

Michigan City Yard, Indiana (MP 226.9)

Bird's-eye-view of the Michigan City Yard. Note the second Michigan City depot on the right. It was destroyed by fire in 1914.

Michigan City, Indiana (MP 228.2)

<u>1850:</u> The MCRR paid for labor to build the new passenger depot.[37]

<u>1853:</u> *The engine house . . . has accommodations for 16 engines. The blacksmith and machine shop, which has been constructed here during the past year, is of stone, and 250 feet long by 65 feet wide.*

<u>1854:</u> *Machine shop completed and fully equipped.*

<u>1862:</u> *The enlargement of engine-house at Michigan City; renewal of the dock in front.*

<u>1864:</u> *Turntable at Michigan City* [completed]. *Shops under supervision of Jacob Losey and will required new boilers this year.*

<u>1868:</u> *New coal house, 150 by 15 feet, with crane and buckets erected; repairs on machine shop, engine house and stock yards.*

<u>1871:</u> *Engine-house floors relaid, and three stalls rebuilt.*

<u>1873:</u> *A new engine-house erected at Michigan City, with 22 stalls, machine-shop and passenger-house. Coal sheds and shutes have been erected made necessary by the large substitution of coal instead of wood for fuel.*

The first Michigan City depot.

<u>1874:</u> *An engine-house was constructed at Michigan City.*

<u>1881:</u> *New Office and Trainmen's House erected at Michigan City.*

<u>1882:</u> *A new passenger house was constructed at Michigan City.*

Furnessville, Indiana (MP 235.9)

This station appears on a 1870 station listing and remains at least through 1905.

Furnessville depot, c. 1920. Note that the building is similar to those at Town Line, Denton, and Wiard's. (Courtesy Charles Conn)

Pierces [MP 238.0]

This Indiana location appears in 1870 through 1874 station listings as a freight station only and is not in 1890 station listings.

Porter (MP 240.0)

This Indiana station appears in 1855 through 1905 station listings and was a crossing for the MCRR and LS&MS. Due to multiple accidents and near misses in this vicinity, an interlocking signal system was installed to protect the crossing in the late 1890s: this was controlled by the tower.

<u>1867:</u> *Passenger house generally repaired.*

Porter depot was replaced by an interlocking tower.

Crisman, Indiana (MP 245.4)

This Indiana station appears on an 1890 station listing; also spelled Chrisman's and Christmans.

Crisman depot, c. 1920. (Courtesy Charles Conn)

Willow Creek, Indiana (MP 246.0)

This Indiana station appears on an 1890 station listing and was a crossing for the MCRR and Baltimore and Ohio Railroad protected by an interlocking signal system controlled from a tower.

Willow Creek depot, c. 1920. (Courtesy Charles Conn)

Lake (MP 249.1)

This location first appears on 1855 station listings. Sometime after 1905 its name was changed to East Gary.

    <u>1854</u>: *New woodshed erected.*

    <u>1860</u>: *Water-house, windmill and framed tower for pumping erected.*

    <u>1865</u>: *New engine-house at Lake for four engines finished.*

    <u>1867</u>: *Passenger houses generally repaired.*

    <u>1868</u>: *Built new freight house and platforms.*

    <u>1871</u>: *One new wind-mill. Passenger-house repaired, with new floors and roof, and addition built on west end.*

Lake depot eventually had its name changed to East Gary.

Tolleston (MP 255.6)

This Indiana location appears in 1870 through 1905 station listings. It was a crossing for the MCRR and Pittsburgh, Fort Wayne, and Chicago Railroad (later owned by the Pennsylvania Railroad). Eventually the crossing was protected with an interlocking switch and signal system, controlled from a tower.

> <u>1862</u>: *New small passenger-house erected.*

Ivanhoe (MP 259.6)

This junction tower first appears on an 1896 station listing and was a crossing for the MCRR, Elgin, Joliet & Eastern Railway and the Indiana Harbor Railroad. It was protected by an interlocking switch and signal system controlled from a tower.

Gibsons (MP 261.0)

This location first appears on an 1855 station listings and remains until at least 1905 as n interlocking switch and signal system controlled from a tower. Sometime after 1890 it became yard operated jointly the MCRR and Indiana Harbor Railroad (predecessor to the Indiana Harbor Belt Railroad).

> <u>1860</u>: *Windmill for pumping erected.*

Hammond (MP 264.4)

Just tenths of a mile east the Illinois state line, this station first appears on an 1890 station listing. More than 100 years later the second Hammond depot was destroyed by arsonists while being prepared for renovation.[38]

The second Hammond depot built in 1902. (Courtesy Hammond Public Library)

Hammond's Bldg (MP 265.5)

This location appears on an 1890 station listing. It apparently was a siding to an icehouse.

Calumet, Illinois (MP 265.9)

This station appears on an 1870 station listing; by 1890 the name changed to Calumet Park. Later it was a junction of the MCRR and the Indiana Harbor, Baltimore and Ohio and Pennsylvania Railroads. The intersection was protected by an interlocking signal system controlled from a tower.

1857: *This account also embraces rebuilding the passenger depot and wood sheds destroyed by fire at Calumet last fall. New passenger house built with cost shared with ICRR.*

Calumet Bridge, Illinois (MP 267.6)

This location appears on an 1896 station listing and was the site of Main Line moveable bridge over the Calumet River.

Kensington, Illinois (MP 271.0)

This station was first established in 1852 at the point where the ICRR and MCRR tracks junctioned. The first depot here, was a joint construction venture by the two railroads, was a two-story, wooden structure that was destroyed by fire in 1877. A long, single-story, wooden building replaced it.

> <u>1878</u>: *New frost-proof tanks, with steam pumps, etc., have been built at Kensington,*

> <u>1881</u>: *Transfer House at Kensington, 800 feet in length erected.*

The MCRR track ended at Kensington. A switch was located just past the station that gave MCRR trains access to the ICRR track for the last 14 miles into Chicago. The following six stations were on that 14-mile stretch and were considered "joint agencies on the road." The depots were owned by the ICRR, but shared space with MCRR ticket agents.

Sixty-third Street (MP 278.3)

Hyde Park (MP 278.7)

Thirty-ninth Street (MP 281.6)

Twenty-second Street (MP 283.6)

Burnside (MP 275.1)

Junction (Grand Crossing) (MP 276.7)

A pencil drawing of the second Kensington depot, c. 1880.

Chicago (MP 285.6)

The MCRR and ICRR formed a partnership to build the great passenger depot in Chicago. Freight houses and other station facilities were individually owned.

1854: *New merchandise house 450 feet long, 60 feet wide of stone nearly completed.*

1855: *Passenger Depot 500 feet long and 167 feet wide completed.*

1860: *Wood-shed at 14 × 90 erected.*

1861: *A new and powerful windmill, for pumping water, has been erected.*

1863: *The engine shed is under charge of Isaac Perry.*

1865: *Building new and commodious freight offices at Chicago.*

1866: *New turntable at Chicago.*

1868: *New wood and coal houses, with crane and buckets; new stationary engine for pumping and small repairs.*

1869: *Addition to wood and coal shed, 80 feet by 30 erected.*

1870: *Additional standing room and capacity for engines at engine house completed.*

1871: *New wood and coal shed, 200 feet long erected. New oil building separate from others built; and new small building, with bunks for engineers finished.*

1873: At Chicago, a freight and office building, 50 ft. by 106, and three stories high erected. All these buildings are first-class, of stone or brick, with slate roofs. At Chicago also, a freight house has been built, of a more temporary character, but of brick, 80 ft. by 496.

1885: *New water tanks, with pumps, etc. finished.*

<u>1893:</u> A new monumental Central Station was completed. Sometime after the last ICRR operated passenger train left the station in the early 1970s, it was torn down.

The MCRR continued to add and delete stations as freight and passenger traffic dictated. Within a few years after 1900, new stations such as Botsford, Miller's and Grand Beach were added to the Main Line. Several others were dropped. The average distance between stations from Detroit to Kensington was 3.1 miles. The largest gaps between stations appeared from Dexter to Chelsea (9.3 miles) and from Michigan City to Furnessville (7.8 miles).

DEPOT OF THE ILLINOIS AND THE MICHIGAN CENTRAL RAILROADS.

The first Chicago depot block print from *Ballou's Pictorial Drawing-Room Companion, April 11, 1857.*

BRIDGE BUILDING AND REPAIR

A portion of the bridge building and repair reports from the MCRR annual reports are presented to show a little about the work and changes over time. For example, on the Main Line, in 1878 a wooden draw-bridge over the Calumet River was replaced by an iron pivot (swing) bridge. It is also interesting to see how the Huron River bridges went from wood pile, to iron truss, then to today's steel deck girder bridges. When the Huron River is low in the summer, one can still see the remnants of the old wooden piles in the riverbed.

The second bridge at Niles, the largest on the road, was completely rebuilt in 1855 ($20,000) and in 1868 was repaired with new deck stringers, new covering and new trestle approaches to the spans at each end. In 1880 an iron bridge was built over the river in preparation for a double track. (Courtesy Ella Sharp Museum)

Here are a few other bridge reports.

<u>1865</u>: *Pile bridge, 100 feet long, erected at Salt Creek. 32 stone culverts put in place of wooden.*

<u>1866</u>: *3 new bridges near Jackson, 1 new bridge near Michigan City and 1 new bridge near State line erected.*

<u>1868</u>: *The bridge over St. Joseph River at Niles, the largest on the road, completely repaired by new deck stringers, new covering and new trestle approaches to the spans at each end. New highway bridge built one mile west of Niles and two bridges raised between Niles and Buchanan. Also, repairs to*

bridges over Kalamazoo River, and to culverts injured by the high water in March. Sixty highway and farm crossing gates made and put up on west division during the year.

W. G. Macomber photo showing a MCRR on-site stone-cutting operation probably for a bridge in Berrien County, c. 1894. (Courtesy McKay-Dole Library in Augusta, Michigan)

1875: *Construction and repairs listed in reports included the following: Wooden Pile Bridge over Trail Creek, at Michigan City (Main Line), 178 feet in length, replaced with Through Iron Truss, Double Track, Pivot Bridge, Stone Abutments and Centre Pier; Wooden Pile Bridge over Huron River, two miles west of Ypsilanti (Main Line), 161 feet 2 inches in length, replaced with a Through Iron Truss Bridge, Stone Abutments; Wooden Pile Bridge over Huron River, west of Fosters (Main Line), 165 feet 4 inches in length, replaced with a Through Iron Truss Bridge, Stone Abutments; Wooden Pile Bridge over the Huron River, east of Delhi (Main Line), 100 feet span, replaced with a Through Iron Truss Bridge, Stone Abutments; In addition to the above, 31 wooden bridges of various lengths have been rebuilt, and 883 feet of bridges filled, requiring 40,844 cubic yards of earthwork.*

1878: *Wooden Pile Bridge over Huron river, near Geddes (Main Line) 117 ft. 6 in. in length replaced with through Iron Truss Bridge, Stone Abutments. Wooden*

Bridge over Jackson Street, Jackson (Main Line), 124 feet in length, replaced with an Iron Plate Girder Bridge, 3 spans, Stone Abutments. Wooden Draw Bridge over Calumet River (Main Line), 178 feet in length, replaced with a through Iron Truss, Double Track Pivot Bridge. In addition to the above, 26 wooden bridges have been rebuilt, and 2,617 feet of bridges filled, requiring 157,710 cubic yards of earth work.

<u>1880:</u> *Included in Bridge Repairs are the following replacements of Wooden Pile Bridges, over Huron River, with Iron Truss Bridges, Stone Abutments: One and one half miles west of Ann Arbor, 127 feet in length; (mile west of Fosters, 120 feet in length; 1 mile east of Delhi, 160 feet in length; mile west of Delhi, 160 feet in length; 1 mile west of Scio, 120 feet in length. In addition to the above, an Iron Bridge 632 feet in length, with Stone Abutments and Piers, has been built over the St. Joseph River, at Niles, for the second track. Twelve Wooden Bridges of various lengths have been rebuilt, and 1,754 feet of Bridges filled, requiring 17,769 cubic yards of earthwork.*

<u>1885:</u> *Stone arch and earth work completed, Big Creek.*

W. G. Macomber photo of driving piles for a MCRR bridge probably at Galien River, c. 1894. (Courtesy McKay-Dole Library, Augusta, Michigan)

CHAPTER 18

THE CHARTER YEARS END

The demise of MCRR's treasured charter was linked to the country's economic depression of 1893–1897 and the political beliefs of Michigan's Republican-Socialist governor, Hazen S. Pingree (1897–1901). The popular three-time Detroit mayor (1889–1897) was first elected on a platform of ending corruption in the city. But early in his term in office, a depression was underway and his focus changed to expanding public welfare programs, creating public works jobs for the unemployed, and using vacant city land for gardens to grow food for the poor. After those successes, he began fighting privately owned utility companies in a belief that such monopolies should be owned by the city.

One of the first monopolies he targeted was the Detroit City Railway Company to lower streetcar fares to three-cents. When that didn't work, he petitioned the legislature for a city-operated railway charter, but was rebuked. It seems such a charter was against state law. Believing that the legislature was controlled by the monopolistic transportation lobby, he took the matter to the state supreme court and again was rebuffed. This action against the Detroit City Railway was a warm-up for what Pingree had in mind for the MCRR after he took office as governor.

Less than a month after becoming governor, Pingree had a house representative present a bill to repeal the charter of the Michigan Central Railroad. The bill passed the house, but it was killed in the senate.

A year later, in February 1898, Pingree attempted to purchase a 1,000-mile mileage book from the MCRR for $20 (2 cents per mile). The ticket agent said no. Pingree knew the state legislature (at the onset of the depression) passed a law regulating the cost of mileage books at two cents per mile. He also knew the MCRR never complied. The Wayne Circuit Court agreed with Pingree.

The MCRR had been worried for some time about the ticket issue. It was the only Vanderbilt-controlled road not issuing the interchangeable thousand-mile tickets. Directors had feared that *by selling such tickets it could be forced by the state authorities of Michigan to sell tickets at 2 cents a mile.*[1]

The MCRR appealed to the state supreme court, which overturned the lower court's decision.

> . . . *the Michigan Central's special charter unquestionably confers the right upon the company to fix its own rates of tolls, and that this is a vested right which cannot be withdrawn by the State without an adequate compensation . . . that the law passed by the Legislature of 1891 regulating the cost of mileage books to 2 cents per mile has no application to the Michigan Central.*[2]

News of Pingree's defeat was covered by newspapers across the country. He vowed to take his case to the U.S. Supreme Court, but never did.[3] Instead, the governor began working on a revised state tax code that would cost the MCRR more than mere ticket money.

In October 9, 1900, Pingree called a special session of the state legislature for the purpose of *considering a joint resolution authorizing submission to the people of a constitutional amendment permitting the taxing of railroads and other corporations on the actual cash value of their property* [ad valorem tax], *instead of on their earnings as at present and to consider the repealing of the special charters held by the Michigan Central, Lake Shore, and Grand Trunk Railroads in Michigan.*[4] The measures passed and nearly 54 years after it was initially granted, the special charter was repealed by Act 2 of the Public Acts of Michigan during this special session.

Over a year later, at a meeting of the stockholders on December 4, 1901, the Company decided not to appeal and resolved to surrender its charter. Ledyard told those in attendance that directors had *decided to give up the road's special charter on December 30 and to operate after that date under the general railroad laws of Michigan, which means a rate of 2 cents per mile on the main line of the road. The rate clerks are already at work rearranging the tariff sheets.*[5]

Engine *Manitou* on a turntable at Jackson, c. 1875.

MCRR shop workers at the Michigan City yard, c. 1900.

The certificate of surrender and incorporation was filed in the office of the Secretary of State, December 30, 1901.

News of the charter's repeal traveled throughout the state with little notice. Passenger concerns about possible ramifications for their great railroad were overshadowed by excitement for a resultant rate decrease. The MCRR would have to drop rates to 2 cents a mile as prescribed by the state's general railroad law. On January 1, 1902, Ann Arbor's rate to Detroit was to drop from $1.14 to 75 cents. *Rate of 75 Cents to Detroit* was the headline of the day.[6]

Apparently seeing the inevitable and trying to make the best of it, months earlier, Ledyard had agreed to work with a special committee appointed by the legislature to discuss the special terms necessary to induce the MCRR to submit to the repeal of their charter. Ledyard was trusted so highly by his peers that the LS&MS and GTR agreed to follow the MCRR's lead. Some of the conditions demanded and given were that an arbiter would assess damages due to the repeal and loss of the charter, the state would pay those damages, and the railroads would have six months to reorganize under Michigan's general railroad laws.

Pingree died in the summer of 1901 while visiting King Edward VII in England. Perhaps his death slowed the process, but after a year

Station agent Plowe relaxing at the Francisco depot, c. 1900.

of waiting to receive damages the MCRR filed a suit by summons in the Wayne Circuit Court against the state of Michigan for $6 million, *resulting from the revocation of the railroad's special charter.*[7]

Two years after Pingree's death, 24 Michigan railroads companies filed suits in U.S. Circuit Court against the state. The suits were meant to block Michigan's auditor *from collecting the new ad valorem tax levied against them by the State of Michigan under the new taxation law. They assert that the so-called ad valorem amendment . . . is repugnant to the Fourteenth Amendment of the United States constitution and discriminates between various kinds of transportation lines.*[8]

Michigan answered back with a suit for nonpayment of taxes. Finally, on June 10, 1910, nearly 10 years after giving up is charter, the fight was over.

> *Mason, Mich. June 10.—The suit of the Michigan Central Railroad, against the State of Michigan for $6,000,000 damages on account of the abrogation of the railroad's special charter, and the suit of the State against the railroad for $4,400,000 back taxes were settled here today. The railroad paid the State $125,000.*[9]

Dexter Depot.
(Courtesy Dexter Historical Society and Museum)

Jackson Depot.
(Courtesy Ella Sharp Museum)

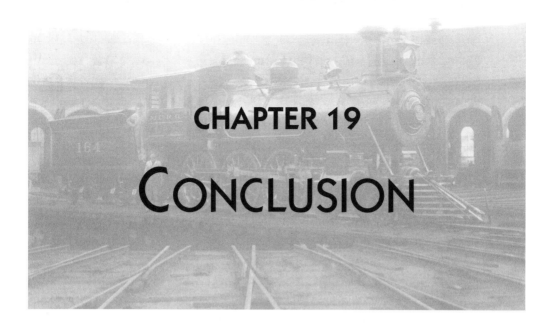

CHAPTER 19

CONCLUSION

While the NYCRR interests had managed the MCRR since 1878 through proxy votes, majority ownership and actual control was not achieved until 1898. During that span the MCRR operated as an autonomous entity, which allowed it to maintain its identity while working as a part of the NYCRR system. One example of that autonomy prior to the charter repeal was the locomotives on temporary loan to NYCRR system lines were all back-shopped (repaired) by the MCRR shops in Jackson. After the charter ended, the autonomy started to fade.

Within two years of the charter's demise, some MCRR forms and documents began to appear printed with "the NYCRR Co. Lessee." A little later, the NYCRR oval began to appear on freight cars. "New York Central System" replaced "Michigan Central Railroad" lettering on tenders, and the only company identity remaining on motive power were the initials "M.C.R.R." printed on the upper coal spill board of the tender. Over the next 30 years the MCRR's identity would fade further away.

In 1906 Ledyard stepped down from the presidency to become chairman of the board of directors. William H. Newman (1907–1908) was his successor. Only three more presidents would lead the MCRR before it was officially leased and controlled by the NYCRR: William C. Brown, 1909–1913; Alfred H. Smith, 1914–1923; and Patrick E. Crowley, 1924–1930.

Developments in technology continued to improve operations along the Main Line. In 1901 the Kinnear track pans (named after Wilson Kinnear, chief engineer of the Detroit River Tunnel) for scooping water at speed without stopping were in place near Dexter. In the next several years, track pans would be in place near Marshall, Lawton, Three Oaks, and Gary, Indiana.

In November 1908, telephones for dispatching trains went into effect between Detroit and Jackson. The Detroit River tunnel was opened in 1910, eliminating the largest impediment to through traffic on the system, and the magnificent Michigan Central Depot on Vernor Avenue at 16th Avenue near Michigan Avenue opened in 1913.

Wrecks continued to plague the MCRR, but they were very few and far between. Perhaps the worst wreck in its history happened on June 22, 1918, when two extra trains collided. An empty troop train ran signals to stop and hit the rear end of the disabled Wallace-Hagenbeck Circus train at Ivanhoe, Indiana. Sixty-seven passengers and one employee were killed.

In 1920 railroad consolidation fever filled boardrooms across the eastern United States. That year Congress passed a law authorizing railroads to consolidate into trunk systems for the purpose of improving efficiency and ensuring the security of short line companies. The ICC was given authority to grant or deny consolidation requests. The New York

The MCRR continued to add and drop stations, c. 1907. This photograph shows the first depot in Gary. (Courtesy Calumet Regional Archives at the Indiana University Northwest Library)

Central was making so much money it wasn't initially interested in changing its operation. The B&O, C&O, and the Pennsylvania, however, were practically crazed by the idea and the NYCRR was pulled into the fight that followed. *The eastern railroad situation became a melee where each one of the big participants tried to do at least three things at once—grab as many prosperous small railroads as possible, shove his opponent away from good roads toward poor ones,* [and] *avoid kicking the ICC (i.e., the public's interests).*[1]

In 1921 the MCRR lost Ledyard. Henry died at Gross Point Farms on May 25. In honor of the man who led the company for 38 years, all trains on the MCRR line stopped simultaneously for 2 minutes. His tribute in the annual report appears in Appendix J.

All the talk about consolidation may have spurred the long-time employees to think about the future of the MCRR. Undoubtedly,

Detroit MCRR depot under construction, c. 1912. (Courtesy Dave Tinder collection, Clements Library, University of Michigan)

those working on the line could see the road's identity disappearing into the Vanderbilt's New York Central Railroad system. In order to preserve memories of Michigan's greatest railroad, 3,700 railroad workers formed the Michigan Central Pioneer Society in June 1921. The club issued pins and conducted an annual reunion and field day. Annual reunions lasted well into the 1950s.

No particular procedure was required for submitting plans to consolidate, so in 1926, the NYCRR gave the ICC their plan to consolidate its principal subsidiaries, the Michigan Central and the Big Four, by leasing them for 999 years. Control of these roads *has rested with the New York Central for some time, and the present move is designed to affect a closer financial and operating union of the lines.*[2]

Stipulations of the lease indicate that it was actually a stockholder payoff of sorts. It called for a dividend of 17.5 percent in June, bringing the total dividend to 35 percent for the year. In addition it called for an annual rental of 3.5 percent on stock and an amount equal to 50 percent on the stock not owned by the NYCRR was paid.[3] It appears that for their vote for the consolidation, the few MCRR stockholders remaining were promised an 18.5 percent increase in earnings.

Everyone seemed happy with the merger at first, but within a few months of the announcement, protests were filed with the Interstate Commerce Commission. The New York Central Securities Corporation and counsel for the minority stockholders of the Big Four filed briefs to stop the move. Their argument against the NYCRR was that the consolidation of two major roads into the Central was unlawful because stockholders were unable to measure their monetary rights. Further, they argued that their rights were violated by *inadequate rental and improper and unjust provisions of the lease.*[4]

In the middle of this public fight for control, the railroad knocked the top off for record earnings. In 1926 gross revenue topped a staggering $95,500,000. Stock dividends were 27.5 percent.[5] Common stock jumped to a staggering $1,100 per share.

The ICC agreed with the petitioners and ruled against the consolidation. They claimed it would not be in the public's interest. Their main concern was that the plan *did not properly safeguard the interests of the short line railroad.*[6]

A couple of months later, the New York Central asked for dismissal of the intervention petitions based on the fact that they were illegal. They believed that requiring the NYCRR to bring the short line roads into the consolidation was not legal under the Transportation Act, and further, the ICC could not approve the plan on condition of including short lines. It had to make its decision based solely on whether the plan was in the public interest.

Around the same time, the death of MCRR director Chauncey M. Depew changed the makeup of the board. General Motors vice president Frederick J. Fisher of Detroit was elected to fill Depew's place.

In the middle of this legal wrangling, something happened outside the business arena that likely helped quell workers' worries about coming takeover and control of the MCRR by the NYCRR, at least for a moment. The company baseball team had beaten the New York Central team to win the regional championship and now they were playing for the railroad world series championship. Their opponent was the team from the Philadelphia Terminal Division of the Pennsylvania Railroad. More than 25,000 attended the event held in Cleveland. It was a one-game playoff and the Pennsylvania team won, 1–0 in a seven-inning pitchers' battle that was called due to rain.

Finally, on January 27, 1929, the ICC approved the NYCRR consolidation plan on the condition they delay the action for six months and they also buy out the petitioning short lines. Those short lines were: Alpena, Boyne City, & Gaylord; the Federal Valley; Chicago,

An 1880 advertisement shows the Main Line and connections.

Attica & Southern; Delaware & Northern; Fonda, Johnstown & Gloversville; Owasco River Railway; Southern New York Railway; Ulster & Delaware; Casey & Kansas; and Kansas & Sidell. Sixty-two other connecting short lines had no objections to the merger. The announcement by the ICC caused a 20-point jump in short line stock values.[7]

When the NYCRR moved immediately to negotiate for the purchase of the short lines, all but the Owasco River Railway balked at the offer. By July they were demanding arbitration, but that wasn't the biggest problem at the moment.

In August, a securities company filed charges against the ICC claiming its decision to allow the consolidation violated antitrust laws. The company also charged the NYCRR, MCRR, and the Big Four (Cleveland, Cincinnati, Chicago & St. Louis) as co-defendants. Their belief was the leases were *against the public interest, contrary to law, oppressive to minority stockholders of the Big Four and the Michigan Central.*[8]

In December the securities company charges were thrown out. The ICC was comfortable with the progress being made on the short line buyout. Because conditions for the consolidation were met, the ICC gave the NYCRR permission to begin the consolidation on February 1, 1930, nearly four years after the company filed the request. The $2 billion consolidation would become the largest ever conducted in the United States.

Part of the ICC conditions provides us with an illustration of how valued the MCRR was at the time as compared with other railroads. The ICC required the NYCRR to meet with arbitrators to set a dollar value on minority-held common stock, which had to be purchased if offered up by stockholders. The NYCRR held 99.315 percent of all MCRR stock, or all but 1,283 shares. The value was fixed at $1,550 per share. The value of a share of the Big Four was fixed at $310 a share.[9]

The last individual MCRR annual report was distributed in 1929. Effective January 2, 1930, earnings and expenses of the railroad would be listed in the annual report of the New York Central Railroad Company. The change was announced in a notice appearing in the annual report of the Cleveland, Cincinnati, Chicago & St. Louis Railway Company, but not the MCRR annual report!

MCRR passes and other railroad documents maintained the road's identity a while longer. The subtitle of the free travel passes changed in 1931 from *Leased and Operated Lines* to *The N.Y.C.R.R. Co., Lessee.* In 1936 the heading became *New York Central System,* with

Michigan Central Railroad printed underneath. About the same time MCRR was removed from depot schedule boards and such, but the name remained on timetables, albeit in a subservient position.

One might ask whether the consolidation was beneficial to the NYCRR. When the new earning statement estimates came out, the company president made this statement:

Had the merger of other railroads with the New York Central been in effect last year, gross operating revenues of the company would have been $590,008,000 instead of $396,917,000, according to a statement by P. E. Crowley, President.[10]

Michiganders never forgot the Old Favorite Line. When the NYCRR, and subsequently the Penn Central, attempted to rename Detroit depot something other than the Michigan Central, their efforts would not stick. It is still the MCRR depot today.

In 1946 officials of the NYCRR recognized the MCRR's 100th anniversary. They printed a centennial celebration color bi-fold with a brief history and pictures of the early officials. The Detroit Historical Society assisted in the celebration by co-sponsoring an exhibit of MCRR material at the Burton Historical Collections. The New York Central also held a celebration at the Book-Cadillac Hotel in Detroit on October 24, 1946, inviting relatives of the former eastern capitalist pioneers who started building the road 100 years before.[11] One such invitation (held by the Bentley Historical Library) came on NYCRR letterhead and read:

> *One hundred years ago the State of Michigan granted a charter to the Michigan Central Railroad in an historic transfer of a great industry from public to private operation.*
>
> *The centennial of that event will be commemorated by a banquet at the Book-Cadillac Hotel, Thursday evening, October 24th, 1846.*
>
> *You are a descendant of Elon Farnsworth, one of the men who in the early days of the Michigan Central did much to build it into the great institution it later became. So it is very fitting that you be a special guest of this railroad that evening.*
>
> *It is with pleasure that I extend to you my personal invitation to be present on this occasion, including the informal reception at 6:30 P.M. in the hotel's FOUNDERS ROOM.*
>
> *Sincerely yours,*
> *C. L. Jellinghaus*
> *Vice President*

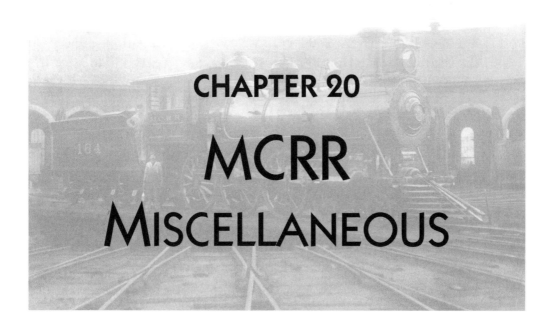

CHAPTER 20
MCRR
MISCELLANEOUS

Here are a few interesting items about the MCRR uncovered during the course of research that didn't fit well within the format of the book, but were too interesting to discard.

1848

The MCRR built a small stationhouse at Davidson Station, about two miles west of the current village of Chelsea. It burned down the same year and a new station was built at Kedron, which was about a half-mile west of Chelsea. It quickly became apparent that Kedron was not as promising a community as nearby Chelsea. Within two years the MCRR selected Chelsea as the site for a new station in 1850.

1848

An early locomotive from the MCRR has survived. An engine named *Alert* was built by Baldwin in 1837. In 1846 it was sold to the Michigan Central where both a tender and cab were added. A couple of years later it was sold to the Galena & Chicago Union Railroad and they renamed it *Pioneer.* The engine is famous for pulling the first train out of Chicago. The 4–2–0 locomotive is displayed without tender on the second floor of the Chicago Historical Society. The tender for the *Pioneer* is on display at a railroad station in Villa Park.

1851

The contract to build the Illinois Central Railroad, which was the longest proposed railroad route in the country at the time, was let to eastern capitalists who owned the Michigan Central Railroad. It required 10,000 workers.

1854

In 1854 the MCRR began transporting orphans from New York to Michigan through a placement program organized by children aid societies in the east. The first train load of 14 boys arrived in Dowagiac in September 1854. These trains continued until 1927. A reenactment of the event took place in 2004, and an orphan train registry has been set up online to gather information about the riders.

1856

The first volunteer fire company at Ypsilanti was organized in 1856, and named the Neptune No. 1. The first engine, a Wright second-class hand pumper, was purchased that same year, with help from the Michigan Central Railroad.

1867

Philo D. Beckwith, of Dowagiac, owned a foundry business and experimented with making heating stoves. His company was floundering until he produced a stove to heat his foundry in 1867. Shortly after, the MCRR found about his stoves and ordered one for each depot between Detroit and Chicago. By 1871, the Round Oak Stove Company was born and it soon became one of the largest stove manufacturers in the world.

1869

Former MCRR employees played a large role in one of our country's best known events—the building of the transcontinental railroad and the golden spike ceremony at Promontory Point, Utah. Jack (1829–1909) and Dan Casement (1832–1881) were brothers employed by the MCRR during the late 1840s and early 1850s building track and bridges. It appears they played a large part in building the ICRR track, which was let by contract to MCRR officials. By the 1860s Jack was the primary track contractor for the Union Pacific Railroad and Dan was his assistant. They built the entire UP track from Fremont, Nebraska to Promontory Point, Utah. Some accounts of the golden spike ceremony claim that Jack finished pounding in the last spike after the dignitaries retired from the scene.

1875

About 137 years ago, MCRR engineers, firemen, brakemen, and conductors used to shop at Drier's Meat Market in Three Oaks. The market is situated near the depot, and when the train stopped for passengers, freight, or water, the workers would run across the street for lunch. Drier's Meat Market opened in 1875, but had operated as a butcher shop by a different owner around the time of the Civil War. It is now a National Historic Site. The ring bologna was a favorite with the MCRR men and you can still buy it today. They even have a MCRR/NYCRR hat collection.

1889

Chief MCRR engineer J. D. Hawks apparently was responsible for the railroad's magnificent station grounds. It was his idea to make MCRR known for having attractive landscaping around their buildings, but gardeners at Ypsilanti and Niles, the two main station greenhouses, took the concept of using greenery to enhance the image further. Ypsilanti and Niles gardeners cut fresh flowers for use in dining cars traveling on the Main Line. They were also known to present cut flowers to women riding on MCRR trains.

The greenhouse at Ypsilanti was the larger operation and provided plants for other stations' gardens. Ypsilanti's gardener John Laidlaw, became internationally famous for his incredible display of plants and floral creations such as designing a full sized locomotive, a replica of the new cantilever bridge at Niagara Falls, and a scale model of the battleship *Maine,* just to name a few. Trains would stop just for passengers to tour the gardens.

Trains stopped at Niles to tour gardener John Gipner's work too. He had seven assistants to help him with tending the greenhouses, flower gardens, and a trout pond. His work was so magnificent, he is credited for Niles earning the nickname of the Garden City. The Ypsilanti and Niles greenhouses operated into the 1920s.

1896

In the 1890s, the MCRR used Hunter Brothers' ice almost exclusively in their dining cars due to its purity of ice. The ice came from Barron Lake, near Niles. Although the ice company closed years ago, Niles still celebrates the Hunter Ice festival each year.

1898

Another example of a former MCRR employee going on to greater success is found in William Haylow, a telegraph operator in Delhi, Michigan. (His handmade business card appears in the memorabilia section of this book.) He was promoted to station agent in Delhi, and by the 1920s he was superintendent of transportation for the Louisville & Nashville Railroad.

1901

One of the last locomotives ordered by the MCRR while the company was still under its original state charter is preserved at the Henry Ford Museum. One of the few remaining Atlantic model (4–4–2) locomotives built by the American Locomotive Company at Schenectady, New York, was delivered to the MCRR in March 1902. It was numbered 254 (then renumbered 7953, and again to 8085) and built to haul fast passenger trains. As car construction materials changed from wood to steel, trains got heavier and longer. The Atlantic model could not handle the increased weight and in 1926 was sold to the Detroit, Toledo & Ironton Railroad Company, which was owned by Henry Ford. Ford rebuilt the locomotive in 1930 and restored it to its original condition before donating it to the museum.

Ypsilanti Station Grounds.

ORIGINAL DETROIT &
ST. JOSEPH RAILROAD
COMMISSIONERS

Major John Biddle, 1792–1859. Biddle was born in Philadelphia, lived in Detroit, and died in White Sulphur Springs, Virginia. He was the speaker of the Michigan house of Representative (1838), president of Farmer's and Mechanics' Bank, trustee of the University of Michigan, and a veteran of War of 1812.

John R. Williams, 1782–1854. Williams was born in Detroit and was a delegate from First District to the constitutional convention of 1835. He was a captain of artillery during the War of 1812. He was a six-time mayor of Detroit, a University of Michigan trustee, and named Detroit street "John R" after himself.

General Charles Larned. A resident of Detroit, Larned Street is named after him. He was a veteran of War of 1812 and a U.S. attorney.

Eurotas P. Hastings. A resident of Detroit, Hastings was president of Bank of Michigan in 1839, auditor general of Michigan from 1840–1842, and started Detroit's first antislavery society. Hastings Street in Detroit and Hastings, Michigan, are named after him.

Admiral Oliver Newberry, 1789–1860. He lived in Detroit and was born in East Windsor, Connecticut. He was a steamboat builder and perhaps Michigan's first millionaire. He bequeathed $2 million to fund Newberry Library, Chicago.

De Garmo Jones, 1787–1846. Jones was born in Albany, New York, and lived in Detroit. He was a businessman who served as mayor of Detroit in 1839 and a state senator in 1840–1841.

James Abbott Jr. 1776–? Abbott lived in Detroit and worked in the fur business and as a long-time city postmaster (1806–1831). Abbott Street in Detroit named after him.

Wm. A. Thompson, ?–1888. He lived in Detroit and died at Salt Lake, Utah.

Dr. Abel Millington, 1787–1838. Dr. Millington was born in Rutland, Vermont, and lived in Ypsilanti. The physician and Washtenaw County Sheriff died St. Charles, Illinois.

Job Gorton. He lived in Ypsilanti and was a farmer.

W. E. Perrine. He lived in Ypsilanti and was a farmer.

John Allen, 1796–1851. Allen both founded and lived in the village of Ann Arbor. He died in the California gold rush.

Anson Brown. ?–1834. Brown served as the city postmaster of Ann Arbor and died in the city cholera epidemic. He also the developed much of lower town, and his 1830 grocery store still stands.

Judge Samuel W. Dexter, ?–1852. He lived in Dexter, the town that was named after him. The judge was also a newspaper owner and editor.

John Gilbert. Gilbert lived and farmed in section 31 of Washtenaw County.

Isaac Crary. A lawyer who lived in Marshall, Crary was the first person from Michigan elected to the U.S. House of Representatives.

He was also responsible for establishing Michigan's education system in 1835.

Judge Caleb Eldred. He lived in Climax, a village in Kalamazoo County. He was a cofounder of Kalamazoo College.

Cyrus Lovell. He lived in Ionia County and was a lawyer, probate judge, and state representative.

Calvin Brittain. He lived in St. Joseph and became commissioner of the St. Joseph Valley Railroad in 1850.

Dr. Talman Wheeler. Dr. Wheeler lived in Berrien County. He became a commissioner of the St. Joseph Valley Railroad and is also known for starting Berrien County's first formal peach orchards in the 1850s.

O. W. Colden. Biographical information about Mr. Colden could not be found.

Appendix B

THE NAME, OCCUPATION, AND LOCATION OF MCRR AGENTS AND ASSISTANTS, JUNE 1848

Name	Occupation	Location
Josiah Dort	Freight Agent	Dearborn
Edgar Howard	Labor	"
James Wilson	"	"
Ephraim Priest	"	"
W. T. Sexton	Freight Agent	Wayne
David P. Cady	Labor	"
Spencer Harmon	"	"
Cornelius Ockford	Freight Agent	Ypsilanti
George Wandless	Labor	"
Charles Keelan	"	"
Frank Davis	"	"
John Pearl	"	"
Alfred Cook	"	"
Hugh Boyle	"	"
Pat Kelly	"	"
Charles Thayer	Freight Agent	Ann Arbor
George Niethamer	Labor	"

Name	Occupation	Location
John Ryan	"	"
Patrick Donahoe	"	"
Timothy O'Connell	"	"
Thomas Fogerty	"	"
E. B. Tyler	Freight Agent	Dexter
John G. Haskins	Labor	"
Barnard Riley	"	"
Patrick Fleming	"	"
Michael White	"	"
Edward Croakin	"	"
S. B. Finn	Freight Agent	Davisons
M. Stevenson	Labor	"
H. M. Esy	"	"
Samuel Barton	"	"
William H. Pease	Freight Agent	Grass Lake
Waterman Baldwin	Labor	"
Henry M. Bunnell	"	"
William H. Walker	"	"
Lucius Barney	Freight Agent	Jackson
John Doudel	Labor	"
George Shaver	"	"
James Cooper	"	"
H. S. Hollister	Freight Agent	Gidleys
Lyman Warren	Labor	"
Jonathan Scott	"	"
Anthony Dunn	"	"
C. Bradbury	Freight Agent	Albion
Peter Conner	Labor	"
George L. Barlow	"	"
Richard Welch	"	"
R. J. B. Moore	"	"

Appendix C

SECTION WORKERS, 1852 (SALARY RANGE: $1.14 TO $1.16 PER DAY)

Name	Occupation	Location
E. P. Warner	Section Repair	Detroit West
S. D. Curtis	"	
Wm. McVey	"	
Anton Kenter	"	
V. Lotterkrous	"	
Casper Bosmer	"	
Adna Merritt	"	Dearborn West
Geo. W. Tucker	"	"
Sholett G. Joslin	"	"
Frederick Morteroust	"	"
Daniel Dibble	"	"
Patrick Downan	"	"
James Simpson	"	Wayne West
George Goldsmith	"	"
Joseph Neale	"	"
John McFarlin	"	"
Alfred Davis	"	Ypsilanti East

Name	Occupation	Location
John Pearl	"	"
John Beggs	"	"
Nicholas Stafford	"	"
C. W. Smith	"	Ypsilanti West
James Monihan	"	"
Henry Blank	"	"
J. Johnson	"	"
N. Asker	"	"
George Mowit	"	"
Henry Taff	"	"
John Sullivan	"	Ann Arbor West
Fredrick Kearns	"	"
Wm. Ryan	"	"
William McElroy	"	"
Patrick Dwyer	"	"
Bart Jones	"	"
Andrew Haven	"	Dexter West
B. Jones	"	"
James Miller	"	"
Pat Bryan	"	"
A. H. Parkhill	"	Chelsea to Francisco
Luke Rigney	"	"
Thos Congdon	"	"
Richard Welch	"	"
Henry Hoover	"	"
Dan Doran	"	"

Appendix D

GREAT RAILROAD CONSPIRACY CASE NAMES

The following list contains the names of those who were accused and arrested of being conspirators. The names that appear in bold indicate those men who were convicted.

Ackeson, John

Barbour, Mills

Barrett, Ephraim A.

Beebe, Eri

Blackburn, Christie

Burnett, Benjamin F.

Cann, John

Champlin, Erastus

Champlin, James

Champlin, Lyman

Champlin, Williard

Corwin, Seba

Corwin, William

Credit, Nathan

Farnham, Ebenezer

Filley, Ammi

Filley, Grandison

Fitch, Abel F.

Freeland, Andrew J.

Gay, George W.

Gleason, Benjamin F.

Gould, Jerome

Grant, Abner

Gunn, William

Hay, Hiram

Hill, Welcome

Hocolm, Harry

Homles, Alonzo

Ladue, John

Lang, William W.

Laycock, Miner T.

Lemm, Napoleon

Lockwood, John A.

Loucks, David

Moulton, Arba N.

Mount, Aaron

Myers, Daniel

Palmer, John

Penfield, Lester

Price, Eben

Price, Richard

Showers, Henry

Smith, Erastus

Stone, Russel

Tyrrell, Jacob

Van Sickle, William

Wakeman, Harvey

Warner, William S.

Welch, John W.

Williams, Orland D.

Engine 32 was called "Rusher" (1858)

Appendix E

LOCOMOTIVE NAMES, 1855

Schedule of LOCOMOTIVES, *Dimensions, &c.*

Name.	Builders.	Diameter of Drivers.	No. of Drivers.	Cylinders.
Bald Eagle,	Amoskeag Co. Manchester,	6 feet,	4	16+20
White Eagle,	" "	"	4	"
Grey Eagle,	" "	"	4	"
Black Eagle,	" "	"	4	"
American Eagle,	" "	"	4	"
Golden Eagle,	" "	5½ feet,	4	"
Flying Cloud,	" "	"	4	"
White Cloud,	" "	6 feet,	4	"
Storm Cloud,	" "	"	4	"
North Wind,	" "	"	4	16+22
East Wind,	" "	"	4	"
South Wind,	" "	"	4	"
West Wind,	" "	"	4	"
Trade Wind,	" "	"	4	"
Whirlwind,	" "	5½ feet,	4	"
Challenge,	M. C. R. R.	"	4	16+20
Defiance,	"	"	4	"
Grey Hound,	Lowell,	6 feet,	4	16+22
Wolf Hound,	"	"	4	"
Fox Hound,	"	"	4	"
Stag Hound,	"	"	4	"
Pioneer,	Hinkley & Drury, Boston,	5 feet,	4	15+18
Comet,	" " "	"	4	"
Torrent,	" " "	"	4	"
Herald,	" " "	"	4	"
Reindeer,	" " "	"	4	"
Antelope,	" " "	"	4	"
May Flower,	" " "	"	4	"
Gazelle,	" " "	"	4	"
Hurricane,	M. C. R. R.	"	4	"
Cataract,	"	"	4	"
St. Joseph,	Lowell,	3 feet,	4	12+18
Jupiter,	Amoskeag Co. Manchester,	4 feet,	6	16+20
Saturn,	" "	"	6	"
Neptune,	" "	"	6	"
Mars,	" "	"	6	"
Pluto,	" "	"	6	"
Twilight,	N. Jersey Loc. Man. Co.	"	6	"
White Bear,	Detroit Loc. Works,	"	6	"
Grizley Bear,	" "	"	6	"
Brown Bear,	" "	"	6	"
Black Bear,	" "	"	6	"
R. Mountain,	Hinkley & Drury, Boston,	"	6	"
Salamander,	" " "	"	6	"
Hecla,	" " "	"	6	"
Ætna,	" " "	"	6	"
Niagara,	" " "	"	6	"
Vesuvius,	" " "	"	6	"

Schedule of LOCOMOTIVES, *continued.*

Name.	Builders.	Diameter of Drivers.	No. of Drivers.	Cylinders.
Peninsula,	M. C. R. R., Detroit,	4 feet,	6	16+20
Goliah,	" "	"	6	"
Washington,	" "	"	6	"
Samson,	" "	"	6	"
Giant,	" "	"	6	"
Lion,	" "	"	6	"
Tiger,	" "	"	6	"
Ajax,	Amoskeag Co. Manchester,	$4\frac{1}{2}$ feet,	4	15+24
Atlas,	" "	"	4	"
Ceres,	" "	"	4	"
Stranger,	" "	5 feet,	4	"
Vulcan,	Hinkley & Drury, Boston,	$4\frac{1}{2}$ feet,	4	15+20
Hercules,	" " "	"	4	"
B. Creek,	" " "	"	4	"
Swallow,	Baldwin,	5 feet,	2	12+18
Alert,	"	$4\frac{1}{2}$ feet,	2	10+18

Appendix F
STATION LISTINGS, 1855

SCHEDULE OF STATIONS, *with their Distance and Rates of Freight and Passenger Fare from Detroit.*

STATIONS.	Miles from Detroit.	Passenger Fare.		Rates of Freight.		
		1st Class.	2d Class.	1st Class.	2nd Class.	3rd Class.
				Cents per 100 lbs.	Cents per 100 lbs.	Cents per 100 lbs.
Detroit,* - - - -	–	–	–	–	–	–
Dearborn,* - - - -	10.1	.30	.25	7	6	3
County House, - -	15.7	.50	–	–	–	–
Wayne,* - - - -	17.5	.55	.45	10	8	5
Sheldons, - - - -	22.2	.75	–	–	–	–
Dentons, - - - -	24.8	.80	–	14	10	6
Ypsilanti,* - - -	29.4	.90	.75	16	11	7
Geddes, - - - -	33 3	1.00	–	18	12	8
Ann Arbor,* - - -	37.4	1.10	.90	20	14	8
Delhi, - - - -	42.6	1.25	–	22	16	10
Scio, - - - -	44.3	1.30	–	23	16	10
Dexter,* - - - -	46.9	1 35	1.05	24	17	11
Chelsea,* - - -	54.4	1.60	1.25	27	20	13
Franciscos, - - -	61.2	1.80	–	30	21	14
Grass Lake,* - -	65.4	1.95	1.50	31	23	15
Leoni, - - - -	68.2	2.00	–	32	23	16
Michigan Centre, -	71.5	2.10	–	34	24	17
Jackson,* - - - -	75.6	2 25	1.75	35	25	18
Sandstone, - - -	81.8	2.45	–	–	–	–
Parma,* - - - -	86.4	2.55	2.00	39	27	20
Concord, - - -	89.1	2.65	–	40	29	21
Bath Mills, - - -	92.0	2.75	–	41	29	22
Albion,* - - -	95.5	2.85	2.20	42	29	23
Marengo, - - -	101.0	3.00	–	43	30	24
Marshall,* - - -	107.3	3 20	2.50	44	31	26
Ceresco, - - - -	112.5	3.35	–	46	32	27
Battle Creek,* - -	120.2	3.50	2.65	47	33	28
Augusta, - - -	129.9	3.70	–	49	35	30
Galesburg,* - - -	134.3	3.80	2.85	50	36	30
Comstock, - - -	139.3	3.90	–	50	38	30
Kalamazoo,* - - -	143.1	4.00	3.00	50	38	30
Mattawau, - - -	155.3	4.25	–	50	40	30
Paw Paw,* - - -	159.4	4.35	3.25	50	40	30
Decatur,* - - -	167.1	4.50	3.40	50	40	30
Dowagiac,* - - -	178.2	4.60	3.50	50	40	30
Pokagon, - - -	184.1	4.70	–	50	40	30
Niles,* - - - -	190.7	4.80	3.60	50	40	30
Buchanan,* - - -	197.0	5.00	–	50	40	30
Terre Coupee,* - -	201.4	5.20	3.95	50	40	30
Chamberlains, - -	210.1	5.50	–	50	40	30
New Buffalo,* - -	217.9	5.75	4.30	50	40	30
Michigan City,* - -	227.5	6.00	4.50	50	40	30
Porter,* - - - -	239.7	6.25	4.70	50	40	30
Lake,* - - - -	248.1	6.40	4.80	50	40	30
Gibsons, - - - -	259.9	6.60	5 00	50	40	30
Junction,* - - -	269.4	6.75	5.00	50	40	30
Chicago,* - - -	284.8	7.00	5.00	50	40	30

* Regular Stations; balance are Flag Stations.

Appendix G

Passengers and Freight
Forwarded from Stations, 1870

Comparative Statement, *showing the Number of Passengers forwarded from each Station during the Years ending May 31, 1869, and May 31, 1870.*

STATIONS.	1870.	1869.	Increase.	Decrease.
Detroit,	140,970½	155,406½	–	14,436
G. T. Junction,	33,781½	20,720	13,061½	–
Dearborn,	7,212	7,304½	–	92½
Inksters,	1,993	2,049½	–	56½
County House,	1,312	1,535½	–	223½
Wayne,	14,539½	14,044½	495	–
Secords,	1,328½	1,272	56½	–
Dentons,	2,842½	2,632	210½	–
Ypsilanti,	34,137½	35,404½	–	1,267
Geddes,	530	634½	–	104½
Ann Arbor,	45,538½	48,150½	–	2,612
Fosters,	1,376½	1,600½	–	224
Delhi,	2,151½	1,750	401½	–
Scio,	1,432	1,305½	126½	–
Dexter,	15,870	16,490	–	620
Chelsea,	9,691½	10,280	–	588½
Franciso,	2,109	2,357½	–	248½
Grass Lake,	8,997	9,530½	–	533½
Leoni,	1,913½	2,144½	–	231
Michigan Central,	1,385½	1,675½	–	290
Jackson,	72,482	66,251½	6,230½	–
Woodville,	715½	615	100½	–
Sandstone,	869	902½	–	33½
Parma,	6,557	7,615½	–	1,058½
Concord,	1,297	1,366½	–	69½
Bath Mills,	389	503	–	114
Albion,	17,040	18,906½	–	1,866½
Marengo,	1,702½	1,740	–	37½
Marshall,	28,000	29,955	–	1,955
Ceresco,	1,796	1,521	275	–

[K.]—*Comparative Statement*—Concluded.

STATIONS.	1870.	1869.	Increase.	Decrease.
Battle Creek, . . .	33,349	33,565½	–	216½
Bedford, ...	144½	258½	–	114
Augusta, ...	7,108½	7,175½	–	67
Galesburg, ...	12,265	12,325	–	60
Comstock, ...	690	905	–	215
Kalamoozo, . . .	65,946½	60,506	5,440½	–
Ostemo, ...	1,633½	1,975	–	341½
Mattawan, ...	6,211	6,131	80	–
Lawton, ...	17,486	18,328½	–	842½
White Oak, . . .	137½	253	–	115½
Decatur, ...	14,611	16,548½	–	1,937½
Tietsorts, . . .	786½	723	63½	–
Dowagiac, ...	16,068½	17,759	–	1,690½
Pokagon, ...	5,145½	5,303½	–	158
Niles, ...	29,263½	31,326	–	2,062½
Buchanan, ...	13,312	14,596½	–	1,284½
Dayton, ...	3,799	4,038	–	239
Galien, ...	4,155½	3,736	419½	–
Averys, ...	2,190½	1,912½	278	–
Three Oaks, . . .	6,899	6,092	807	–
New Buffalo, . . .	7,646½	4,472	3,174½	–
Corymbo, ...	1,142½	788½	354	–
Michigan City, . . .	28,709	25,544	3,165	–
Furnessville, . . .	926	787½	138½	–
Porter, ...	1,798	1,681½	116½	–
Lake, ...	3,002	2,804½	197½	–
Tolleston, ...	1,075	892½	182½	–
Gibsons, ...	1,581	1,158	423	–
Calumet, ...	1,800½	1,525½	275	–
Chicago, ...	115,894	96,816½	19,077½	–
Joliet & N. I. Railroad, .	845½	859½	–	14
Totals, . . .	865,582½	846,452½	19,130	–

[J.]

COMPARATIVE STATEMENT, *showing the Number of Tons of Freight forwarded from each Station during the years ending May 31, 1869, and May 31, 1870.*

STATIONS.	1870.	1869.	Increase.	Decrease.
Detroit,	182,222	172,732	9,490	–
G. T. Junction,	23,395	8,300	15,095	–
Dearborn,	969	2,554	–	1,585
Inksters,	315	399	–	84
Wayne,	2,273	1,854	419	–
Secords,	8	89	–	81
Dentons,	2,094	2,502	–	408
Ypsilanti,	10,343	9,326	1,017	–
Geddes,	24	8	16	–
Ann Arbor,	8,694	8,933	–	239
Kelloggs,	159	165	–	6
Fosters,	189	183	6	–
Farmers,	797	795	2	–
Delhi,	5,681	4,213	1,468	–
Scio,	1,146	554	592	–
Dexter,	10,968	10,302	666	–
Chelsea,	5,498	5,194	304	–
Francisco,	883	1,212	–	329
Grass Lake,	5,401	5,056	345	–
Leoni,	351	171	180	–
Michigan Centre,	65	27	38	–
Jackson,	67,969	52,940	15,029	–
Woodville,	2,591	3,577	–	986
Sandstone,	–	620	–	620
Parma,	3,814	3,038	776	–
Concord,	1,143	1,570	–	427
Bath Mills,	460	706	–	246
Newburg,	231	316	–	85
Albion,	6,968	5,059	1,909	–
Marengo,	1,630	1,235	395	–
Marshall,	11,746	14,077	–	2,331

Comparative Statement—Continued.

STATIONS.	1870.	1869.	Increase.	Decrease.
Ceresco, ...	2,828	1,155	1,673	–
Battle Creek, . . .	12,582	11,036	1,546	–
Augusta, ...	4,633	5,876	–	1,243
Galesburg, ...	3,032	3,587	–	555
Comstock, ...	1,069	1,442	–	373
Kalamazoo, . . .	28,427	20,747	7,680	–
Ostemo, ...	512	504	8	–
Mattawan, ...	3,977	5,782	–	1,805
Lawton, ...	13,405	13,494	–	89
White Oak, . . .	18	9	9	–
Decatur, ...	10,000	9,893	107	–
Tietsorts, ...	333	108	225	–
Dowagiac, ...	8,858	10,494	–	1,636
Pokagon, ...	1,294	2,160	–	866
Niles, ...	8,999	11,897	–	2,898
Buchanan, ...	3,937	4,458	–	521
Dayton, ...	1,053	1,130	–	77
Wilsons, ...	1,038	539	499	–
Galien, ...	3,063	1,956	1,107	–
Averys, ...	2,428	2,569	–	141
Three Oaks, . . .	3,006	4,037	–	1,031
New Buffalo, . . .	4,932	3,112	1,820	–
Corymbo, ...	1,321	536	785	–
Michigan City, . . .	39,321	39,297	24	–
Furnessville, . . .	3,787	4,558	–	771
Pierces, ...	304	307	–	3
Porter, ...	5,511	4,288	1,223	–
Lake, ...	350	512	–	162
Tolleston, ...	54	49	5	–
Gibsons, ...	80	67	13	–
Calumet, ...	54	68	–	14
Chicago, ...	218,168	229,920	–	11,752
Joliet and N. Ind. Railroad,	77,369	89,541	–	12,172
Totals, ...	823,770	802,835	20,935	–

Appendix H

TYPES AND NUMBER OF SHOP EMPLOYEES, 1870

TABLE G.

Statement showing the numbers and occupation of Employees at the different Shops on the line of the Road in this Department.

OCCUPATION.	Detroit.	Marshall.	M. City.	Chicago.	Total.
Superintendent, . . .	1	–	–	–	1
Clerk, ...	1	–	–	–	1
Draughtsman, . . .	1	–	–	–	1
Time Keeper, . . .	1	1	1	–	3
Master Mechanics, . .	–	1	1	–	2
Engine Dispatchers, . .	1	1	1	1	4
Machinists, ...	42	25	23	1	91
Copper and Tinsmiths, .	14	2	2	–	18
Flue Setters and Caulkers, .	2	2	2	–	6
Tender and Truck Rep'rers,	6	3	2	–	11
Boiler Makers, . . .	9	3	5	–	17
Helpers, ...	5	3	4	–	12
Bolt Cutters, . . .	2	1	1	–	4
Carpenters, . . .	8	2	1	–	11
Pattern Makers, . . .	1	1	1	–	3
Laborers, ...	9	11	8	2	30
Blacksmiths, . . .	8	4	4	1	17
Helpers, ...	9	4	5	2	20
Painters, ...	3	1	1	–	5
Stationary Engineers, . .	2	1	1	–	4
Stationary Firemen, . .	1	–	–	–	1
Engine Wipers, . . .	7	10	9	6	32
Locomotive Engineers, .	38	31	17	7	93
Locomotive Firemen, . .	38	31	17	7	93
Watchmen, . . .	3	4	3	2	12
Apprentices, . . .	18	3	6	–	27
Boiler Washers, . . .	1	1	1	–	3
Drayman, ...	–	–	1	–	1
	231	146	117	29	523

Appendix I
Passengers and Earnings, 1847–1870

STATEMENT, *showing the Number of Passengers carried on the Michigan Central Railroad since its ownership and organization by the present Company, and the Earnings from the same.*

YEARS ENDING MAY 31,	No. of Passengers.	Passenger Earnings.
1847, ...	41,223	$74,163 08
1848, ...	73,656	138,649 53
1849, ...	96,070	197,767 56
1850, ...	152,672	368,436 70
1851, ...	191,852	490,119 68
1852, ...	221,200	581,477 24
1853, ...	247,552	589,489 32
1854, ...	357,936	855,917 94
1855, ...	503,774	1,246,409 90
1856, ...	550,780	1,497,854 61
1857, ...	593,630	1,610,415 75
1858, ...	461,957	1,321,039 56
1859, ...	361,527	938,609 39
1860, ...	324,422	803,507 97
1861, ...	327,775	775,228 53
1862, ...	308,829	724,915 48
1863, ...	447,362	889,682 28
1864, ...	645,759	1,262,415 07
1865, ...	852,889	1,771,813 60
1866, ...	902,826	2,061,335 05
1867, ...	823,474	1,824,225 75
1868, ...	786,405	1,721,506 97
1869, ...	846,452	1,795,806 11
1870, ...	865,582	1,914,921 75
Totals, ...	10,985,604	$25,455,708 82

Appendix J

TRIBUTE TO HENRY LEDYARD, 1921

[The following tribute appeared in MCRR's 1921 annual report.]

At a meeting of the Board of Directors of The Michigan Central Railroad Company held at the Grand Central Terminal June 15, 1901, the President announced the death of Mr. Henry B. Ledyard, Chairman of the Board of Directors of the company, whereupon the following minute was adopted and directed to be entered upon the records of the company and a copy engrossed and sent to the family: THE President announced with sincere regret the death of Henry B. Ledyard, Chairman of the Board of Directors of this company, at his home in Detroit, Michigan, on the 25th day of May, 1921; whereupon the following was presented and adopted: We, the Directors of The Michigan Central Railroad Company, mourn the death of our Chairman, Henry B. Ledyard. He was an outstanding figure in American life and won distinction as a soldier, engineer and railroad executive. He had the inspiration of a distinguished ancestry. His grandfather was Lewis Cass, one of the foremost statesmen of his time, and he also was a member of the family of Chancellor Livingston of New York. He graduated at West Point with high rank in his class and won recognition and promotion in the army during the Civil War. When peace came, Mr. Ledyard decided that his duty was to devote his talents, rare equipment and experience to the upbuilding of the country by the extension and improvement of its railroads. He became an engineer on the Northern Pacific in 1870 and afterwards entered the service of the Chicago Burlington & Quincy Railroad Company. He rose rapidly from a clerk to Assistant General Superintendent and Chief Engineer and then to General Superintendent. In 1874 he joined The Michigan Central Railroad Company as Assistant General Superintendent and Chief Engineer. The next year he became General Superintendent, two years afterwards General Manager, and six years in this service led to his advancement to the Presidency of the company. Mr. Ledyard's training at West Point and in the army had taught him the value of discipline and efficiency. His close contact with the employees in his different positions in the railway service gave him such knowledge of the force that he was able also to secure loyalty to himself and the company with good workmanship. During his twelve years as President the Michigan Central Railroad was almost made over, and its terminal facilities so enlarged that it was able to care for the unexpected demands of the Great War. He designed and carried through the construction of the tunnel under the Detroit River, which has done so much for interstate commerce. During his forty-seven years with this company, Mr. Ledyard was not only interested in the extraordinary growth and extension of American railroads, but took an active part in their development. Mr. Ledyard's life at Washington with his grandfather made him acquainted with the famous people of a most interesting period in our history. He had been in close relations with the great captains of industry. His reminiscences were valuable and most interesting. A large-hearted, big-brained, cultivated man was our late associate and friend who endeared himself to all. We extend to his family our deepest sympathies.

Appendix K

LIST OF MCRR OFFICERS, 1846–1930

Year	President	Superintendent	Treasurer
1846	John M. Forbes	John W. Brooks	George B. Upton
1847	John M. Forbes	John W. Brooks	George B. Upton
1848	John M. Forbes	John W. Brooks	George B. Upton
1849	John M. Forbes	John W. Brooks	George B. Upton
1850	John M. Forbes	John W. Brooks	George B. Upton
1851	John M. Forbes	John W. Brooks	George B. Upton
1852	John M. Forbes	John W. Brooks	George B. Upton
1853	John M. Forbes	John W. Brooks	George B. Upton
1854	John M. Forbes	Edwin Noyes	Isaac Livermore
1855	John M. Forbes	Reuben N. Rice	Isaac Livermore
1856	John M. Forbes	Reuben N. Rice	Isaac Livermore
1857	Forbes/Brooks	Reuben N. Rice	Isaac Livermore
1858	John W. Brooks	Reuben N. Rice	Isaac Livermore
1859	John W. Brooks	Reuben N. Rice	Isaac Livermore
1860	John W. Brooks	Reuben N. Rice	Isaac Livermore
1861	John W. Brooks	Reuben N. Rice	Isaac Livermore
1862	John W. Brooks	Reuben N. Rice	Isaac Livermore
1863	John W. Brooks	Reuben N. Rice	Isaac Livermore

1864	John W. Brooks	Reuben N. Rice	Isaac Livermore
1865	John W. Brooks	Reuben N. Rice	Isaac Livermore
1866	John W. Brooks	Reuben N. Rice	Isaac Livermore
1867	Brooks/Joy	Rice/Sargent	Isaac Livermore
1868	James F. Joy	Homer E. Sargent	Isaac Livermore
1869	James F. Joy	Homer E. Sargent	Isaac Livermore
1870	James F. Joy	Homer E. Sargent	Isaac Livermore
1871	James F. Joy	Homer E. Sargent	Isaac Livermore
1872	James F. Joy	Homer E. Sargent	Isaac Livermore
1873	James F. Joy	Homer E. Sargent	Isaac Livermore
1874	James F. Joy	Homer E. Sargent	Isaac Livermore
1875	James F. Joy	Sargent/William B. Strong	Isaac Livermore
1876	James F. Joy	Strong/Ledyard	Benjamin Dunning
1877	Joy/Sloan	Henry B. Ledyard	Benjamin Dunning
1878	Samuel Sloan/ Vanderbilt	Henry B. Ledyard	Cornelius Vanderbilt
1879	William H. Vanderbilt	Henry B. Ledyard	Cornelius Vanderbilt
1880	William H. Vanderbilt	Henry B. Ledyard	Cornelius Vanderbilt
1881	William H. Vanderbilt	Henry B. Ledyard	Cornelius Vanderbilt
1882	William H. Vanderbilt	Henry B. Ledyard	Cornelius Vanderbilt
1883	Vanderbilt/Ledyard	Ledyard/Brown	Henry Platt
1884	Henry B. Ledyard	Edwin C. Brown	Henry Platt
1885	Henry B. Ledyard	Edwin C. Brown	Henry Platt
1886	Henry B. Ledyard	Edwin C. Brown	Henry Platt
1887	Henry B. Ledyard	Edwin C. Brown	Henry Platt
1888	Henry B. Ledyard	Edwin C. Brown	Henry Platt
1889	Henry B. Ledyard	Edwin C. Brown	Henry Platt
1890	Henry B. Ledyard	Edwin C. Brown	Henry Platt
1891	Henry B. Ledyard	Robert Miller	Henry Platt
1892	Henry B. Ledyard	Robert Miller	Daniel A. Waterman
1893	Henry B. Ledyard	Robert Miller	Daniel A. Waterman
1894	Henry B. Ledyard	Robert Miller	Daniel A. Waterman
1895	Henry B. Ledyard	Robert Miller	Daniel A. Waterman
1896	Henry B. Ledyard	Richard H. L'Hommedieu	Daniel A. Waterman

1897	Henry B. Ledyard	Richard H. L'Hommedieu	Daniel A. Waterman
1898	Henry B. Ledyard	Richard H. L'Hommedieu	Edwin D. Worcester
1899	Henry B. Ledyard	Richard H. L'Hommedieu	Edwin D. Worcester
1900	Henry B. Ledyard	Richard H. L'Hommedieu	Edwin D. Worcester
1901	Henry B. Ledyard	Richard H. L'Hommedieu	Edwin D. Worcester
1902	Henry B. Ledyard	Richard H. L'Hommedieu	Edwin D. Worcester
1903	Henry B. Ledyard	Richard H. L'Hommedieu	Edwin D. Worcester
1904	Henry B. Ledyard	Richard H. L'Hommedieu	Charles F. Cox
1905	Henry B. Ledyard	Henry A. Worchester	Charles F. Cox
1906	Henry B. Ledyard	Henry C. Nutt	Charles F. Cox
1907	William H. Newman	Sheldon W. Brown	Charles F. Cox
1908	William H. Newman	Sheldon W. Brown	Charles F. Cox
1909	William C. Brown	Sheldon W. Brown	Charles F. Cox
1910	William C. Brown	Sheldon W. Brown	Charles F. Cox
1911	William C. Brown	Sheldon W. Brown	Milton S. Barger
1912	William C. Brown	Sheldon W. Brown	Milton S. Barger
1913	William C. Brown	Sheldon W. Brown	Milton S. Barger
1914	Alfred H. Smith	Sheldon W. Brown	Milton S. Barger
1915	Alfred H. Smith	Sheldon W. Brown	Milton S. Barger
1916	Alfred H. Smith	Edmond D. Bronner	Milton S. Barger
1917	Alfred H. Smith	Edmond D. Bronner	Milton S. Barger
1918	Alfred H. Smith	Edmond D. Bronner	Milton S. Barger
1919	Alfred H. Smith	Edmond D. Bronner	Milton S. Barger
1920	Alfred H. Smith	Edmond D. Bronner	Milton S. Barger
1921	Alfred H. Smith	Edmond D. Bronner	Walter Hackett
1922	Alfred H. Smith	Edmond D. Bronner	Walter Hackett
1923	Alfred H. Smith	Edmond D. Bronner	Walter Hackett
1924	Patrick E. Crowley	Edmond D. Bronner	Walter Hackett
1925	Patrick E. Crowley	Edmond D. Bronner	Walter Hackett
1926	Patrick E. Crowley	Henry Shearer	Walter Hackett
1927	Patrick E. Crowley	Henry Shearer	Walter Hackett
1928	Patrick E. Crowley	Henry Shearer	Walter Hackett
1929	Patrick E. Crowley	Henry Shearer	Walter Hackett
1930	Patrick E. Crowley	Henry Shearer	Walter Hackett

Appendix L

MICHIGAN CENTRAL TIMELINE OF SIGNIFICANT EVENTS, 1846–1901

1846   MCRR Company buys railroad from the state of Michigan

1848   First new track laid

1849   *May Flower* steamship built; track to Michigan City completed

1850   Detroit terminal completed; freight depot burns

1851   All 60-lb. heavy T rail in place; Great Conspiracy Trial ends

1852   Track completed to Chicago

1853   MCRR leaders build Soo Locks

1854   MCRR linked with Great Western at Windsor; *May Flower* sinks

1855   Use of telegraph begins

1856   Gross earnings top $1 million

1857   MCRR North Shore Line steamers permanently docked

1858   Depots at all stations now completed as new or rebuilt
        from state structures

1862   First use of coal burning locomotives; Detroit square
        engine house burns

1863   Brotherhood of Locomotive Engineers founded at Marshall
        by MCRR workers

1864   MCRR appears on cover of *Harper's Weekly* national magazine

1865   Lincoln funeral train passes on MCRR; Detroit freight depot burns

1866   President Johnson travels length of MCRR giving speeches

1867   MCRR joins Blue Line shippers; refrigerator & Pullman Palace Cars added

1868   First use of steel rails

1870   First use of air brakes; Detroit River Transit Co. formed (for the tunnel)

1871   Chicago fire destroys MCRR buildings

1872   Gross earnings top $5 million

1873   First use of Miller compression platforms and vestibule canopies

1875   MCRR joins U.S. Fast Mail

1878   Boston ownership era ends; New York & Vanderbilt era begins

1880   Push begins to build showcase depots for Chicago Exposition

1883   Canada Southern alliance begins; Great Western ties cut

1884   First MCRR ferry built (the *Michigan*); CSR gains Main Line status

1885   First use of vaccination car for employees

1887   MCRR partnership builds Grand Hotel on Mackinac Island

1888   First year all locomotives burn coal

1889   First year coaches lit with incandescent lights

1896   Use of payroll car ends; employees now paid by check

1898   New York Central Railroad gains full control of the MCRR

1901   First track pan at Kinnear opens near Dexter; State charter ends

Appendix M

STATIONS ADDED AND DELETED, 1850 TO 1896

Mile Post* Detroit	Annual Report Stations 1850	Annual Report Stations 1855	Annual Report Stations 1870	Annual Report Stations 1874	Station Listing 1896	Depot Agent 1896	County Location
0	Detroit	Detroit	Detroit	Detroit	Detroit	G. Chamberlin	Wayne Co., MI
2.2					Bay City Junction	None	Wayne
2.9					Stockyard	Wm. Hurd	Wayne
3.9			G. Trunk Junction		West Detroit	J. Shinnick	Wayne
7.3					**Junction Yard**	J. Maire	Wayne
					Townline	None/Prepaid	Wayne
10.2	Dearborn	Dearborn	Dearborn	Dearborn	Dearborn	E. Howe	Wayne
13.6			Inkster		Inkster	Mrs. S. Harrison	Wayne
15.2	County House	County House	County House	County House	**Eloise**	S. Keenan	Wayne
17.5	Wayne	Wayne	Wayne	Wayne	Wayne	H. Colburn	Wayne
18.0					Wayne Junction	None/Prepaid	Wayne
21.0			Secord	Secord		NA	Wayne
22.2	Sheldon	Sheldon			Sheldon	None/Prepaid	Wayne
24.8	Denton	Denton	Denton	Denton	Denton	T. Moon	Wayne
26.7					Wiard's	None/Prepaid	Wash.
29.4	Ypsilanti	Ypsilanti	Ypsilanti	Ypsilanti	Ypsilanti	B. Damon	Wash.
32.1	Lowell					NA	Wash.
33.3	Geddes	Geddes	Geddes	Geddes	Geddes	W. Weed	Wash.
37.3	Ann Arbor	Ann Arbor	Ann Arbor	Ann Arbor	Ann Arbor	H. Hayes	Wash.
38.8			Kellogg	Kellogg		NA	Wash.
40.5	Foster's		Foster's	Foster's	Foster's	Wirt Cornwell	Wash.
41.9	Farmer's			Farmer's		NA	Wash.
43	Delhi	Delhi	Delhi	Delhi	Delhi	C. Slimmer	Wash.
44.2	Scio	Scio	Scio	Scio	Scio	J. Deubel	Wash.
46.9	Dexter	Dexter	Dexter	Dexter	Dexter	W. Clark	Wash.
54.2	Chelsea	Chelsea	Chelsea	Chelsea	Chelsea	Wm. Martin	Wash.
61.2	Francisco	Francisco	Francisco	Francisco	Francisco	C. Plowe	Jackson
65.3	Grass Lake	Grass Lake	Grass Lake	Grass Lake	Grass Lake	P. Willis	Jackson
68.3	Leoni	Leoni	Leoni	Leoni	Leoni	F. Barber	Jackson

71.7	Michigan Centre	Michigan Centre	Michigan Centre	Michigan Centre	Michigan Centre	A. Crittenden	Jackson
74.5					Jackson Junction	None/Prepaid	Jackson
75.6	Jackson	Jackson	Jackson	Jackson	Jackson	H. W. Scott	
78.8			Woodville	Woodville		P. A. Hahn	Jackson
81.8	Sandstone	Sandstone	Sandstone	Sandstone	**Trumbull**	NA	Jackson
85.4	Gidley's	**Parma**	Parma	Parma	Parma	C. Strand	Jackson
89.2	Concord	Concord	Concord	**North Concord**	North Concord	G. Lewis	Jackson
92.3	Bath Mills	Bath Mills	Bath Mills	Bath Mills	Bath Mills	None/Prepaid	Jackson
94.2	Newburg Mills				Newburg Mills	None/Prepaid	Jackson
95.9	Albion	Albion	Albion	Albion	Albion	Geo. French	Calhoun
101.2	Marengo	Marengo	Marengo	Marengo	Marengo	J. Wilkinson	Calhoun
107.7	Marshall	Marshall	Marshall	Marshall	Marshall	C. Gifford	Calhoun
109.7	Emerald Mills					NA	Calhoun
112.9	Ceresco	Ceresco	Ceresco	Ceresco	Ceresco	C. Smith	Calhoun
114.5			Whites	Whites	**Wheatfield**	S. Wholihan	Calhoun
119.9					Nichols	T. Barry	Calhoun
120.8	Battle Creek	Battle Creek	Battle Creek	Battle Creek	Battle Creek	Geo. Sadler	Calhoun
126.3				Bedford	Bedford	None/Prepaid	Calhoun
130.4	Augusta	Augusta	Augusta	Augusta	Augusta	Frank Fitch	Calhoun
134.8	Galesburgh	Galesburgh	Galesburgh	Galesburgh	Galesburgh	W. Smith	Kal.
139.7	Comstock	Comstock	Comstock	Comstock	Comstock	O. Loveland	Kal.
143.4					Kalamazoo Junction	W. Thompson	Kal.
143.6	Kalamazoo	Kalamazoo	Kalamazoo	Kalamazoo	Kalamazoo	E. Gates	Kal.
149.4			Ostemo	Ostemo	Ostemo	Mrs. Rickard	Kal.
155.9		Mattawan	Mattawan	Mattawan	Mattawan	B. Payn	Kal.
159.9	Paw Paw	Paw Paw	**Lawton**	Lawton	Lawton	L. Waldorff	Van Bur.
161.9			White Oak	White Oak		NA	Van Bur.
167.6	Decatur	Decatur	Decatur	Decatur	Decatur	M. Barron	Van Bur.
172.9			Tietsorts	Tietsorts	**Glenwood**	C. Chase	Cass

Mile Post* Detroit	Annual Report Stations 1850	Annual Report Stations 1855	Annual Report Stations 1870	Annual Report Stations 1874	Station Listing 1896	Depot Agent 1896	County Location
178.8	Dowagiac	Dowagiac	Dowagiac	Dowagiac	Dowagiac	E. Alliger	Cass
184.9		Pokagon	Pokagon	Pokagon	Pokagon	Frank Fitch	Cass
191.6	Niles	Niles	Niles	Niles	Niles	F. Barron	Berrien
192.8					West Niles	None/Prepaid	Berrien
197.8	Buchanan	Buchanan	Buchanan	Buchanan	Buchanan	A. Peacock	Berrien
202.4	Terra Coupee	Terra Coupee	**Dayton**	Dayton	Dayton	A. Weaver	Berrien
204.0			Wilsons			NA	Berrien
205.4			Galien	Galien	Galien	E. Simmons	Berrien
209.2					Barnett Siding	None/Prepaid	Berrien
210.0			Avery	Avery	Avery	None/Prepaid	Berrien
211.2		Chamberlain	**Three Oaks**	Three Oaks	Three Oaks	W. Green	Berrien
218.3	New Buffalo	New Buffalo	New Buffalo	New Buffalo	New Buffalo	G. Waite	Berrien
222.9			Corymbo	Corymbo	Corymbo	None/Prepaid	LaPort Co., IN
226.9					Michigan City Yard	None/Prepaid	LaPort
228.2	Michigan City	Michigan City	Michigan City	Michigan City	Michigan City	Wm. Thons	LaPort
235.9			Furnessville	Furnessville	Furnessville	N. Williams	Porter
238.0			Pierces	Pierces	Pierces	NA	Porter
240.0	Porter	Porter	Porter	Porter	Porter	H. Ruggles	Porter
245.4					Crisman	F. Mahns	Porter
246.0					Willow Creek	W. Rechtenwall	Porter
249.1	Lake	Lake	Lake	Lake	Lake	C. Moore	Lake
255.6			Tolleston	Tolleston	Tolleston	J. Staff	Lake
259.6					Ivanhoe	None/Prepaid	Lake
261.0	Gibson	Gibson	Gibson	Gibson	Gibson	NA	Indiana
264.4					Hammond	O. Mallett	Lake
265.5					Hammond Bldg	NA	Lake
265.9			Calumet	Calumet	**Calumet Park**	None/Prepaid	Cook Co. IL
267.6					Calumet Bridge	None/Prepaid	Cook
271.0	Kensington				Kensington	C. West	Cook

Appendix M   **317**

MCRR TRACK ENDS

Milepost			Station	Agent	County
273.8			Burnside	None	Cook
275.7	Junction		Chg. to Grand Crossing	T. Collins	Cook
			63rd Street	J. Funk	Cook
279.2			Hyde Park	I. Manley	Cook
281.1			39th Street	N. Farrin	Cook
283.2			22nd Street	V. Labbe	Cook
			Union Stock Yard	D. Cotter	Cook
285.6	Chicago	Chicago	Chicago	W. Mather	Cook

NOTES

CHAPTER 1

1. James H. Lanman, *History of Michigan* (New York: Harper & Brothers, 1859), p. 239.

2. Frank W. Stevens, *The Beginnings of the New York Central Railroad* (New York: G. P. Putnam, 1926), p. 8.

3. *Michigan Free Democrat* (Detroit), August 7, 1855, p. 3. This likely explains the route going through the villages represented by prominent men in Ypsilanti, Ann Arbor, Delhi, Dexter, Chelsea, Marshall, *etc.*

4. George C. Bates, "The Beginning of the Michigan Central Railroad," *Michigan Pioneer and Historical Collections*, XXII (1893), p. 349.

5. Franklin Ellis & Crisfield Johnson, *History of Berrien and Van Buren Counties, Michigan* (Philadelphia: D. W. Ensign & Co., 1880), p. 52.

6. Ray Haddock, "The Railroad of Michigan," *Atlas of the State of Michigan* (1873), p. 17.

7. *Ibid.*, p.17.

8. Alvin Harlow, *Road of the Century: The Story of the New York Central* (New York: Creative Age Press, Inc., 1947), p. 214.

9. *Ibid.*, p. 214.

10. Ray Haddock, p. 17.

11. *Ibid.,* p. 17.

12. Robert J. Parks, *Democracy's Railroads Public Enterprise in Jacksonian Michigan* (Port Washington: Kennikat Press, 1972), p. 91.

13. *Michigan Free Democrat,* August 7, 1855, p. 3.

CHAPTER 2

1. Haddock, p. 18. The most popular stagecoaches in the country were the Troy and the Concord coaches, made in Troy, New York, or Concord, New Hampshire.

2. James F. Joy, "The Railroad History of Michigan," *Michigan Pioneer and Historical Collections,* Vol. XXII (1892), p. 293.

3. *Detroit Journal and Courier,* February 6, 1838, p. 2.

4. Robert J. Parks, *Democracy's Railroads: Public Enterprise in Jacksonian Michigan* (New York: National University Publications, 1972), p. 93. This document was heavily relied on for this chapter and is a "must read" for anyone interested in the period of state involvement in railroads.

5. O. W. Stephenson, *Ann Arbor: The First Hundred Years* (Ann Arbor: The Ann Arbor Chamber of Commerce, 1927), p. 331.

6. *Ibid.,* p. 307.

7. *Ibid.,* p. 332.

8. George N. Fuller, *Messages of the Governors of Michigan, Vol. I* (Lansing: The Michigan Historical Commission, 1925), p. 276–277.

9. Manuscript undated, unpublished: *The Railroad.* Dexter Area Historical Society & Museum, Dexter, Michigan.

10. Genealogical Society of Washtenaw County, *Family History Capers,* Vol. 26, no. 1 (2002), p. 5.

11. *Detroit Free Press,* July 3, 1841, p. 2.

12. Norma McAllister (local historian), undated notes, Dexter Area Historical Society & Museum, Dexter, Michigan.

13. Stephenson, p. 332.

14. Letter dated August 25, 1842, to Mr. & Mrs. Daniel Sullivan in Erie, Pennsylvania from Jeremiah Cummings, Marengo, Michigan.

15. *The American Railroad Journal and General Advertiser for Railroads, Canals, Steamboats, Machinery and Mines,* February 7, 1846, p. 86.

16. *Detroit Advertiser* (about Marshall), November 25, 1845, p. 3; and *Detroit Advertiser* (about Kalamazoo), February 3, 1846, p. 2.

17. Larry B. Massie & Peter J. Schmitt, *Kalamazoo: The Place Behind the Products* (California: American Historical Press, 1995), p. 38.

18. Elon Farnsworth (the first MCRR treasurer) papers, Bentley Historical Library, Ann Arbor, Michigan.

19. Massie & Schmitt, *Kalamazoo,* p. 41.

20. Robert J. Parks, *Democracy's Railroads: Public Enterprise in Jacksonian Michigan* (New York: National University Publications, 1972), p. 101. This document was heavily relied on for this chapter and is a "must read" for anyone interested in the period of state involvement in railroads.

21. Harlow, p. 218.

22. *The American Railroad Journal and General Advertiser for Railroads, Canals, Steamboats, Machinery and Mines,* February 7, 1846, p. 84.

23. Haddock, p. 18.

24. George N. Fuller, p. 512.

25. James F. Joy, p. 301.

26. *Ibid.*

27. *Michigan Free Democrat,* August 17, 1855, p. 2.

CHAPTER 3

John W. Brooks, *Report Upon the Merits of the Michigan Central Railroad as an Investment for Eastern Capitalists* (New York: Van Norden & Amerman, Printers, 1846). This document is referenced exclusively in this chapter.

CHAPTER 4

John W. Brooks, *Report Upon the Merits of the Michigan Central Railroad as an Investment for Eastern Capitalists* (New York: Van Norden & Amerman, Printers, 1846). This report also includes the Michigan Central Railroad charter.

1. Clarence M. Burton, *The City of Detroit, Michigan* (Detroit: S. J. Clark Publishers, 1922), p. 691.

2. James F. Joy, *Railroad History of Michigan,* Michigan Historical Collections, Vol. 22 (1893), p. 301.

3. Henry Greenleaf Pearson, *An American Railroad Builder: John Murray Forbes* (Boston: The Riverside Press Cambridge, 1922), p. 26. Forbes had a falling out with Daniel Webster over Webster's support of the 1851 Fugitive Slave Act.

4. MCRR 100th year anniversary booklet, printed by the New York Central Railroad, p. 3.

CHAPTER 5

1. James F. Joy, p. 295. At least one reason to doubt Joy's memory about Sturgis backing out of his tentative commitment to join the 25 other investors is the record of Sturgis attending a meeting that discussed the time and location of the first official meeting of MCRR owners (Bentley Historical Library).

2. Sarah Forbes Hughes, *Letters and Recollections of John Murray Forbes* (Cambridge: Houghton Mifflin, 1899), p. 119.

Note: A good portion of birth, death, and related information was provided by New England Historic Genealogical Society from the Massachusetts Vital Records, 1841–1910, and the Mount Auburn Cemetery, Cambridge, Massachusetts.

CHAPTER 6

1. Elon Farnsworth Papers, Bentley Historical Library.

2. Clarence M. Burton, *The City of Detroit, 1701–1922,* (Detroit: S. J. Clarke Pub. Co., 1922), p. 692. *Note:* George C. Hopper wrote his memories of the Civil War called "From Beverley Fork to Bottoms Bridge with the 1st Michigan Infantry from May 1st to June 6th, 1864" (1913). He was wounded in action at Gaines Mill, Virginia, June 27, 1862, and wounded and taken prisoner at Manassas, Virginia, August 30, 1862.

3. *Detroit Free Press,* March 13, 1894.

4. George B. Catlin, *The Story of Detroit* (Detroit: the Detroit News, 1923), p. 416.

5. Document at Dexter Area Historical Society & Museum ("The Railroads") as compared to MCRR Payroll records, June 30, 1848.

6. *Jackson County History,* 1878.

7. C. H. Salmons & C. H. Frisbee, *The Burlington Strike* (Aurora: Bunnell and Ward, 1889), p. 471.

8. Letter dated August 24, 1847, to J. W. Brooks in Detroit from Levi Wilson, Boston, Massachusetts.

9. Letter dated March 29, 1849, to J. W. Brooks in Detroit from B. P. Reynolds, Misawaka, Illinois.

10. *Sunday Morning Patriot,* December 15, 1901 (Henry Hall), Dexter Area Historical Society & Museum, Dexter, Michigan.

11. Edward K. Warren Foundation, *The Region of Three Oaks* (LaPorte: Plimpton Press, 1939), p. 120.

12. Nicholas Marsh, *Remembering Delhi Mills* (Ann Arbor: Braun & Brumfield, 1985), p. 19.

Note: The other quotations and related information in this chapter came from The First Annual Report of the Directors of the Michigan Central Railroad Company to the Stockholders, June 1847, Detroit; printed by Charles Wilcox, 1847 (University of Michigan Historical Collections). All other quotations not footnoted in this book are from the MCRR annual reports that cover the years being discussed.

CHAPTER 7

1. MCRR Construction Distribution Ledger B, July 1848–July 1851, p. 176.

2. *Illustrated London News,* February 9, 1850, p. 1.

3. *Shoves Detroit Directory* (Detroit: Free Press Book & Job Printers, 1852), pp. 13–14.

4. MCRR Construction Distribution Ledger, p. 23.

5. *Ibid.,* p. 273.

6. *Ibid.,* p. 7.

7. *Ibid.,* p. 280.

8. Henry Hall (1887), p. 5.

9. Letter dated December 1, 1847, to J. W. Brooks in Detroit, from John M. Forbes in Boston.

10. MCRR Construction Distribution Ledger, p. 580.

11. James F. Joy, p. 304.

12. *New York Daily Tribune,* October 13, 1848, p. 1.

13. *Detroit Free Press,* June 19, 1849, p. 1.

14. Edward K. Warren Foundation, *The Region of Three Oaks* (LaPorte: Plimpton Press, 1939), p. 120.

15. *Detroit Free Press,* March 7, 1892, p. 13.

16. MCRR Construction Distribution Ledger, 1849, p. 276.

17. Edward K. Warren Foundation, *The Region of Three Oaks* (La-Porte: Plimpton Press, 1939), p. 121.

18. *Ibid.,* p. 121.

19. *Ibid.,* p. 127.

20. *Ibid.,* pp. 122–123.

CHAPTER 8

1. The MCRR Construction Distribution Ledger B, July 1848–July 1851.

2. Pauline A. Pinckney, *American Figureheads and Their Carvers* (Port Washington, NY: Kennikat Press, 1940), p. 101. Jeremiah Dodge and son Charles J. Dodge were in partnership (1833–1839) and worked together on a face carved for the *U.S.S. Constitution.* They also collaborated on the only other piece of their known figure-head work, Hercules, which was carved for the ship *Ohio* and now resides in the Peabody Museum in Salem, Massachusetts (*Shipcarvers of North America,* by M.V. Brewington, Barre Publishing Co. Barre, Massachusetts, 1962, p. 48). Charles has other non-figurehead sculptures surviving that attest to his abilities. One example is the carved wooden bust of his wife currently at the Brooklyn Museum of Art (New York).

3. Floyd Russell Dain, "The Michigan Central Railroad and the Michigan *May Flower,*" *Detroit in Perspective,* Vol. 2, no. 1 (Autumn 1973), p. 45.

4. All descriptions of the *May Flower* accoutrements, pay, and insurance come from the MCRR Construction Distribution Ledger B.

5. William L. Bancroft, *Memoir of Capt. Samuel Ward* (1892), p. 5.

6. C. H. Salmons and C. H. Frisbie (1889), p. 471.

7. William L. Bancroft (1892), p. 4.

8. Broadside, MCRR, 1852.

9. *New York Times,* November 25, 1854, p. 2.

10. Harlan Hatcher, *The Great Lakes* (New York: Oxford University Press, 1944), p. 236.

11. Fred Irving Dayton, *Steamboat Days* (New York: Tudor Publishing, 1939), pp. 402–411.

12. James Dale Johnston, *Johnston's Detroit City Directory* (Detroit: Fleming & Co. 1857), pp. 120–121.

13. Harlan Hatcher, *Lake Erie* (New York: The Bobbs-Merrill Company, 1945), p. 131.

14. Milo M. Quaife, *Lake Michigan* (New York: The Bobbs-Merrill Company, 1944) p. 197.

15. *The History of Berrien and Van Buren Counties, Michigan* (Philadelphia: Ensign & Co., 1880), p. 51.

16. *Ibid.*, p. 52.

17. Official List of Officers and Agents, No. 68 (MCRR), October 9, 1896, p. 16.

18. *Dexter Leader,* month & day unknown, 1881.

19. *History of Berrien and Van Buren Counties, Michigan* (1880), p. 52.

CHAPTER 9

1. MCRR Construction Distribution Ledger B, May 1850, p. 507.

2. *Ibid.*, p. 590.

3. James F. Joy, p. 304.

4. Letter dated August 1, 1851, to Brooks in Detroit from Forbes in Boston.

5. John F. Stove, *History of the Illinois Central Railroad* (New York: Macmillan Publishing Co. Inc., 1975), p. 31.

6. James F. Joy, p. 305.

7. John F. Stove, p. 32.

8. George H. Merriam, "A Man of Large Experience: Edwin Noyes and Railroad Development of Maine," *Railroad History* 156 (Spring 1887), p. 11.

9. J. Jay Myers, *American History,* Vol. XXXVI, no. 3 (August 2001), p. 65. Harvey kept his title of canal agent, but was only allowed to handle supplies and payroll. History credits Harvey with building the canal, in part, because his later memoirs about the construction ignores Brooks altogether. Although Brooks never looked for credit for his accomplishments, he should be credited with building the St. Mary's Canal Locks.

10. *History of Berrien and Van Buren Counties* (1883), p. 267.

11. Robert B. Ross & George B. Catlin, *Landmarks of Detroit: A History of the City* (Detroit: Evening News Association, 1898), p. 416.

12. Henry Russel, *Argument in Favor of the High Bridge at Detroit, Michigan* (Detroit: 1896), p. 9.

13. James F. Joy, p. 296.

14. John F. Stove (1975), p. 81.

CHAPTER 10

1. *National Railroad Journal.*

2. MCRR Construction Distribution Ledger B.

3. Frisbee (1877).

4. Henry Hall, Dexter Area Historical Society & Museum.

5. Martin J. Hershock, "Free Commoners by Law: Tradition, Transition, and the Closing of the Range in Antebellum Michigan," *The Michigan Historical Review,* Vol. 29 (Fall 2003), p. 97.

6. *The Jackson Citizen,* November 10, 1851.

7. Charles V. DeLand, *History of Jackson County, Michigan* (Logansport, IN: B. F. Bowen, 1903), p. 154.

8. *Ibid.,* p. 157.

9. Charles Hirschfield, *The Great Railroad Conspiracy: The Social History of a Railroad War* (The Michigan State College Press, 1953).

10. Martin J. Hershock, p. 98.

11. *Ibid.*

12. Robert B. Ross & George B. Catlin, *Landmarks of Detroit: A History of the City* (Detroit: The Evening News Association, 1898), p. 415.

CHAPTER 11

1. Wilber H. Siebert, *The Underground Railroad from Slavery to Freedom* (Glouchester: Russell & Russell, 1967), p. 136.

2. Washington Gardner, *History of Calhoun County* (New York: Lewis Publishing Co., 1913), p. 84. Quotes editor Barnes's interview from the *Sunday Morning Call.*

3. Jon H Yzenbaard, "The Crosswhite Case," *Michigan History Magazine,* Vol. LIII, no. 2 (Summer 1969), pp. 131–143.

4. *Detroit Tribune* (The Death of George DeBaptiste) January 17, 1887, p. 2, Clarke Historical Library, Central Michigan University, Mt. Pleasant, Michigan.

5. Sarah Forbes Hughes, *Letters and Recollections of John Murray Forbes,* p. 171.

6. *Ibid.,* p. 285.

7. Edward Waldo Emerson, "James Murray Forbes," *The Atlantic Monthly,* September, 1899, p. 390.

8. James Morris Morgan, "Commerce Destroying Aboard the Georgia," *The Atlantic Monthly,* March 1917, p. 338.

9. Isabel Anderson, *Under the Black Horse Flag,* p. 38.

10. *American Local History Network,* Elijah McCoy, African American Inventor and resident of Eloise, Michigan.

CHAPTER 12

1. Sarah Forbes Hughes (1899), p. 165.

2. C. H. Salmons & C. H. Frisbee (1899), p. 472.

3. *New York Times,* February 9, 1855.

4. *Detroit Advertiser,* November,1856. It was a piece of the cable originally intended to be used at Newfoundland, and was the first really successful submarine telegraph cable laid in any water. *Michigan History Magazine,* Vol. XXIV (Winter 1940), p. 83.

5. Sarah Forbes Hughes (1899), p. 168.

6. *Ibid.,* p. 169.

7. Clarence M. Burton (1922), p. 694.

8. Letter from M. Miles, *Michigan History Magazine,* no. 3 (July 1924), p. 393.

9. *Detroit Free Press,* March 6, 1892, A. B. Priest Interview, p. 1.

10. C. H. Salmons & C. H. Frisbee (1889), p. 473. The first meeting of the Brotherhood was at the home of William D. Robinson, an MCRR engineer from Marshall, who is considered the organization's founder. Some of those who attended the first few organizational meetings included Henry Hall, J. C. Thompson, John Brown, Sam Keith, Linus Keith, Thomas Nixon, Sam Amlar, Thomas Faulkner, Henry Lathrop, and Thomas Van Wormer.

11. *Johnston's Detroit City Directory* (1861), p. 48.

12. *Detroit Free Press,* April 17, 1892, George C. Hopper Interview, p. 1.

13. *Chicago Tribune,* August 8, 1860, p. 1.

14. *New York Times,* June 8, 1863, p. 1.

15. Jno. Robertson, *Michigan in the War* (Lansing: George & Co., State Printers, 1882), p. 69.

16. *Detroit Free Press,* April 17, 1892, p. 1.

17. *Ibid.*

18. *Dexter Leader,* August 1896.

19. Information provided by the Michigan City Public Library, *Historic Sites of LaPorte County,* document, 2006, p. 7.

20. *History of Jackson County, Michigan* (Chicago: Inter-state Publishing Co., 1881), p. 558.

21. C. H. Salmons & C. H. Frisbee (1889), pp. 475–476.

22. Robert B. Ross & George B. Catlin, p. 821.

23. *Ibid.,* p. 472.

24. *New York Times,* September 6, 1866, p. 1.

25. *Dexter Leader,* July 1872.

26. Robert L. Frey, *Encyclopedia of American Business History and Biography: Railroads in the Nineteenth Century* (New York: Bruccoli Clark Layman, Inc., 1988), p. 33.

27. *Ibid.,* p. 35.

CHAPTER 13

1. *Chapin's Ann Arbor City Directory,* p. 32.

2. *Clark's Detroit City Directory,* p. 448.

3. *Dexter Leader,* September 1869.

4. James Joy, p. 295.

5. *New York Times,* November 8, 1870.

6. *Ibid.,* March 9, 1870.

7. *Ibid.,* March 26, 1875.

8. *Ibid.,* October 9, 1875.

9. *Michigan Historical Collections,* Vol. 22, p. 351.

CHAPTER 14

1. *Sunday Morning Patriot,* December 15, 1901 (Henry Hall).

2. *Ibid.*

3. *Ibid.*

4. *Ibid.*

5. *Ibid.*

6. C. H. Salmons (1889).

7. *New York Daily Times,* May 12, 1852.

8. *Ibid.,* April 20, 1852.

9. *Ibid.,* July 5, 1852.

10. *Ibid.,* April 30, 1853.

11. *Ibid.,* November 10, 1856.

12. William Sloane Kennedy, *Wonders and Curiosities of the Railway* (Chicago: S. C. Griggs & Co., 1884), pp. 84–85.

13. *New York Times,* January 31, 1869.

14. *Detroit Free Press,* July 20, 1870.

15. *Ibid.*

16. *New York Times,* October 12, 1879.

17. *Ibid.,* August 25, 1886.

18. *Ibid.,* March 29, 1888.

19. *Ibid.,* October 14, 1893.

CHAPTER 15

1. *New York Times,* June 26, 1877.

2. *Ibid.*

3. Robert L. Frey (1988), p. 208.

4. *New York Times,* June 12, 1877.

5. *Ibid.,* June 25, 1878.

6. *Ibid.*

7. *The Decatur Republican,* November 11, 1937.

8. *The Washington Post,* September 3, 1882.

9. *The New York Times,* June 6, 1883.

10. *Ibid.*

11. The MCRR had been crossing the GWR bridge since it was completed in 1855 and it was the company's only access to Buffalo. When the GTR built their bridge in 1873, the old GWR bridge was dismantled (1877).

12. Floyd W. Mundy, *The Earning Power of Railroads, 1918–1919* (New York: Middleditch Co., 1919), p. 290.

CHAPTER 16

1. *New York Times,* July 26, 1877.
2. *Ibid.,* August 28, 1877.
3. *Scientific American Supplement,* February 23, 1889, pp. 1–2. The *Transfer* II was actually just named the *Transfer,* which was painted on the side in white. To distinguish between the *Transfer* running at Gross Isle and the *Transfer* running between Detroit and Windsor, a (II) was added to the later.
4. Henry Russel, *Argument in Favor of the High Bridge at Detroit, Michigan* (Detroit: 1896), p. 15.
5. *Ibid.,* December 22, 1884.
6. *Ibid.,* May 7, 1886.
7. *Dexter Leader,* October 1885.
8. *New York Times,* May 7, 1886.
9. *Ibid.,* May 5, 1887.
10. *Ibid.,* April 11, 1889.
11. Letter, *Michigan History Magazine,* Vol. VIII (1924), pp. 400–401.
12. *New York Times,* April 11, 1889.
13. *Dexter Leader,* May 1889.
14. *New York Times,* April 30, 1891.
15. *Dexter Leader,* 1893.
16. *Washington Post,* September 25, 1893.
17. *Dexter Leader,* February 22, 1895.
18. *Detroit Free Press,* October 1, 1895.
19. *Dexter Leader,* August 1896.
20. *New York Times,* October 24, 1895.
21. *Dexter Leader,* May 1898.
22. Silas Farmer, *The History of Detroit* (Detroit: Farmer & Co., 1889), p. 1063.

CHAPTER 17

1. George B. Catlin, "Oliver Newberry," *Michigan History Magazine,* Vol. XVIII (1934), p. 22.
2. Information obtained from Jim Harlow and Meintz: *Michigan Railroads and Railroad Companies,* March 1, 2007.

3. Information obtained from Jim Harlow and *Poor's Manual of the Railroads,1894,* November 24, 2006

4. Information obtained from Jim Harlow and *Poor's Manual of the Railroads, 1924,* April 27, 2005

5. Jim Harlow also contributed information from various documents in his collection about the following MC stations in this chapter: Wayne Junction, Jackson Junction. Nichols, Kalamazoo Junction, Willow Creek, Tolleston, Gibson, Calumet Park and others.) August 24, 2006.

6. Walter Romig, *Michigan Place Names* (Detroit: Wayne State University Press, 1986), p. 617.

7. MCRR Construction Distribution Ledger B, June 1849, p. 356.

8. O. W. Stephenson, *Ann Arbor: The First Hundred Years* (Ann Arbor: The Ann Arbor Chamber of Commerce, 1927), p. 307.

9. MCRR Construction Distribution Ledger B, June 1849, p. 356.

10. Manuscript circa 1880, unpublished: *The Railroad.* Dexter Area Historical Society & Museum, Dexter, Michigan.

11. MCRR Construction Distribution Ledger B, June 1849, p. 356.

12. *Ibid.,* August 1850, p. 504.

13. *Ibid.,* June 1851, p. 629.

14. *Ibid.,* July 1851, p. 640.

15. Chapman (1881), p. 758.

16. MCRR Construction Distribution Ledger B, October 1850, p. 558.

17. Chapman (1881), p. 758.

18. MCRR Construction Distribution Ledger B, December 1849, p. 446.

19. Michigan Historical Marker.

20. Memorial Report Jackson County, *Michigan Pioneer and Historical Collections,* Vol. 21 (1892), p. 163.

21. MCRR Construction Distribution Ledger B, June 1850, p. 507.

22. *Ibid.,* p. 558.

23. *Ibid.,* April 1851, p. 613.

24. *Ibid.,* p. 558.

25. *Ibid.,* January 1849, p. 243.

26. *Ibid.,* March 1849, p. 284.

27. *Detroit Free Press,* May 26, 1849.

28. *Michigan Historical Collections,* Vol. 21 (1892), p. 84.

29. Larry B. Massie & Peter J. Schmitt, *Kalamazoo: The Place Behind the Products* (California: American Historical Press, 1995), p. 38.

30. MCRR Construction Distribution Ledger B, August 1848, p. 57.

31. *The Decatur Republican* November 11, 1937.

32. MCRR Construction Distribution Ledger B, December 1848, p. 200.

33. *Ibid.,* November 1848, p. 165.

34. *Ibid.,* March 1849, p. 284.

35. *Ibid.,* December 1848, p. 200.

36. *Ibid.,* December 1848, p. 200.

37. *Ibid.,* July 1850, p. 526.

38. *Flashback,* Hammond Historical Society, February 2003, p. 2.

CHAPTER 18

1. *New York Times,* January 9, 1897.

2. *Ibid.,* October 4, 1898.

3. *Ibid.,* October 5, 1898.

4. *Washington Post,* October 10, 1900.

5. *New York Times,* December 5, 1901.

6. *Ann Arbor Courier-Register,* December 25, 1901.

7. *New York Times,* December 28, 1902.

8. *Ibid.,* March 28, 1903.

9. *Ibid.,* June 11, 1910.

CHAPTER 19

1. *Time Magazine,* January 14, 1929.

2. *Washington Post,* June 10, 1926.

3. *Ibid.*

4. *New York Times,* March 29, 1927.

5. *Ibid.,* June 17, 1927.

6. *Ibid.,* June 3, 1927.

7. *Ibid.,* January 1, 1929.

8. *Ibid.,* August 24, 1929.

9. *Ibid.,* March 1, 1930.

10. *Ibid.,* March 14, 1931.

11. *Farnsworth Papers.*

BIBLIOGRAPHY

The following resources were used in this project and are recommended for the libraries of those interested in the history of the MCRR.

Floyd Russell Dain, "The Michigan Central Railroad and the Michigan *May Flower*," *Detroit in Perspective,* Vol. 2, no. 1 (Autumn 1973). This magazine article is one of the few resources on MCRR steamships.

Chas. E. Fisher, "The Michigan Central Railroad," *Railway and Locomotive Historical Society Bulletin,* no. 19, Boston, Massachusetts, 1929. This 31-page bulletin gives a brief summary of MCRR annual reports up to Joy's presidency.

Robert L. Frey, *Encyclopedia of American Business History and Biography: Railroads in the Nineteenth Century* (New York: Facts on File, 1988). This book provides biographical information on MCRR officials not found elsewhere.

Alvin Harlow, *Road of the Century: The Story of the New York Central* (New York: Creative Age Press, Inc., 1947). This book includes a chapter that provides an interesting but brief overview of MCRR history.

Charles Hirschfield, *The Great Railroad Conspiracy: The Social History of a Railroad War* (Michigan State College Press, 1953). This book covers the full story of the MCRR conspiracy.

Sarah Forbes Hughes, *Letters and Recollections of John Murray Forbes* (Cambridge: Houghton Mifflin, 1899). This book provides insight into the early days of the MCRR through the writings of its first president.

Graydon M. Meintz, *Michigan Railroads & Railroad Companies* (East Lansing: Michigan State University Press, 1992). This book lists all railroad companies incorporated in the state of Michigan, with the corporate history of the largest railroad systems; also includes a brief history of Michigan's railroad history.

Graydon M. Meintz, *Michigan Railroad Lines,* 2 vols. (East Lansing: Michigan State University Press, 2005). This book lists the date every railroad line in the state was constructed, and its disposition.

Robert J. Parks, *Democracy's Railroads: Public Enterprise in Jacksonian Michigan* (Port Washington: Kennikat Press, 1972). This book provides a comprehensive look at state ownership of the railroad.

Henry Greenleaf Pearson, *An American Railroad Builder: John Murray Forbes* (New York: Houghton Mifflin, 1911). This biography provides insight into the history of the MCRR by understanding the man who was most responsible for financing the building of the road.

Alvin F. Staufer, *New York Central's Early Power, Volume II 1831–1916* (Carrollton, OH: Carrollton Standard Printing Co., 1967). This book provides information on MCRR locomotives not available elsewhere.

Robert D. Tennant, Jr., *Canada Southern Country* (Erin, Ontario: Boston Mills Press, 1991). This history of the CSR provides a nice overview of its connection to the MCRR, plus a comprehensive look at building the Detroit River tunnel.

For those looking for a broad overview, the following book is a basic primer of general Michigan railroad history.

Willis F. Dunbar, *All Aboard: A History of Railroad in Michigan* (Grand Rapids: Eerdman's Publishing Co., 1969).

Michigan Central Station, Kalamazoo.

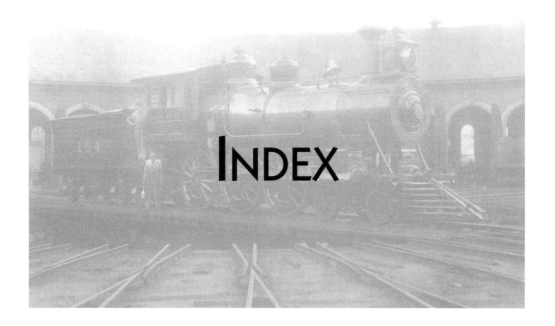

INDEX

Note: This *name and place* index does not include entries appearing on lists found in the appendices, nor does it include page listings for cities/towns with over 50 entries.